WOMEN MAKING MODERNISM

UNIVERSITY PRESS OF FLORIDA

Florida A&M University, Tallahassee
Florida Atlantic University, Boca Raton
Florida Gulf Coast University, Ft. Myers
Florida International University, Miami
Florida State University, Tallahassee
New College of Florida, Sarasota
University of Central Florida, Orlando
University of Florida, Gainesville
University of North Florida, Jacksonville
University of South Florida, Tampa
University of West Florida, Pensacola

Women Making Modernism

EDITED BY
ERICA GENE DELSANDRO

University Press of Florida
Gainesville · Tallahassee · Tampa · Boca Raton
Pensacola · Orlando · Miami · Jacksonville · Ft. Myers · Sarasota

25 24 23 22 21 20   6 5 4 3 2 1

The Library of Congress has cataloged the printed edition as follows:
Names: Delsandro, Erica Gene, editor.
Title: Women making modernism / edited by Erica Gene Delsandro.
Description: Gainesville : University Press of Florida, 2020. | Includes
    bibliographical references and index. |
Identifiers: LCCN 2019013070 (print) | LCCN 2019018136 (ebook) | ISBN
    9780813057309 (ePDF) | ISBN 9780813066172 (cloth : alk. paper)
Subjects: LCSH: Modernism (Literature) | Women and literature.
Classification: LCC PN56.M54 (ebook) | LCC PN56.M54 W66 2020 (print) | DDC
    809/.892870904—dc23
LC record available at https://lccn.loc.gov/2019013070

The University Press of Florida is the scholarly publishing agency for the State University
System of Florida, comprising Florida A&M University, Florida Atlantic University,
Florida Gulf Coast University, Florida International University, Florida State University,
New College of Florida, University of Central Florida, University of Florida, University of
North Florida, University of South Florida, and University of West Florida.

University Press of Florida
2046 NE Waldo Road
Suite 2100
Gainesville, FL 32609
http://upress.ufl.edu

CONTENTS

FIGURES

Introduction

Making a Feminist Modernist Studies

ERICA GENE DELSANDRO

Women Making Modernism stands as a corrective to the consistent tension between feminist studies and modernist studies. Since the "relationship between modernism and modernity was elementally shaped by women, feminists, and feminist women," it stands to reason, as Urmila Seshagiri reminds us, that "feminist method[s] *should* be as indispensable to the study of modernism as women were to the movement's multiple strands."[1] And yet despite waves of feminism in the academy, this is not the case. Rather, feminism remains ancillary even in the expanded arena of new modernist studies.[2]

This volume makes the case for feminism's necessity in modernist studies, arguing that without an integrated feminist approach our modernism is irresponsible at best and dishonest at worst. And the contributors included here take as their cue the renewed fervor around feminist inquiry in literary studies in the academy—exemplified by the new feminist literary studies journal, *Feminist Modernist Studies (FMS),* launched in 2018—and beyond. We, like Madelyn Detloff in her essay for the inaugural double issue of *FMS*, "write from a space of distress."[3] As feminists, our distress is "the result of contextual, cultural, temporal, and geographic positionality," reading, teaching, and writing in an environment that feels all too familiar.[4] According to Detloff, feminists perceive this familiarity as being in the "Sisyphe position": confronting the "unfortunately repetitive, seemingly unwinnable task . . . of rolling a giant boulder . . . up a hill so that it does not career down and crush the things one values" (36). The boulder represents patriarchy's innumerable exclusionary hierarchies and their attendant constraints and oppressions, and feminist modernists find themselves once again struggling to keep them at bay. (Arguably, this labor never ceases but rather ebbs and flows in intensity and urgency.) And because there is no one way to push the boulder up the hill, readers of this collection will not find one singular argument about the state or fate of feminist modernist studies nor one singular method for succeeding once and for all to secure the boulder atop the hill.

Rather, collectively we assert the value of amplifying the reality of women's contributions to modernism by exploring a myriad of women writers through a diverse set of approaches. Along the way, many of our authors engage in self-reflection, taking into account their personal histories, social locations, and anxieties, thus bridging the arbitrary division, long enforced by patriarchal postures of intellectualism, between the academic and affective self. Thus, the Sisyphe position is "generative," embodying a willfulness that, as Sara Ahmed explains, "involves persistence in the face of being brought down."[5] Consequently, the essays in this volume are intended as sources of generation, encouraging scholars and teachers to stretch their critical feminist imaginations toward discovery and possibility, revision and reinvention.[6]

In order to generate a more feminist—and by extension, more honest and responsible—modernist studies, we eschew the "hermeneutics of suspicion," a phrase coined by Paul Ricoeur, which has come to represent a practice of textual engagement that positions the reader as an adversary to the text. Like a detective or a secret agent, the suspicious reader is always seeking to uncover hidden ideologies, reveal implicit biases, and disrupt the placid surfaces of the unassuming novel, poem, or short story. This approach is deeply indebted to high theory and its impact on the academy through the late twentieth- and early twenty-first century. Not only shaping the way we read and the scholarship we produce, the hermeneutics of suspicion has dominated the way we think of the profession, so much so, that, for many, becoming a scholar means becoming appropriately suspicious. This is unsurprising since suspicious academics are the "serious" and "rigorous" scholars whose work, as Jack Halberstam notes, is applauded and privileged in professional arenas ranging from conference roundtables and department colloquiums to search committees and editorial boards.[7] Halberstam challenges the dominance of suspicion and its attendant power: "Indeed terms like *serious* and *rigorous* tend to be code words . . . for disciplinary correctness; they signal a form of training and learning that confirms what is already known according to approved methods of knowing, but they do not allow for visionary insights or flights of fancy" (6). In Rita Felski's words, this "critical mood" "shortchange[s] the significance of art by focusing on the 'de' prefix (its power to demystify, destabilize, denaturalize) at the expense of the 're' prefix: its ability to recontextualize, reconfigure, or recharge perception."[8] Not only do we shortchange the significance of art and literature but also we shortchange ourselves as scholars, confirming "what is already known" at the cost of visionary insights.

This volume strives for an approach that is motivated by discovery, empathy, and excitement. It responds to Felski's challenge in *The Limits of Critique* to "revitalize and reimagine" interpretation and follows in the footsteps of feminist literary scholarship that has, as Felski explains, "cranked up the level of positive affect and literary enthusiasm" by "reclaiming the work of women writers, attending to overlooked genres, forms, and themes, triggering waves of excitement, recognition, and curiosity" (10, 29). Considering that feminists "were among the first critics to emphasize the affective dimensions of interpretation, to talk about reading as an embedded practice, to conceive of literature as a means of creative self-fashioning," it only seems right that we turn to feminism to "revitalize and reimagine" modernist studies (29).

In so doing, the essays in this volume are not as interested in what secrets scholars can reveal hidden in the texts we read or what counter-ideologies authors have smuggled into their work—the orientation of a suspicious approach. Rather, the essays in this volume are eager to explore modernist women writers and their work in order to imagine a fresh approach to modernism—the orientation of openness. Instead of excavating, defamiliarizing, and disrupting, the scholars included here intend to open, offer, and amplify.[9] Moreover, the authors in this volume are committed to scholarly introspection: the orientation of openness through which they approach their examination of modernist women writers is also at play in their reflection on our collective feminist project, illustrating the political tensions that infuse our reading postures and writing processes.

With its power to revitalize and reimagine, feminism as a mode of reading might be akin to what Halberstam characterizes as low theory. Aiding us in the creation of "a grammar of possibility," low theory is not just a "mode of accessibility" but also a kind of "theoretical model that . . . refuses to confirm the hierarchies of knowing that maintain the *high* in high theory."[10] Leveraging feminism to reinvigorate modernist studies, this volume is careful to avoid the hierarchies of knowledge that have traditionally dominated modernist studies, such as canonicity and iconicity. The structural trap of iconicity has been a long-held approach for feminist scholars seeking to pave a way for women authors in a male-dominated modernism. When faced with a canon of male icons, feminist modernist scholars have tended to create female icons that vie for the critical attention historically bestowed upon their male counterparts and, ideally, that secure a place in the male-dominated modernist canon. Not a surprising approach, since, as Seshagiri explains, "the process of canon-formation—and deformation, and reformation—constitutes the simplest and yet most complex act in feminist scholarship about modernism."[11] Although perhaps a necessary strategy when the reigning accounts of modernism overlooked women's contribution almost completely, the significant presence of female icons within modernist studies currently begs feminist thinkers to stretch their imaginative muscles.[12] The continued reliance on the icon as a scholarly strategy only reproduces an exclusive view of the field, a view in which icons loom large, either shining their literary light on other, lesser-known modernists who, in their association with an icon, come into view, or casting their shadows over the messier, more complicated networks of contestation and affiliation obscuring a more robust—and arguably, more feminist—vision of modernism.[13]

Examining the gender politics of the modernist canon demonstrates the ways that iconicity has narrowed the field of modernist women writers. Virginia Woolf and Gertrude Stein, the first women writers whose work was considered canonical, have been championed by feminist scholars who diligently fought for their inclusion in the histories, anthologies, and companion literature that supports the teaching of modernism. From their inclusion in graduate seminars to the monographs that appear each year, their iconicity in the academy is unquestionable. Woolf, unlike most of her male counterparts, has even secured a place in popular culture, thanks to feminist scholars and common readers alike. Although certainly a victory over male-dominated modernism, Woolf's and Stein's icon status is not necessarily a victory over canonicity. In fact, their unassailable place in the modernist canon only reinforces the ideology of canon formation, an ideology dependent upon exclusion and hierarchy that, ultimately, limits our view of and restricts our access to modernist literature and culture.

Our approach in this volume is to offer alternative ways of reading and models of scholarship that challenge the exclusion and hierarchy of canonicity. Inspired by Caroline Levine's work, *Forms: Whole, Rhythm, Hierarchy, Network*, which "makes a case for expanding our usual definition of form in literary studies to include patterns of sociopolitical experience," we think of modernist women writers and thinkers in terms of arrangements rather than in hierarchies (2). Levine's approach, which draws both on Karl Marx and Michel Foucault, asks us not to separate the sociopolitical from the literary. While many thinkers and writers have attempted such a fusion,[14] what distinguishes Levine's work is its persistent refusal to set one group of conditions or thoughts against another, thus troubling the reign of perhaps the most dominant form, the binary.[15]

Rather, Levine gathers populations of various pieces—be they objects, political conditions, writers, literary texts, or abstract concepts—and then reads the gathering closely. For example, the gathering could be doorknobs, diamonds, and a Victorian novel, or the formation of bodies into compliant masses and the configuration of a historical moment into a revolution. She does not ask what diamonds or doorknobs tell us about the traditionally viewed historical moment, but instead investigates what interesting abstract and concrete realities are rendered visible when this particular collection is gathered together. Each constituent element, of course, invites its own close reading, but for Levine, the most generous and productive analysis is born from the links among the elements, revealing new alignments and, consequently, new forms. Reading these forms closely helps us escape the tired tyrannies of exclusion and hierarchy—restricted by binary structures—and imagine new, fertile configurations and groupings.

Reading the configurations and groups is so productive, argues Levine, because forms have *affordances*: each form contains certain constraints and allows for particular possibilities, and when they affiliate the constraints and possibilities shift and change. Thus, we can ask, "what potentialities lie latent—though not always obvious—in aesthetic and social arrangements?"[16] For example, gender, when used as a *hierarchy*, ranks and excludes. As in traditional modernist studies, writing by men has been privileged and writing by women subordinated, often to the extent of exclusion, or worse, erasure. However, what if gender is understood not as a binary with an embedded hierarchy, but as a *whole*? As a *whole*, gender becomes a container culling together and giving form to texts that, and writers who, might otherwise be perceived as unassociated and underval-ued. When leveraged as a *whole*, gender creates a new sociopolitical arena, a constellation of women writers. In contrast to the canon, gender as a *whole* shapes without ranking, setting parameters that enable an alterna-tive view of modernism, one in which networks emerge as a relevant form, connecting and affiliating outside the valuing imperative traditionally as-sociated with gender when employed as a hierarchical binary.

Not only can something like gender be a form but also it can be some-thing like a network, that would seem, at first blush, to favor formless-ness over form. However, an interdisciplinary approach to network theory has begun to show "how these connective configurations follow knowable rules and patterns" (6, 7).[17] Although we do not pursue particular exam-ples of *networks* as rigorously as Levine does in her book, we do take seri-ously the sociopolitical reality of "the overlapping of multiple networks" in our investigation of women modernists in order to reposition women writers as more than just *contributors* to, but as *makers* of modernism (115). To understand women writers as constitutive of modernism is to perceive them and their work as integral to the *networks* of modernist production: more than mothers or muses, auxiliary or ancillary, modernist women writers are nodes in the *network* of modernism, conduits and creators. In this volume, we explore the way in which women modernists cultivated, sustained, challenged, and revised their roles in the literary and cultural networks that scholars such as Wesley Beal argue are part of the material reality of the modernist experience.[18]

Caroline Levine's thinking motivates the essays in this volume because it compels us to imagine how we can bring *together* a clutch of writers, objects, and alliances—rather than *separating* them into binary categories such as inside and outside, high modernism and middlebrow, history and literature—and to ask how ordering, patterning, and shaping creates are-nas that can simultaneously coexist, contradict, and complement. Rather than employing gender as a *hierarchy* of division, for example, as tradi-tional modernist studies has done for so long, and instead of employing canonicity as a *whole*, creating insiders and outsiders, the scholars in this volume seek to imagine various *networks* that constitute modernist studies, *networks* that often interrupt, sometimes assist, and occasionally super-sede the established patterns of order that have given shape to modernism through the academically endorsed institution of modernist studies. This approach is the antithesis of canon formation in that it opens up the canonical narratives in new ways for political analysis and invites new ways of ordering, patterning, and shaping. Such an approach does not produce a wholesale rejection of institutionally endorsed forms such as iconicity and canonicity. Instead, as demonstrated by the essays in this volume, it encourages readers to perceive what these traditional forms *afford* us as readers and scholars of modernism.

Our contributors thus reject suspicion in favor of an orientation of openness as mentioned earlier. Rather than reinforce such "wide-spread critical habits" that, according to Eve Sedgwick, are "perhaps by now nearly synonymous with criticism itself," this collection seeks to explore various other ways of reading that exist alongside, working with and against, more suspicious scholarly orientations.[19] Our goal here is not to evaluate the history of suspicious reading within modernist studies, nor is it to usher in a new, singular interpretive mode that feminist modernist scholars should employ. Rather, by including a diverse selection of reading practices and interpretive postures, by placing more traditional critical essays alongside theoretical think pieces, we hope to challenge the dominance of suspicious reading, illustrating its position as *one mode among many* that feminist modernist scholars utilize in their literary-political projects. And this is the hallmark of an orientation of openness: instead of reinforcing the paranoid approach Sedgwick questions, we champion a robust reading practice that invites and entertains various interpretative modalities, employing both proximity and distance, both depth and surface, to leverage the metaphors populating the discourse of criticism and theory today. Such an orientation of openness is eager and curious, it advocates and imagines, it believes in and engages with. It encourages us to entertain other ways of reading, other stances, postures, and moods.[20]

Ironically, these new ways of reading, stances, postures, and moods rely on what has been characterized as both the most traditional and hierarchical of tools: close reading. Dressed in the clothes of New Criticism, close reading had promised to reveal the worthiest of writing, for if we, as readers, pay close enough attention, scrutinize the rhythms and nuances carefully enough, the aesthetic and transcendental elements—the "richness" of great literature—would rise to the surface, emerging from the mundanity in which lesser literature is mired. Yet it is this very "richness," as Heather Love explains, that is deeply embedded in concepts of privilege.

Love notes that "there is perhaps no term that carries more value in the humanities than 'rich,'" whereas literary richness demands "the figure of the privileged messenger or interpreter" to mine the "complexity and polyvalence" of a text, revealing the "warmth and depth of experience" secreted within its pages.[21] Literary richness, in this sense, requires that a superior reader be actively engaged in the hermeneutics of suspicion. However, Love argues that instead of seeking only to unearth through close reading the secrets hidden deep in the text, scholars might also attend to what is in plain sight, leveraging description and summary as tools of analysis.

Heather Love's advocacy for "close attention" foregrounds description over interpretation in an effort to disrupt the value system embedded in the concept of "richness" as it emerged from New Critical practices. As a queer theorist, Love is quite aware that New Critical ways of reading are the product of certain scholars (white, cisgender, male) during a particular cultural moment (pre– and post–World War II) when English Departments were building institutional prominence among the sciences and social sciences. For the New Critics, the canon of great literature was constituted primarily by works written by heterosexual, cisgender, white men whose class or social status positioned them as cultural arbiters. Consequently, to associate close reading with New Critical practices is to imbue it with not only a suspicious approach to texts but also a suspicious—and thus exclusionary—approach to writers that do not fit the traditional patriarchal archetype of the author. Not surprisingly, New Critical close reading inevitably produced what Jane Gallop calls a "rather restricted canon of traditional literature, almost exclusively written by men of European descent."[22] Close reading has often reinforced the same tired conclusion that Sandra Gilbert and Susan Gubar made famous many years ago, "the patriarchal notion that the writer 'fathers' his text just as God fathered the world."[23] And although, thanks to decades of feminist scholarship, the reign of the author-as-father archetype has been dismantled, this long-dominant conception has shaped the gender politics of literary studies, broadly, and of modernism, particularly.

Close reading, however, can be adapted to new purposes; it need not rely on suspicion to reveal the interfaces, correspondences, and positions of relief or contrast that become visible when we think about literary forms. Levine offers a revisioning of close reading when she looks beyond the horizon of the book into the sociopolitical contexts that produced it (in the past) and that frame it (in the present). She argues that "tracking shapes and arrangements" that are not confined to the literary text involves "a kind of close reading, a careful attention to the forms that organize texts, bodies, and institutions." Such a practice would seek out "pattern over meaning, the intricacy of relations over interpretive depth." Levine advocates that it is time to build on what "literary critics have traditionally done best—reading for complex interrelationships and multiple, overlapping arrangements." She proclaims that we must "*export* those practices, to take our traditional skills to new objects—the social structures and institutions that are among the most crucial sites of political efficacy."[24]

Caroline Levine's recalibration of close reading is so compelling because of her willingness to move beyond canonicity—a New Critical concept if there ever was one—and recognize the political power of unexpected and often overlooked alliances, affiliations, and networks. Moreover, these connections or nodes of overlap need not be exclusively text-based. Close reading requires us to read not only the text but also the text in relation to the sociopolitical realities it shapes and reflects. In this manner, feminist modernist scholars are validated in their project of reclamation and revision, a project dependent upon close examination of the material conditions of women writers in the first half of the twentieth century. And feminist modernist scholars are encouraged to continue their work, expanding it to include an examination of the material conditions of feminist modernist scholarship in the early twenty-first century.

Therefore, it is not surprising that this volume includes more than traditional close readings of women-authored texts. Our orientation of openness is represented in the myriad of subjects and themes addressed: patronage, competition, and mentorship; portability, secondhand clothing, and self-fashioning, to name a few. Generational divides are traversed and literary categories questioned. What might be read as singular—an author as icon, a text as canonical—is presented as constituent of a broader literary landscape. Additionally, several essays in this volume place our work as feminist modernist scholars today in direct conversation with the authors and texts under examination, thus illuminating the extra-textual, political potential of close reading. The volume also addresses the sociopolitical realities of the academy—graduate school curriculums, publishing, promotion and tenure—that feminist modernist scholars negotiate. We want to encourage feminist modernist scholars to recognize the formal limitations of the story as it stands—and has stood for so long—and seek out fresh affordances and affiliations, revealing modernism and women modernist anew.

Emily Ridge explores such fresh affordances in the first essay of the collection, "Writing Modernist Women: Toward a Poetics of Insubstantiality." Ridge looks closely at the trope of portability in modernist literature and extols the insubstantiality that portability grants women writers. In so doing, Ridge offers an alternative to the discourse of weightiness that undergirds the politics of canonicity. Which authors are *substantial* enough to be included in the canon? Which women writers deserve to be given their due *weight* in discussions of canonicity? Similarly, Celia Marshik advocates for an object studies approach to modernist literature in service of repositioning canonical and non-canonical texts. "Modernism and Middlebrow through the Eyes of Object Studies" is the first of several theoretical think pieces included in this volume. Rather than taking as her subject a particular text, trope, or writer, Marshik reflects on her own process of employing object studies, examining the tools it provides, the challenges it poses, and the discoveries it makes possible. Jane Garrity, in "The Haunting of Mary Hutchinson," follows suit, investigating the conflation of Mary Hutchinson's much-admired fashion sense with her writing. An unfortunate conflation according to Garrity, who argues that it amplified a conservative conception of femininity derived from gendered assumptions about artificiality and adornment. A complement to both Ridge's and Marshik's analysis, Garrity engages questions of substance and style, attending to the way the assessment of women's adorned bodies, evaluated through patriarchal rubrics, ultimately worked against their literary contributions, as in the case of Mary Hutchinson, forcing them to haunt, instead of headline, our histories of modernism.

In "Peggy Guggenheim's and Bryher's Investment: How Financial Speculation Created a Female Modernist Tradition," Julie Vandivere takes a cue from Levine's work by examining networks of capitalist exchange and investment that influenced modernist modes of patronage. Vandivere's essay is motivated by the question: who pays for art that is deliberately unmarketable? Modernist literature, unlike its Victorian predecessor, wore its unmarketability as a badge of honor, and although this posture arguably increased the status of male-authored modernism, it often acted as a hindrance to women writers who were trying not only to make their artistic mark but also to make a living in a patriarchal literary arena. By tracing the practices of patronage of Bryher and Peggy Guggenheim, Vandivere offers a way to view modernist affiliations as both (vexed) feminist investments and (often risky) financial exchanges.

Allison Pease follows up Vandivere's essay—and anticipates Catherine W. Hollis's chapter on Emma Goldman—by drawing our attention to the division between major and minor authors in modernist studies. In her reflective analysis in "Bringing Women Together, in Theory," Pease examines not only hierarchies within modernist studies but also her own research process, suggesting that if we want a level playing field we might want to act as if the playing field is already level. For Pease, there is an exciting, equalizing potential in the convergence between feminist theory and feminist literary criticism, even if this convergence forces us to raze the foundations of modernist hierarchies—the very hierarchies with which feminist modernist scholars have been trying to ascend—and, to appropriate modernism's most misquoted catchphrase, "make it new."[25]

Newness is a theme in Catherine W. Hollis's chapter, "Emma Goldman among the Avant-Garde." Hollis engages with themes central to the field's understanding of modernism: youth, newness, freshness, and provocativeness. For Hollis, these aspects of modernism manifest in and come to bear upon intergenerational relationships among women, highlighting a particularly feminist lens through which to read networks of modernist production among women. Melissa Bradshaw's essay, "Fantasies of Belonging, Fears of Precarity," complements Hollis's exploration of Emma Goldman's vexed but fruitful relationships with younger, more modernist women by attending to the multifaceted gender politics leveraged by women writers vying for position within male-dominated literary networks. Although Amy Lowell and Edith Sitwell take center stage in Bradshaw's analysis, her work is enriched by a meta-reflection that recognizes our complicity in crafting the narratives that constitute modernist studies. Constructive and hopeful, Bradshaw models the kind of self-reflection that we deem necessary for feminist modernist studies not only to survive but also to thrive.

In order for academics to meet and exceed the challenges posed by our current sociopolitical realities—shrinking budgets in the humanities, the importance of interdisciplinary research, the inescapable presence of a consumerist discourse to describe higher education—scholars must examine both our complicity in the problems and our contribution to the solutions. For feminist modernist scholars, this means reimagining the stories we tell about modernism. In "Virginia Woolf and Mina Loy: Modernist Affiliations," Erica Gene Delsandro focuses on two modernist women writers who are rarely addressed in tandem and, by bringing them together, proposes alternative ways of reading that privilege affiliations and resonances. In so doing, Delsandro advocates for more inclusive and expansive reading practices that invite readers—scholars and students alike—to remake modernism in their scholarship and in their classrooms.

Our volume concludes with Madelyn Detloff's essay, "Iconic Shade . . . and Other Professional Hazards of Woolf Scholarship." Detloff examines the effects of canonicity on feminist modernist scholarship and the material realities of higher education in an era of neoliberal instrumentalization. Employing Virginia Woolf as an example, Detloff weighs the advantages and disadvantages of the author's unassailable position in the modernist canon, ultimately advocating that we look to Woolf as a canon maker and a canon breaker, learning from her missteps and incorporating her successful strategies into our own feminist toolbox.

The essays in this collection reveal a rich constellation of female affiliations—intellectual, artistic, scholarly, and otherwise—necessary for the continued efficacy of modernist studies. In other words, what this collection hopes to do is nothing short of revising the story we tell about modernism by reimagining how we tell it. Such a close reading of unconventionally grouped objects, texts, people, and approaches offers us a way to revise: a practice not unfamiliar to feminist studies. Ultimately, a return to the revisionary ethos of feminism's earlier academic incarnation might benefit modernist studies at this moment. Revision, to quote Adrienne Rich's 1971 Modern Language Association presentation, is "the act of looking back, of seeing with fresh eyes, of entering an old text from a new critical direction."[26] And in addition to looking back onto old texts and old narratives of modernism, our contributors would add, we must also look forward to a future in which feminist modernist studies flourishes, ensuring a field that is dynamic, robust, and inclusive.

Adopting Rich's peroration to our present moment, Felski proposes a series of verbs—curating, conveying, criticizing, composing—to characterize what the humanities do in the early twenty-first century, a period in which humanistic study, as much as feminist study, finds its purpose and contribution under scrutiny.[27] What is at stake is nothing less than the survival of feminist modernist studies. Again, as Rich reminds us, revision "is for woman more than a chapter in cultural history"; it is "an act of survival."[28] Nearly fifty years after Rich's literary-feminist manifesto and long after feminism's second wave has ebbed, feminist modernist scholars have proven their success at surviving by engaging various interpretative practices, at times suspicious and at times open, at times close and at times distant, championing ways of reading that give meaning not only to our scholarship but also to our lives and experiences, our histories and futures.

Notes

1. Seshagiri, "Mind the Gap!," 3 (emphasis mine). In contextualizing the special online edition of *Modernism/modernity* dedicated to feminist modernist studies, Seshagiri reveals that during its twenty years the journal has never dedicated an issue to a single modernist woman writer nor to modernist women writers as a group. Although feminist scholarship might be contained within specific issues, "the artists, critics, and philosophers named for intellectual colloquy . . . are all Anglo-European men. There are no women" (7). The aporia, Seshagiri's word, between women's role in creating modernism and their absence in modernist studies, is the "gap" that feminist modernist scholars must mind (3). Feminism, she declares, "cannot afford complacency" (4).

2. The concept of a new modernist studies was circulating in the 1990s, coalescing in the formation of the Modernist Studies Association (MSA) in 1998 and its attendant conference and journal (*Modernism/modernity*). Perhaps the most well-known portrayal of this shift in scholarly and institutional direction was outlined (retrospectively) by Douglas Mao and Rebecca Walkowitz in their 2008 *PMLA* article, "The New Modernist Studies." In this essay, they discuss the "invention" of the MSA and characterize modernist studies since then under the rubric of "expansion" (737). Since the emergence of new modernist studies, the field certainly has expanded in many directions: transnational, cosmopolitan, postcolonial, and queer are all adjectives now commonly preceding modernism. Similarly, attention to objects and affect—just to name a few recent scholarly touchstones—have been providing scholars with fresh methodological approaches to modernist texts. And yet, despite all this expansion—and a rich period of recovery work by feminist scholars—women modernists, with a few exceptions, remain understudied and undervalued. The present volume seeks not only to add another study to the still-too-short list of predecessors that have focused on women writers but also to read across and against diversities of sexuality, ability, class, and race; age and ideological differences; major and minor author distinctions. In this context, it is imperative to acknowledge directly where we fall shortest of our goals, that is,

in diversity across race. As mentioned above, feminism does not benefit from complacency. Those of us involved in this collection extend our gratitude to Holly Laird for helping us articulate this sentiment so clearly.

3. Detloff, "Strong-Armed Sisyphe," *Feminist Modernist Studies* 1, nos. 1–2 (2018): 36. The first edition of *FMS* appeared in 2018. The inaugural editor, Cassandra Laity, writes in her introduction, "Toward Feminist Modernisms," that she "was told by a major press that *Feminist Modernist Studies* was 'not needed' and librarians would not 'know how to classify it.'" Such a response necessitates the question Laity rightfully raises: "how scholarship on modernism and feminism/gender/sexuality could be simultaneously unnecessary (e.g., already done, fully integrated into modernist studies) and not recognizable as a category of academic study?" This paradox is not new to feminist scholars of modernism who have frequently noted "that gender issues are either largely omitted, summarily added on, or—within feminist scholarship—subsumed under modernism's broader intellectual expansions" (1).

4. As Detloff elaborates:

Rolling a rock up a hill over and over again is frustrating, but it gives one strong arms. I know many women and other marginalized people who learn to keep the rock rolling with one arm while attending to daily business with the other. I don't mean to dismiss occasions when the weight of the rock is crushing, and I certainly don't mean to imply that the task is easy, merely that when one is fighting the same (or at least remarkably similar) battles over and again, the terrain—the slope of the hill, the heft of the rock—becomes familiar. ("Strong-Armed Sisyphe," 37)

5. Ibid., 39; Ahmed, *Willful Subjects*, 2.

6. In advocating generation, imagination, and renewal, we do not intend to neglect or reject the past. Rather, as feminist modernist scholars, we are keenly attuned to those who came before us and whose groundbreaking, field-shifting feminist interventions constitute the foundation upon which we stand: Sandra Gilbert and Susan Gubar's *Madwoman in the Attic*; Shari Benstock's *Women of the Left Bank*; Bonnie Kime Scott's *Gender of Modernism*; Mary Lynn Broe and Angela Ingram's *Women's Writing in Exile*; Carol Ascher, Louise DeSalvo, and Sara Ruddick's *Between Women*; Rita Felski's *The Gender of Modernity*; and many more. Their work and commitment resonate throughout this volume.

7. Halberstam, *Queer Art of Failure*, 6.

8. Felski, *Limits of Critique*, 20, 17.

9. As Susan Stanford Friedman reminds us in her response to Felski in the *PMLA* "Theories and Methodologies" section dedicated to *The Limits of Critique*, feminist studies, grouped with "interdisciplines of cultural studies," is under

examination as much as poststructuralist theory. Friedman, "Both/And," 344. However, what Felski attends to and Friedman affirms is that feminist studies negotiated suspicious reading with other reading postures, moods, and approaches. Other scholars in the "Theories and Methodologies" section, like Diana Fuss, articulate their reluctance to deprioritize critique in "a new age of what can only be called an outlandish indifference to truth," asserting the necessity to continue certain suspicious practices in the name of truth and social justice. Fuss, "But What about Love?," 353. Heather Love, perhaps, strikes a productive balance when she explains that "Felski argues that moving beyond critique is not a matter of moving beyond politics, but it is an attempt to articulate a political vision that does not rely on negativity." Love, "'Critique Is Ordinary,'" *PMLA* 132, no. 2 (March 2017): 369.

10. Halberstam, *Queer Art of Failure*, 16.

11. Seshagiri, "Mind the Gap!," 12.

12. The number of single-author monographs that take a female modernist as their subject stand to assure us that early feminist scholars succeeded in their goals; Woolf, H.D., and Stein, for example, now sit comfortably alongside James Joyce, T. S. Eliot, and E. M. Forster in the modernist pantheon. Thanks to the pioneering work of scholars like Shari Benstock, Bonnie Kime Scott, and Marianne DeKoven (among others), modernist studies is certainly more truthful in its accounting of who was making modernism.

13. Jane Garrity's "Modernist Women's Writing" argues that feminist modernist scholars today should not be satisfied with the professional status quo in which only a select few modernist women writers are included in the books, articles, and syllabi that constitute modernist studies, despite the optimism that accompanied Douglas Mao's and Rebecca Walkowitz's declaration in 2008 that we are firmly in the age of new modernist studies. Moreover, Garrity addresses the question of the category "women writers" in her essay, and we refer readers to her compelling argument for the continued use of the gendered category as this collection shares and advocates the perspective articulated within while also validating the important work of deconstruction and queer studies in shining a critical light on the limitations of the concept of woman. Garrity, "Modernist Women's Writing," 15–29.

14. Foucault is one such thinker. Levine shares Foucault's emphasis on "the arrangements that structure everyday experience" (*Forms*, xiii). However, whereas Foucault felt that the arrangements converged into large and encompassing power structures, Levine feels that they are also constantly creating contradicting and colliding forms of infinite variety and shape. Instead of only seeking to indict and disrupt structures, feminist modernist scholars, following Levine, should pay close attention to the way forms affiliate and reorient, thus seeking

their affordances. In this manner, scholars in this volume take on an approach that privileges discovery, open to perceiving what other imaginative and powerful forms emerge. Ultimately, we might argue that Levine's project differs from Foucault's in its optimism.

15. A binary is structured by two elements in a three-part relationship to each other: oppositional, interdependent, and hierarchical.

16. Levine, *Forms*, 6–7.

17. Levine references the work of Bruno Latour numerous times in her text and notes. She cites Latour's passing suggestion that "fiction writers often do a better job than sociologists at capturing social relations because they are free to experiment, offering a 'vast playground to rehearse accounts of what makes us act'" (*Forms*, 19). With such a sympathetic perspective on fiction, Latour, a primary developer of actor-network theory, lends himself to Levine's project, which reimagines more traditional literary formalism with attention to network theory in its various manifestations. As Levine explains: "Networks are useful, Bruno Latour suggests, because they allow us to refuse metaphysical assumptions about causality in favor of observing linkages between objects, bodies, and discourses. . . . By tracing the actual and possible paths that forms follow, we can practice a large-scale cultural studies method that starts not by presuming causality, but rather by attending to specific patterns of contact between forms" (113).

18. Beal claims that the "dialectic of fragment and totality" is modernism's most "durable feature." For Beal, this dialectic is an "open tension" and is the very "cultural logic of modernism." Furthermore, the network, "the figure by which fragment and whole are mediated," becomes a vehicle for "imagining new models of community." See *Networks of Modernism*, 3.

19. Sedgwick, "Paranoid Reading and Reparative Reading, or, You're So Paranoid, You Probably Think This Essay Is About You," in *Touching Feeling*, 124. Sedgwick's essay ushered in a range of assessments that examine dominant literary critical practices, such as Stephen Best and Sharon Marcus's special issue of *Representations*, "Reading 'The Way We Read Now'" in 2009.

20. Felski, paraphrasing Yves Citton, anticipates "the emergence of another regime of interpretation: one that is willing to recognize the potential of literature and art to create new imaginaries rather than just denounce the mystifying illusions." Felski, *Limits of Critique*, 187.

21. Love, "Close but not Deep," 371, 373, 371.

22. Gallop, "Ethics of Reading," 13. Gallop revisits the practice of close reading in her essay, "The Historicization of Literary Studies and the Fate of Close Reading," but whereas Love seeks to replace critique's dependence on close reading with the practice of close attention, Gallop encourages us to return to the "most valuable thing English ever had to offer," that which "transformed us from

cultured gentleman into a profession: close reading." Gallop, "Historicization of Literary Studies," 183. For Gallop, close reading is not unlike Love's close attention or surface reading as advocated by Best and Marcus in their "Surface Reading: An Introduction," from the special issue of *Representations* mentioned above.

23. Gilbert and Gubar, *Madwoman in the Attic*, 4.

24. Levine, *Forms*, 23.

25. The phrase "make it new" is popularly employed as the quintessential modernist catchphrase, and credit is regularly given to Ezra Pound for its articulation. And yet, as Michael North reveals in his book *Novelty: A History of the New*, Pound's relationship to this phrase is one mediated by (mis)translation and has very little to do with the modernist literary milieu in which he was a prominent impresario. An excerpt from North's book detailing the phrase's provenance can be found online in *Guernica* (https://www.guernicamag.com/the-making-of-making-it-new/).

26. Rich, "When We Dead Awaken," 35. This essay was first published in 1972 in *College English*. Although representative of second wave feminism and early feminist trends in literary criticism, Rich's employment of revision as a feminist strategy, methodology, and reading practice finds resonance with our current moment in the academy in regard to the position and function of feminist approaches. In terms of modernist studies, our evocation of Rich does not seek to return scholars to a pre-queer studies, pre-*Gender Trouble* era, but rather aims to highlight the dynamic nature of feminism, emphasizing its ability to respond robustly to the changing forms of patriarchal dominance.

27. Felski, introduction to *New Literary History*, 216. Felski introduces the special issue of *New Literary History* dedicated to Bruno Latour's work, and her theorization of "composition" derives from Latour's manifesto "An Attempt at a 'Compositionist Manifesto,'" published in *New Literary History* in 2010.

28. Rich, "When We Dead Awaken," 35.

Works Cited

Ahmed, Sara. *Willful Subjects*. Durham, NC: Duke University Press, 2014.

Beal, Wesley. *Networks of Modernism: Reorganizing American Narrative*. Iowa City: University of Iowa Press, 2015.

Best, Stephen, and Sharon Marcus. "Surface Reading: An Introduction." *Representations* 108 (2009): 1–21.

Detloff, Madelyn. "Strong-Armed Sisyphe: Feminist Queer Modernism Again . . . Again." *Feminist Modernist Studies* 1, nos. 1–2 (2018): 36–43.

Felski, Rita. *The Limits of Critique*. Chicago: University of Chicago Press, 2015.

———. Introduction to *New Literary History* 47, nos. 2–3 (Spring–Summer 2016): 215–29.

Friedman, Susan Stanford. "Both/And: Critique and Discovery in the Humanities." *PMLA* 132, no. 2 (March 2017): 344–51.

Fuss, Diana. "But What about Love?" *PMLA* 132, no. 2 (March 2017): 352–55.

Gallop, Jane. "The Ethics of Reading: Close Encounters." *Journal of Curriculum Theorizing* (Fall 2000): 7–17.

———. "The Historicization of Literary Studies and the Fate of Close Reading." *Profession* (2007): 181–86.

Garrity, Jane. "Modernist Women's Writing: Beyond the Threshold of Obsolescence." *Literature Compass* 10, no. 1 (2013): 15–29.

Gilbert, Sandra M., and Susan Gubar. *The Madwoman in the Attic: The Woman Writer and the Nineteenth-Century Literary Imagination*. 2nd ed. New Haven: Yale University Press, 2000.

Halberstam, Jack (Judith). *The Queer Art of Failure*. Durham, NC: Duke University Press, 2011.

Laity, Cassandra. "Editor's Introduction: Toward Feminist Modernisms." *Feminist Modernist Studies* 1, nos. 1–2 (2018): 1–7.

Levine, Caroline. *Forms: Whole, Rhythm, Hierarchy, Network*. Princeton: Princeton University Press, 2015.

Love, Heather. "Close but not Deep: Literary Ethics and the Descriptive Turn." *New Literary History* 41, no. 2 (2010): 371–91.

———. "'Critique Is Ordinary.'" *PMLA* 132, no. 2 (March 2017): 364–70.

Mao, Douglas, and Rebecca L. Walkowitz. "The New Modernist Studies." *PMLA* 123, no. 3 (2008): 737–48.

North, Michael. *Novelty: A History of the New*. Chicago: University of Chicago Press, 2013.

Rich, Adrienne. "When We Dead Awaken: Writing as Re-Vision." In *On Lies, Secrets, and Silence: Selected Prose 1966–1978*, 33–49. New York: W. W. Norton, 1979.

Sedgwick, Eve. *Touching Feeling: Affect, Pedagogy, Performativity*. Durham, NC: Duke University Press, 2003.

Seshagiri, Urmila. "Mind the Gap!: Modernism and Feminist Praxis." *Modernism/ modernity* 2, no. 2 (2017).

Writing Modernist Women

Toward a Poetics of Insubstantiality

EMILY RIDGE

> [Mary Carmichael] had a sensibility that was very wide, eager and free. . . .
> It ranged, too, very subtly and curiously, amongst almost unknown or unre-
> corded things; it lighted on small things and showed that perhaps they were not
> small after all.
>
> (Virginia Woolf, *A Room of One's Own*)

Critical discussions of the modernist canon often turn around questions
of substantiality; which writers should, for example, be deemed weighty
enough for inclusion in this esteemed category? Feminist endeavors to
rethink modernist hierarchies have just as often involved claiming due
weight for neglected female writers.[1] However, this essay will take a different tack by claiming that the very terminology employed to establish such
hierarchies of value was, in fact, critiqued by modernist women writers
themselves during the period in question; such writers were concerned
with interrogating less the failure to view women's writing as substantial
enough in itself than the intuitive association of value with the idea of
substance, enacting a subversive turn toward the insubstantial as a way of
questioning our understanding of value itself. To borrow Susan Stewart's
terms, the "miniature," evocative of interior and subjective "space and
time," was given precedence in these works over the "gigantic," evocative
of the "abstract authority of the state and the collective, public life," in
ways that "interrupt[ed] the everyday hierarchical organization of detail."[2]

Such an interruption is, indeed, pointedly enacted in the most well-known feminist treatise of that era, Virginia Woolf's *A Room of One's Own* (1929), in which a gendered politics of scale is implicitly delineated. From the outset, Woolf offers up the instigating idea for her extended polemic in miniature terms: "Alas, laid on the grass, how small, how insignificant this thought of mine looked; the sort of fish that a good fisherman puts back into the water so that it may grow fatter and be one day worth cooking and eating" (7). Like her imagined incarnation of the contemporary woman writer, Mary Carmichael, Woolf lights, again and again, on "small things" in association with female creative practice (92). She goes on to liken, for example, the underencouraged woman writer to the "furtive, timid and small" counterpart of a "glossy, bold and big" experimental rat, while novels written by female novelists who attempted to defer to a masculine system of values are scattered in the manner of "small pock-marked apples in an orchard, about the second-hand bookshops of London" (54, 75). A similar descriptive logic informs *Three Guineas* (1938) a decade later, in which Woolf apologizes for the "smallness of the contribution" in the closing paragraph (367). In both texts, the alleged "small size" of the female brain in established scientific discourse is also highlighted.[3]

Such a logic works in marked contrast to her descriptive renderings of masculine constructs. Here, the scale shifts. As the narrator's small and insignificant thought lands on the grass of an Oxbridge bank in *A Room of One's Own*, it is surrounded by buildings, constructed by and for men, described as "magnificent" and "massive" (10, 11). The link between scale and gender is consolidated more firmly when the narrator visits the British Museum, the celebrated dome of which becomes a "huge bald forehead" containing what is later pronounced as the "enormous body of masculine opinion to the effect that nothing could be expected of women intellectually" (28, 55).

Far from damning her own work and those works of other women writers with faint praise in conforming to such a scale, Woolf subjects the scale itself to question in ways that conflict in terms of purpose and motivation. On the one hand, she interrogates its accuracy. A scale, in allowing for expanding and diminishing degrees, is made to be distorted. "Women have served all these centuries as looking-glasses," she notes, "possessing the magic and delicious power of reflecting the figure of man at twice its natural size" (37). Men's achievements, it is implied, are not as "enormous" as they might think and women's, by extension, more substantial or might very well become just as substantial as men's under the right circumstances. Accordingly, though Mary Carmichael might range with curiosity "amongst almost unknown or unrecorded things," as observed in the above epigraph, Woolf goes on to caution that "no abundance of sensation or fineness of perception would avail unless she could build up out of the fleeting and the personal the lasting edifice which remains unthrown" (92). Here, the woman writer is urged to aspire to the imposing architectural proportions of the male writer, if in her own distinct style, in order to show that the "small things . . . were not small after all." Yet, on the other hand, and more subtly, the same writer is urged to reconsider the value system embedded within such a scale. This endeavor requires not the enlargement of small things, an act equally vulnerable to the charge of distortion, but a new understanding of the alternative power of the insubstantial.

Indeed, what emerges from Woolf's essay, above all, is the cumulative impression that insubstantiality has its own distinct advantages. The narrator's instigating thought is distinguished by its very smallness and insignificance, and these qualities make it difficult to pin down, due both to its miniature aspect and its concentrated energy. Far from being allotted the monumental stature perceived in the surrounding Oxbridge infrastructure, this original thought, which, as Woolf suggests, provides the key to the essay as a whole, is defined by discretion rather than display, as well as a kind of slippery dynamism:

> I will not trouble you with that thought now, though if you look carefully you may find it for yourselves in the course of what I am going to say.
>
> But however small it was, it had, nevertheless, the mysterious property of its kind—put back into the mind, it became at once very exciting, and important; and as it darted and sank, and flashed hither and thither, set up such a wash and tumult of ideas that it was impossible to sit still. (7)

This energy, as described, is passed to the narrator who is prompted to walk "with extreme rapidity across a grass plot" only to encounter a Beadle who reminds her that access to the plot in question is reserved for Fellows and Scholars only (7). Not long after, she is refused entry at the doors of a "famous library," a refusal that likewise sets her in motion in order to pass the time before lunch (10).

The essay is, in fact, far more mobile in emphasis than the title would have us believe, as Rachel Bowlby points out:

> It might seem outlandish to think of *A Room of One's Own*, which is all about the importance of an inside, personal space for the woman writer, as having any connection with the links between women, walking and writing in Woolf's work. Yet the book is structured throughout by an imaginary ramble.[4]

This imaginary ramble, unbounded by aims and structures and thus transgressive in its course, promises insights beyond the imposing yet rigid scope of the library that "sleeps complacently and will, so far as [Woolf is] concerned, so sleep forever" (*Room,* 10). "What idea it had been which had sent me so audaciously trespassing," she asks herself after her encounter with the Beadle, "I could not now remember" (8). It is the very insubstantial nature of this originary idea that confers both an audacious mobility and elusiveness to the unfolding discussion, alerting the reader to the complacency and potential deficiencies of a more macroscopic vision.

Virginia Woolf here outlines a poetics of insubstantiality that, as I argue, comes to inform modern women's writing on multiple levels from the late nineteenth century. This disruptive fixation on insubstantiality forms part of a wider shift toward portability during this period that saw, as Zygmunt Bauman has described in *Liquid Modernity,* "a remarkable reversal of the millennia-long tradition" of cherishing durability in favor of "the smaller, the lighter, the more portable" (14, 13). Women were precursors to men in steering such a reversal, having long been forced to cherish their portable possessions without access to a more durable stake in society.[5] Before it became a choice worth making, they were portable by default, and certain "new" women learned to use this status to their advantage.

The fixation on insubstantial elements, particularly in characterizing the modern female subject, can also be aligned with a broader aesthetic move away from realistic forms that served to represent, as Stewart discusses, not everyday life but "its hierarchization of information."[6] It is an alignment that gives credence to Gail Cunningham's assertion of the complex interconnections between the "emancipation of women and the emancipation of the English novel."[7] Indeed, the emergence of modernist writing was driven by the same kind of anti-hierarchical impetus that prompted women to question the structures that framed their experiences, both lived and represented, as well as the types of knowledge and discourse that were privileged at the expense of others.

However, such interconnections have often been obscured by the prevalent association of modernism with the production of what Paul K. Saint-Amour has recently caricatured as a kind of "muscular idol smashing and warrior masculinity."[8] If such a warrior masculinity equally enacted a revolt against realism's hierarchization of information, it staged such a revolt in gigantic terms, making monumental claims about its own obliteration of the monumental structures of the past. In describing, by contrast, a "weak modernism," Saint-Amour sets out to complicate such "masculine-gendered" constructions, with a specific aim in mind: "to leave off theorizing weakness as a failure, absence, or function of strength and instead to theorize *from* weakness as a condition endowed with traits and possibilities of its own" (438, 439). This conception of "weak modernism" forms part, as Saint-Amour acknowledges, of a new wave of "modest" criticism, deriving from work in queer, gender, and disability studies (439).

The following essay undertakes a similar line of inquiry. Focusing on a selection of female protagonists in works by writers as diverse as Dorothy Richardson, Cicely Hamilton, Edith Wharton, and Jean Rhys, among others, the essay will trace the development of a shared poetics of insubstantiality in relation to the evolution of modern female subjectivity in literature from early to high modernism. In other words, it will show that ideas, images, and objects pertaining to the insubstantial were foregrounded in terms of their active potential rather than their reductiveness as a way of exposing and undercutting, as opposed to consolidating, an existing value system.

Smallness

Virginia Woolf's attention to smallness, in material as much as conceptual terms, was, in part, a reaction to a perceptible Victorian infatuation with greatness. "I hate great men," Ralph Denham declares in an oft-cited passage from *Night and Day* (1919), pursuing the point further: "The worship of greatness in the nineteenth century seems to me to explain the worthlessness of that generation" (12). This was far from being an isolated instance of critique, and such sentiments recur, in remarkably similar terms, in women's writing at this time. In the very same year, Miriam Henderson can be found to articulate a comparable dismissal in *The Tunnel* (1919), the fourth installment of Dorothy Richardson's novel sequence *Pilgrimage* (1915–1967), in response to a book recommendation:

> "Oh, how interesting," she said insincerely when she had read *Great Thoughts from Great Lives* on the cover. . . . I ought to have said I don't like extracts. "Lives of great men all remind us We can make our lives sublime," she read aloud under her breath from the first page. . . . I ought to go. I can't enter into this. . . . I hate "great men," I think. (2: 283)

Not long after, May Sinclair's *The Life and Death of Harriett Frean* (1922), sets out to painstakingly illustrate that the worship of great men could have the very opposite of a "sublime" effect. The eponymous Harriett is shown to be steeped in a patriarchal cult of greatness from a young age: "Sometimes she or her mother read aloud, Mrs. Browning or Charles Dickens; or the biography of some Great Man, sitting there in the velvet-curtained room or out on the lawn under the cedar tree" (39). This form of worship, it is implied, contributes to her destructive and long-drawn-out sacrifice to an outdated Victorian ideology of feminine self-denial over the course of the novel.

Like Woolf, both Richardson and Sinclair respond by shifting attention to the other end of the scale. Miriam's instinctual recoil from the idea of the "great" man goes hand in hand with her own endeavor to represent what she later calls, in *Deadlock* (1921), the "small existence of single lives."[9] It is one such single life that she portrays in the form of Miriam Henderson, and she makes no pretence of attributing "greatness" to Miriam's story. On the contrary, *Pilgrimage* is an exploration of what it means to be small, deliberately presenting, as such, an *anti*-great life. The same is true of Sinclair. She is careful to spotlight Harriett's infantile smallness as her defining characteristic on her deathbed in the closing paragraphs of the novel: "She was lying at the bottom of her white-curtained nursery cot. She felt weak and diminished, small, like a very little child."[10] Even more than *Pilgrimage*, *The Life and Death of Harriett Frean* forms an insubstantial riposte to those weighty biographical testaments to masculine achievement; the book, in itself, is slight in size, especially in comparison to Richardson's. An important distinction must be made between Sinclair and Richardson in this respect. Sinclair's critique of masculine constructions of greatness focuses on the ensuing contraction of prospects for women, and Harriett's progression to an ultimate state of childlike negligibility, while forming the subject of the book, is conceived as a regrettable outcome. Richardson, however, asks how and why smallness came to be a pejorative category. The very length of *Pilgrimage* suggests that Richardson's concern is to demonstrate, in a very hands-on way, that the small things, to reinvoke Woolf, are not small after all. As a composite piece, it seems to preemptively confirm Gaston Bachelard's phenomenological observation that "one of the powers of attraction of smallness lies in the fact that large things can issue from small ones."[11]

Dorothy Richardson also shows, on occasion, an interest in smallness of the Sinclair variety, but only insofar as this serves her ultimate aim of dismantling constructions of greatness. Even when Miriam experiences frustration when confronted with the spectacle of "small and cringing" women (women not unlike Harriett Frean), it is an inquisitive frustration: "Who made them so small and cheated and for all their smiles so angry?" (*Pilgrimage,* 1: 436). She seeks to understand these perceived attributes, in part, as a means of exposing those men who "[know] nothing of the contrast between the small figure and the big arrogance" (3: 456). H. G. Wells, in the long-acknowledged guise of Hypo G. Wilson in *Pilgrimage,* is the subject of one such exposure.[12] Miriam directly applies the designation "great man" to Hypo, as she prepares to meet him along with his wife, Alma, for the first time in *The Tunnel*. This meeting immediately alerts Miriam to the distortions of scale that accompany perceptions of greatness, finding that her expectations dwarf the actuality of the man: "That extraordinary ending of fear of the great man at the station. Alma and the little fair square man not much taller than herself, looking like a grocer's assistant" (2: 110). Indeed, Miriam's eventual refusal of Hypo's pervading influence signals the triumph of one "small figure" over one "great man," while *Pilgrimage* itself, in purporting to resist dominant modes of "masculine realism," as Richardson would go on to explain in a 1938 foreword (1: 9–12), was "explicitly developed," in the words of Elisabeth Bronfen, "in opposition to the novels of H. G. Wells" (1: 9).[13]

Yet, Wells's own work shows that he was well attuned to the distinctive capability of the "small figure" in contrast to the "big arrogance," a capability that was to be feared as much as disparaged. His 1909 novel, *Ann Veronica,* concerning the feminist rebellion of its eponymous heroine, offers a striking visualization of this contrast, using unsettlingly combative terms of representation:

> Were I a painter of subject pictures, I would exhaust all my skill in proportion and perspective and atmosphere upon the august seat of empire, I would present it grey and dignified and immense and respectable beyond any mere verbal description, and then in vivid black and very small, I would put in those valiantly impertinent vans, squatting at the base of its altitudes and pouring out a swift straggling rush of ominous little black objects, minute figures of determined women at war with the universe.
>
> Ann Veronica was in their very forefront. (180)

Although the novel as a whole outwardly manifests sympathy toward Ann Veronica's struggle, the terms in which that struggle is described (of which the above passage is but one example) disclose ambivalence. While the "august seat of empire" exceeds "mere verbal description" in its given pre-eminence, those "minute figures" of female resistance are mired, for Wells, in a sort of descriptive malaise. It is as if Wells cannot make up his mind as to whether those miniature figures should be viewed with admiration or condescension. They are characterized as valiant and "determined" yet "impertinent." They are "vivid" and "ominous" in the threat that they pose yet their "squatting" postures and "straggling" ant-like movements point to an animalesque waywardness and inconsequentiality that is no match for the impervious might of the "universe." Indeed, the end of the novel sees Ann Veronica's ultimate withdrawal from this struggle as she settles down to a family life that seems to encapsulate the greyness, dignity, immensity, and respectability she originally rose up against, "hedged about with discretions—and all this furniture—and successes!" (257). The ending of the novel aside, this earlier subject picture nonetheless implies a growing awareness and apprehension as to the potential impact of small-scale affronts to the existing power structure at this time.

Such a power structure was predicated on a disproportionality of wealth. This is a point that remains unexpressed in any direct way in the Wells passage, but it is acutely realized by Woolf in envisaging the "foundation of gold and silver" upholding the Oxbridge architecture in all its splendor in *A Room of One's Own* and emphasized by Richardson in detailing Miriam's financial insecurity in pursuing her deliberately anti-great course of independent adventure.[14] The immense advantage of that "august seat of empire" over those little black figures in *Ann Veronica* is, above all, a function of proprietorial distribution and scope. It is the appropriation of property and land on a grand scale that makes an empire what it is, and, by extension, it is the withholding of proprietorial power that fosters the small-scale guerrilla style actions that Wells imagines.

This facet of the contrast between greatness and smallness is exposed most strongly when male characters are shown to fear, not the potential implications of minute rebellious upsurges, but the prospect of themselves becoming "small." In *The Life and Death of Harriett Frean*, for example, Harriett's mother expresses concern for a family friend who has, like their own family, lost a great deal of his wealth and thus the trappings that go with it: "He can't be happy without his big house and his carriages and his horses. He'll feel so small and unimportant" (86). The inference is clear: proprietorial loss confers the stigma of smallness in this scheme, a stigma to be avoided where possible.

However, the stigma of proprietorial smallness is also shown to confer a new perspective. An anxiety similar to that expressed by Harriett's mother is articulated by a central male protagonist, Captain Bretherton, in an earlier play by feminist playwright Cicely Hamilton, *Diana of Dobson's* (1908), a play which sets out to expose the sexual double standards that underlie pecuniary evaluations of worth: "Hang it all, it makes a man feel so small when he realizes that he hasn't any market value at all" (138). The play narrates the events that transpire from the sudden good fortune of a poorly paid shop worker, Diana Massingberd. Upon inheriting a £300 legacy from an aunt, she makes the decision to live large for a single month, indulging in the short-term fantasy of a luxurious lifestyle rather than adopting the more prudential course of putting the money by as a safety net. In embarking on an extravagant holiday in Switzerland, she is courted by the hard-up yet high-living Bretherton who presumes her to be a widow of some means. When the precariousness of her actual financial situation is revealed at the end of act 2, he accuses her of having behaved like an "adventuress" in feigning a fortune she did not have (130). She returns the insult—"For if I'm an adventuress, Captain Bretherton, what are you but an adventurer?"—by alleging that his romantic interest lay solely in her perceived fortune: "And what, pray, have you to offer to the fortunate woman in exchange for the use of her superfluous income? Proprietary rights in a poor backboneless creature who never did a useful thing in his life!" (130).

Hamilton here neatly reverses the gender roles in the conventional marital exchange, thus revealing the dubious empowerment allotted to the average woman through marriage. Act 3 sees Bretherton attempt, for the most part unsuccessfully, to prove his ability to work for a living, and it is at this juncture that he observes the diminishment of his own "market value," lacking the necessary skillset to earn that value effectively. Finding himself homeless, he again encounters Diana who has, herself, fallen on hard times. It is in this scaled-down capacity that their romance rekindles on terms of equivalence. Subtitled "A Romantic Comedy in Four Acts," the subversive romantic climax arrives in this play through a meeting of minds that involves the hero's reduction to smallness as opposed to the usual narrative scenario involving the heroine's elevation to a sham proprietorial security through an advantageous marriage. Bretherton must "feel so small," in the sense of proprietorial insubstantiality, to be in a position to enter into any kind of empathetic and egalitarian relationship with Diana. Insubstantiality is not simply redemptive for Bretherton; it allows for a different kind of vision and experience of the world, a vision and experience that was just beginning to be roundly embraced for its potential by modern women writers.

Lightness

One crucial effect of proprietorial loss or reduction was the accompanying lack of the responsibility attached to possession. If smallness offered new perspectives and subjects for discussion, the removal of durable attachments in favor of a lightness in weight enabled ease of movement. Women had, in fact, traditionally been associated with material levity, largely due to their long-standing proprietorial disenfranchisement, which highlighted, in Jordanna Bailkin's words, "a perceived division between masculine worth and feminine insubstantiality."[15]

Many modernist women writers were highly conscious of such associations and their implications. In Woolf's *Night and Day*, for example, Katharine Hilbery is shown to balk at the idea of being held up for scrutiny by Ralph Denham:

> She had a view of him as a judge. She figured him sternly weighing instances of her levity in this masculine court of inquiry into feminine morality and gruffly dismissing both her and her family with

some half-sarcastic, half-tolerant phrase which sealed her doom, as far as he was concerned, for ever. (206)

For all Denham's disregard for greatness, he is posited here as a man of substance, bolstered by the law. His power is attributed to his capacity to "weigh," and, in this imagined courtroom, feminine levity is construed as a moral flaw.

Yet, in the context of a broader social system that traditionally allotted the moral high ground to those with proprietorial responsibilities, women's presumed levity was also an imposition of the law in that most women in the western world had been denied full property rights until the late nineteenth century. As Deborah Wynne has argued, "less substantial property" assumed importance for women in the nineteenth century precisely because it presented a substitute for more significant forms of ownership largely denied to them: "such things could be as important as real property to Victorian women, functioning as tangible aids to identity at a time when for men the identity of the property owner conferred voting rights."[16]

At the same time, the identity of the property owner also conferred rigid boundaries, and literary works by early twentieth-century women writers increasingly follow the trajectory of a gradual awakening, on the part of a female protagonist, to the limited perspective and redundant values of that "masculine court of inquiry." In her nonfictional critique of the contemporary marriage market, *Marriage as a Trade* (1909), written the year after *Diana of Dobson's*, Hamilton conceived of women's freedom in terms of a new and experimental levity, which involved a reordering of values:

> To no man, I think, can the world be quite as wonderful as it is to the woman now alive who has fought free. . . . Her traditions have fallen away from her, her standard of values is gone. The old gods have passed away from her, and as yet the new gods have spoken with no very certain voice. The world to her is in the experimental stage. She grew to womanhood *weighed down* by the conviction that life held only one thing for her; and she stretches out her hands to find that it holds many. She grew to womanhood *weighed down* by the conviction that her place in the scheme of things was the place of a parasite; and she knows (for necessity has taught her) that she has feet which need no support. She is young in the enjoyment of

her new powers and has a pleasure that is childish in the use of them. (30)

Just as an insignificant idea prompts an audacious mode of mobile transgression for Woolf in *A Room of One's Own*, for Hamilton, an embrace of levity means entering into an "experimental stage" involving "new powers" and "childish" pleasure. (Note, again, the emphasis on smallness in the latter adjective.)

Growth for the modern woman entails, in Hamilton's account, the shedding of unnecessary weight. This is a metaphorical levity in that she is referring to established "traditions" and "values." Yet it also has a literal component in the very material implications of this act of eschewing a previous value system. If the woman's place in the old scheme of things had been the "place of a parasite," this implies a dependency on the hospitality of men within their designated property. Stepping outside of that scheme required the abandonment of a proprietorial security that was also an acknowledgment of its artificiality; to be a parasite is to experience a vicarious form of ownership in that the benefits of ownership are accrued at another's expense. "Had [the Victorian woman] not rather sacrificed herself to her own security?" George Dangerfield would go on to ask in a discussion of suffragette activism during this period.[17]

As Hamilton describes, the modern woman, by contrast, was compelled to sacrifice herself to insecurity. But Hamilton's remarks are penetrating in more ways than one. This implied sacrifice to insecurity taps into a broader movement away from landed property as the prime signifier of social dominance, a shift from solid to liquid modernity, in Bauman's terms: "Travelling light, rather than holding tightly to things deemed attractive for their reliability and solidity—that is, for their heavy weight, substantiality and unyielding power of resistance—is now the asset of power."[18] Such a development can be further understood as an outcome of what Tim Cresswell has described as the rise of a "nomadic" over a "sedentarist metaphysics" in the modern western world.[19] This new manifestation of power in line with an emerging nomadic metaphysics was tentatively explored by a range of writers, male and female, during this period, but women's writing yields particular insights given the historical resonances of lightness for women, as observed, producing an experimental poetics of insubstantiality that is peculiarly feminine.

Edith Wharton's *The Reef* (1912) is one pertinent example of a novel that attempts to come to terms with this new form of power, thus touching on the possibilities of such a poetics. It is centrally concerned with the problem of character interpretation in an evolving age of fluidity, more specifically the character who has no visible material ties. In this, a portable woman, Sophy Viner, is pitted against a domestic woman, Anna Leath, the mistress of Givré, formerly the estate of her deceased husband, in France. The novel charts the gradual revelation of a two-week Parisian affair in the recent past between Anna's newly intended, George Darrow, and Sophy, now governess in Anna's house and engaged to her stepson, Owen. This revelation raises the question of how Sophy should be judged for her part in the affair. It seems that this is a question that Wharton herself is at pains to answer, something remarked upon by Stephen Orgel: "as the novel proceeds, it is clear that Wharton knows less and less how she wants to view the characters she has created."[20]

From the outset, Sophy is associated with her luggage (it is in the attempt to locate her lost trunk that Darrow is first drawn into an involvement with her), while Anna is associated with the figure of the house. These are symbolic as well as objective associations in both instances:

Ordinarily Darrow would have felt little disposed to involve himself in the adventure of a young female who had lost her trunk; but at the moment he was glad of any pretext for activity. . . .

"You've lost a trunk? Let me see if I can find it."

It pleased him that [Sophy] did not return the conventional "Oh, *would* you?" Instead she corrected him with a laugh—"Not *a* trunk, but *my* trunk; I've no other—" (*Reef,* 11)

Though [Anna] could still call up that phase of feeling [the sense of possibility on first arrival, newly married, to the house] it had long since passed, and the house had for a time become to her the very symbol of narrowness and monotony. Then, with the passing of years, it had gradually acquired a less inimical character, had become, not again a castle of dreams, evoker of fair images and romantic legend, but the shell of a life slowly adjusted to its dwelling: the place one came back to, the place where one had one's duties, one's habits and one's books, the place one would naturally live in till one died: a dull house, an inconvenient house, of which one knew all the defects, the shabbiness, the discomforts, but to which one was so used that one could hardly, after so long a time, think one's self away from it without suffering a certain loss of identity. (66)

Wharton generates a seemingly clear distinction between these two figures, upheld through opposing sets of defining keywords and impressions. Sophy is poised on the side of youth and adventure. Despite her youth, she is suspected of having an "avowed acquaintance with the real business of living" (22). Anna, in contrast, is attributed an innocent kind of maturity and poised on the side of duty and habit. Further to this, Sophy is, as Robin Peel points out, "described in terms that emphasize her insubstantiality,"[21] her liaison with Darrow represented, by him, as a "moment's folly . . . a flash of madness" while the relationship between Darrow and Anna is seen as "no light thing" (231, 91–92).

It is worth noting here the repeated play on the idea of "lightness" throughout. The hypocritical Darrow, for example, feels himself slide into the pose of an "amateur actor's in a light part" as he initially attempts to conceal the history of his relationship with Sophy (117). As the truth begins to emerge bit by bit, he remarks rather disparagingly upon Anna's treatment of the situation with a "lightness that seemed to his tight-strung nerves slightly, undefinably overdone" (152). It is as if "lightness," in gesturing toward an immateriality or an immaterial existence, is somehow unreal, even dishonest. Traveling light, and without stable reference points, would seem to signal moral abandon here, an association further evoked in Darrow's earlier sense of disgust as he sits in his Parisian hotel bedroom toward the end of the brief affair with Sophy, "exactly ten days since his hurried unpacking had strewn it with the contents of his portmanteaux" (60). We are told, moreover, that "these traces of his passage had made no mark on the featureless dullness of the room, its look of being the makeshift setting of innumerable transient collocations" and that the room, in effect, begins to take "complete possession" of his mind instead (60, 61). Darrow's identity is effaced here in conjunction with the usurpation of his proprietorial power. Correspondingly, the frameworks of trunk and house ostensibly point to the qualities of insubstantiality (immoral) and substantiality (moral), respectively.

Or do they? Are these divisions really so clear-cut? If Sophy is associated with her luggage, we must remember that this association is pointedly

introduced from Darrow's narrative perspective when, in the opening section of the text, they come across one another at Calais, Sophy having run
away from her employer, Mrs. Murrett. In the shock of later rediscovering
Sophy at Anna's house, he has "an almost physical sense of struggling for
air, of battling helplessly with material obstructions" (114). If we trace the
textual source of this gut reaction in the book, we find that such material
obstructions refer indeed to actual luggage: "A porter, stumbling against
Darrow's bags, roused him to the fact that he still obstructed the platform,
inert and encumbering as his luggage" (5). This is the manner in which
Darrow is first externally presented to the reader at the very beginning of
the novel. Darrow's instinctive response to Sophy, as he later encounters
her, is drawn directly from this scene, and he merges her in memory with
his own encumbering baggage.

Yet Sophy's own trunk has gone astray, and such a scenario demands,
it is implied, a new conception of character, as their initial conversation
about her situation reveals:

> "The truth is, we quarrelled," she broke out, "and I left last night
> without my dinner—and without my salary."
> "Ah—" he groaned, with a sharp perception of all the sordid dangers
> that might attend such a break with Mrs. Murrett.
> "And without a character!" she added, as she slipped her arms into
> the jacket. "And without a trunk, as it appears—" (18)

The word "character" here refers, on a surface level, to Mrs. Murrett's recommendation letter, involving judgment on her moral qualities, but the
word gestures equally to Sophy's very personhood. How to give Sophy a
character? This is a question the novel progressively addresses. It involves,
in the first place, relocating her trunk, a process that sets the wheels of the
plot in motion. But attaching Sophy to something concrete proves inadequate. In fact, the more Darrow attempts to understand and to define
her, the more he comes up against his own self-created obstructions: "She
might be any one of a dozen definable types, or she might—more discon-
certingly to her companion and more perilously to herself—be a shifting
and uncrystallized mixture of them all" (50).

Darrow's categorial confusion regarding Sophy anticipates Anna's difficulties when she later comes to "recognize kindred impulses in a character
that she would have liked to feel completely alien to her" (253). Indeed,
Anna's own "shell of a life slowly adjusted to its dwelling" is rendered

fragile by the intrusion of Sophy. That very phrase directly invokes an exchange between Madame Merle and Isabel Archer in Henry James's *The Portrait of a Lady* (1881) as to how far a person's "shell" should contribute to our understanding of their character. For Madame Merle, "one's self— for other people—is one's expression of one's self; and one's house, one's clothes, the books one reads, the company one keeps—these things are all expressive" (186–87). How far should the "shell" be taken into account in any discussion of an individual character? The figure of Sophy offers a case study in the exploration of this question, both for Anna, within the novel, and for Wharton, at an authorial remove. There is a very real sense in *The Reef* of an attempt, on Wharton's part, to interrogate set categories, to account for "alien" impulses, to confront artistically the "shifting and uncrystallized mixture" of character types. Is the woman with no ties a woman of any substance at all, and, if so, of what kind of stuff is she made? If the novel does not provide a clear answer to this question, what is abundantly apparent is that new female characters were emerging whose insubstantial qualities could no longer be neatly dismissed within a "masculine court of inquiry into feminine morality," to reinvoke Woolf. Sophy's perceived levity is attributed a power that rattles the domestic certitudes of those around her, exposing a "sedentarist metaphysics" in the process of giving way.

In the years to follow, a new fascination with the insubstantial, in the form of lightness, comes to shape the direction of modernist women's writing. A 1920 entry in Katherine Mansfield's journal, which offers a succinct sketch of a woman named Marie, suggests her awareness that a preoccupation with the evanescent qualities of human character is to go against the descriptive grain:

> *October.* She is little and grey with periwinkle—I feel inclined to write periwinkle—blue eyes and swift, sweeping gestures. Annette said she is "une person tres superieure—la verve d'un cocher," and "qu'elle a son appartement a Nice. . . . Mais, que voulez-vous? La vie est si chere. On est force." But Marie does not look like any of these imposing, substantial things. She is far too gay, too laughing, too light, to have ever been more than a gather in the coachman's hat. As to an *appartement,* I suspect it was a chair at a window which overlooked a market.

Throttling, strangling by the throat, a helpless, exhausted little black silk bag.

But one says not a word and to the best of one's belief gives no sign. I went out into the gentle rain and saw the rainbow. It deepens; it shone down into the sea and it faded: it was gone. The small gentle rain fell on the other side of the world. Frail—frail. I felt Life was no more than this.[22]

In this new scheme, human experience is "frail" and fleeting, the universe a fading rather than an imposing backdrop.

In Woolf's *Mrs. Dalloway* (1925), Clarissa Dalloway is shown to "advanc[e], light, tall, very upright" toward the flower stand to purchase the flowers that will come to stand for all that is transient and delicate about human experience, a transience and delicacy the novel attempts to capture from the opening line (9). Like Sophy, the translucent yet elusive quality of Clarissa's character—"so transparent in some ways, so inscrutable in others"—forms the subject of the book (67). Jean Rhys's work is populated by mobile female characters who are distinguished by their very lightness, as articulated by Sasha Jensen in *Good Morning, Midnight* (1939): "I am empty of everything. I am empty of everything but the thin, frail trunks of the trees and the thin, frail ghosts in my room" (48). "Life is curious," she goes on to note, "when it is reduced to its essentials" (73). It is exactly such a reduction to essentials, beyond the extensive accoutrements of a domestic life, that many of these writers were intent on examining.

That a number of negative and parodic incarnations of portable women appeared in the same period—from Lucy Tantamount in Aldous Huxley's *Point Counter Point* (1928) with her "living modernly's living quickly" philosophy to the fabulously wealthy yet houseless Mrs. Rattery in Evelyn Waugh's *A Handful of Dust* (1934)—implies both a wider apprehensiveness about this literary development as well as the persistence of a "sedentarist metaphysics" with its accompanying system of value judgment.[23] Indeed, Rhys's writing is less concerned with celebrating insubstantiality, in the mode of Mansfield and Woolf, than with exploring what it means to be a small, mobile figure in the face of a normative substantiality: "Walking in the night with the dark houses over you, like monsters" (28). This is a normative substantiality that, by 1939, had *not* quite gone away. Yet, neither had this new poetics of insubstantiality, and its impact is marked. In damning what she saw as the "feminine fatuity" of contemporary female-authored romances in her well-known 1856 essay, "Silly Novels by Lady Novelists," George Eliot continually returns to the term "frothy" as indicative of all that is abject about this style of writing (301, 305, 306). It is testament to the radical influence of this new and peculiarly feminine poetics that the endeavor to capture all that is "frothy" and flimsy about human experience became an artistic priority rather than an incrimination.

Finally, the very act of tracing the evolution of such a poetics confirms its anti-hierarchical impetus; as I hope to have shown, to follow insubstantial tropes across modernist women's writing is to overturn traditional modes of literary categorization, revealing unexpected affinities among writers of diverse social and cultural backgrounds and forging instructive connections among texts of differing literary styles, origins, and reputations. It is an approach that allows for the kind of "ferment and recombination . . . among elements" that can occur within a theoretical model of "weak modernism," as outlined by Saint-Amour.[24] As such, it also establishes, with a nod to Caroline Levine's recent discussion of formal affordances, the paradigm of network over hierarchy. For Levine, whose discussion can be extended to critical as much as literary models, "hierarchies organize literary texts' investments in certain values or characters over others" while "networks link national cultures, writers, and characters."[25] Her choice of verbs—to organize/to link—registers a crucial distinction here. If an organizational impetus has long directed literary critical energies, the affordances of a more connective model are under-explored.

For a start, the network allows us to see texts as part of sympathetic rather than combative dialogues across space and time, generating an overarching vision of an inclusive authorial/textual community rather than a canon. It allows, moreover, for the unanticipated exchange, bringing Hamilton into conversation with Woolf, Wharton with Rhys, and so on. The aim, as with any conversational approach, is not to order and arrange but to exchange views on a given topic and to remain receptive, through this process, to the kinds of unforeseen insight that arise in open forms of dialogue. This is a dialogue in which marginal and canonical texts or authors necessarily play equal roles. But further, such an approach can shed fresh light on those previously elevated canonical works. In this specific case, it enables us to view *A Room of One's Own* less as a singular masterpiece than as a contribution to an ongoing intertextual discussion, in the way that it responds to and picks up on the many tropes and figures in circulation in women's writing in the preceding years. Above all, communities and networks are made up of small, disparate, mobile parts, evading the lure of a monolithic structural center. An account of the formation of a poetics of insubstantiality—a poetics that, as I have shown, is likewise oriented away from any centrist structure of power—is particularly well served by such a critical paradigm.

Notes

1. The question of the relationship of women writers to the modernist canon is a long-standing subject of debate, one that feminist critics are still grappling with, as evidenced by the launch, in 2018, of a new journal, *Feminist Modernist Studies,* which aims to carve a space for discussions of modernist women's writing neglected elsewhere. For an overview of the diversity of approaches to this question from the 1970s, see Harrison and Peterson, Introduction to *Unmanning Modernism,* vii–xv. For a more recent intervention that takes account of new directions in modernist studies, see Fernald, "Women's Fiction," 229–40.

2. Stewart, *On Longing,* xii, 27.

3. Woolf, *A Room of Own's Own,* 30. See also Woolf, *Three Guineas,* 360–61.

4. Bowlby, *Still Crazy,* 16.

5. See, for example, Wynne, *Women and Personal Property,* 15–52.

6. Stewart, *On Longing,* 26.

7. Cunningham, *New Woman,* 3.

8. Saint-Amour, "Weak Theory, Weak Modernism," 437.

9. Richardson, *Pilgrimage,* 3: 211.

10. Sinclair, *Life and Death,* 184.

11. Bachelard, *Poetics of Space,* 108.

12. Hypo Wilson is well known to have been based on H. G. Wells, with whom Richardson had an affair lasting approximately two years and resulting in a miscarriage.

13. Bronfen, *Art of Memory,* 231. Bronfen was referring to the work of Stephen Heath in offering this observation. Heath, it is worth noting, further provides an excellent account of the intertextual exchanges between *Pilgrimage* and *Ann Veronica.* See Heath, "Writing for Silence," 126–47.

14. Woolf, *A Room of One's Own,* 12.

15. Bailkin, *Culture of Property,* 25.

16. Wynne, *Women and Personal Property,* 10.

17. Dangerfield, *Strange Death,* 146.

18. Bauman, *Liquid Modernity,* 13.

19. Cresswell, *On the Move,* 26.

20. Orgel, introduction to *The Reef*, viii–ix.
21. Peel, *Apart from Modernism*, 169.
22. Mansfield, *Journal of Katherine Mansfield*, 219.
23. Huxley, *Point Counter Point*, 282; Waugh, *A Handful of Dust*, 97–98.
24. Saint-Amour, "Weak Theory, Weak Modernism," 451.
25. Levine, *Forms*, 21.

Works Cited

Bachelard, Gaston. *The Poetics of Space*. Translated by Maria Jolas. New York: Orion, 1964.

Bailkin, Jordanna. *The Culture of Property: The Crisis of Liberalism in Modern Britain*. Chicago: University of Chicago Press, 2004.

Bauman, Zygmunt. *Liquid Modernity*. Cambridge: Polity, 2000.

Bowlby, Rachel. *Still Crazy After All These Years: Women, Writing and Psychoanalysis*. London: Routledge, 1992.

Bronfen, Elisabeth. *Dorothy Richardson's Art of Memory: Space, Identity, Text*. Translated by Victoria Appelbe. Manchester: Manchester University Press, 1999.

Cresswell, Tim. *On the Move: Mobility in the Modern Western World*. New York: Routledge, 2006.

Cunningham, Gail. *The New Woman and the Victorian Novel*. London: Macmillan, 1978.

Dangerfield, George. *The Strange Death of Liberal England*. New York: Capricorn, 1961.

Eliot, George. "Silly Novels by Lady Novelists." In *Women and Romance: A Reader,* edited by Susan Ostrov Weisser, 301–6. New York: New York University Press, 2001.

Fernald, Anne E. "Women's Fiction, New Modernist Studies, and Feminism." *Modern Fiction Studies* 59, no. 2 (Summer 2013): 229–40.

Hamilton, Cicely. *Diana of Dobson's: A Romantic Comedy in Four Acts*. 1908. Edited by Diana F. Gillespie and Doryjane Birrer. Peterborough, UK: Broadview, 2003.

———. *Marriage as a Trade*. 1909. Detroit: Singing Tree, 1971.

Harrison, Elizabeth Jane, and Shirley Peterson. Introduction to *Unmanning Modernism: Gendered Re-Readings*, vii–xv. Edited by Elizabeth Jane Harrison and Shirley Peterson. Knoxville: University of Tennessee Press, 1997.

Heath, Stephen. "Writing for Silence: Dorothy Richardson and the Novel." In *Teaching the Text*, edited by Susanne Kappeler and Norman Bryson, 126–47. London: Routledge and Kegan Paul, 1983.

Huxley, Aldous. *Point Counter Point.* 1928. London: Chatto and Windus, 1934.

James, Henry. *The Portrait of a Lady.* 1881. London: Penguin, 2003.

Levine, Caroline. *Forms: Whole, Rhythm, Hierarchy, Network.* Princeton: Princeton University Press, 2015.

Mansfield, Katherine. *The Journal of Katherine Mansfield.* Edited by J. Middleton Murray. London: Constable, 1954.

Orgel, Stephen. Introduction to *The Reef,* by Edith Wharton, vii–xxiii. Edited by Stephen Orgel. Oxford: Oxford University Press, 1998.

Peel, Robin. *Apart from Modernism: Edith Wharton, Politics, and Fiction before World War I.* Cranbury, NJ: Fairleigh Dickinson University Press, 2005.

Rhys, Jean. *Good Morning, Midnight.* 1939. London: Penguin, 1969.

Richardson, Dorothy. *Pilgrimage.* 4 vols. London: Dent and Cresset, 1938.

Saint-Amour, Paul K. "Weak Theory, Weak Modernism." *Modernism/modernity* 25, no. 3 (August 2018): 437–59.

Sinclair, May. *The Life and Death of Harriett Frean.* 1922. London: Virago, 1980.

Stewart, Susan. *On Longing: Narratives of the Miniature, the Gigantic, the Souvenir, the Collection.* Durham, NC: Duke University Press, 1992.

Waugh, Evelyn. *A Handful of Dust.* 1934. Harmondsworth, UK: Penguin, 1951.

Wells, H. G. *Ann Veronica.* 1909. Edited by Sylvia Hardy. London: J. M. Dent; London: Everyman, 1993.

Wharton, Edith. *The Reef.* 1912. Edited by Stephen Orgel. Oxford: Oxford University Press, 1998.

Woolf, Virginia. *A Room of One's Own.* 1929. London: Penguin, 2000.

———. *"A Room of One's Own" and "Three Guineas."* Edited by Morag Shiach. Oxford: Oxford University Press, 2008.

———. *Mrs. Dalloway.* 1925. London: Vintage, 2004.

———. *Night and Day.* 1919. London: Penguin, 1992.

Wynne, Deborah. *Women and Personal Property in the Victorian Novel.* Farnham, UK: Ashgate, 2010.

2

Modernism and Middlebrow through the Eyes of Object Studies

CELIA MARSHIK

Ever since the publication of Bonnie Kime Scott's monumental *The Gender of Modernism* in 1990, feminist modernist scholars have been attuned to an expanded constellation of modernist men and women who wrote, published, and corresponded about literary work that was (more or less) experimental and directed at a highbrow readership. In the following decade, other scholars directed attention to the array of writers who wrote for middlebrow and popular audiences and yet, at times, engaged in dialogue with or about modernism. Work by Nicola Humble, Faye Hammill, and Bob Scholes, among others, has introduced the new modernist studies to writers such as E. M. Delafield, Dornford Yates, Rosamond Lehmann, and many additional authors who were once popular.[1] Their projects, at once acts of recovery and analyses of how different brows understood themselves and one another, have challenged the tendency to treat different cultural registers—work written for distinct, if sometimes overlapping, audiences—entirely separately. And yet, the undoubted differences of audience, publishers, and even assumptions about artistry[2] make it challenging to work across the brows. How can we link up writers like Stella Gibbons, who openly satirizes Freudian thought in *Cold Comfort Farm* (1932), with a writer like H.D., who chronicles her experience of analysis in *Tribute to Freud* (1956)? Is it possible to realign scholarly projects so they range across James Joyce but also P. G. Wodehouse, William Faulkner but also Dorothy Canfield Fisher?

Fifteen or more years ago, such questions were seldom posed. Like most scholars who attended graduate school in the 1990s, I was trained in high modernism, and my dissertation and first book explored how five modernist authors managed a culture of censorship. I wrote about Virginia Woolf and Jean Rhys but also Dante Gabriel Rossetti, George Bernard Shaw, and James Joyce; in retrospect I see that this project, in which chapters assess one author at a time, came out of a training that had started to absorb the lessons of *The Gender of Modernism* but that had not yet begun to consider what light middlebrow and mass culture might shed on research questions. Without exposure to that archive, we could not even *ask* the kinds of questions that would let different registers engage in meaningful dialogue.

My second book was, in contrast, inspired by two basic questions: why do so many characters in British fiction wear mackintoshes, and why do bad things happen to them? I was able to pose these questions because of my familiarity with high modernism. My work on the mac started with Joyce, Woolf, and Rebecca West, but focusing on an *object* and wanting to make claims about that object's cultural work required linking up a variety of writers. It brought me to Humble, Hammill, and Scholes, and through them to a range of texts I had not yet read. And thinking about an object through an expanded archive lead me to a realization about method: if I wanted to make claims about evening gowns, how they were understood, worn, woven into plots, and challenged, I could not look at high modernism alone.

My second book (*At the Mercy of Their Clothes: Modernism, the Middlebrow, and British Garment Culture*) argues that specific items of clothing figure a profound discomfort about the relation between persons and things in the early twentieth century. At times, clothing becomes all but human; humans, in contrast, are thingified—deprived of the capacity for action and agency that we normally attribute to persons. This approach provides one way of opening up the relationship between high modernists and their contemporaries. In this essay, I provide examples from my work on secondhand clothing to demonstrate how an object-oriented approach illuminates middlebrow authors as well as how such an approach repositions canonical modernist texts. I then touch on the tools that make this kind of work possible, the challenges it poses, and the theorists who have helped me along the way.

Following an Object: Secondhand Clothing

Representations of secondhand clothing in the early twentieth century highlight an economy of subjectivity mediated through used garments. Characters that donate or sell their clothing part with more than mere material: their things take part of the donor with them. And those who buy cast-offs discover that they become auxiliary to the original owner of the attire as garments serialize characters in the first wearer's image. Representations of used garments figure a limited economy: the hierarchy between subject and object—between wearer of garments and the garments themselves—is leveled or at least realigned as humans become absorbed and influenced by their dress. Equally important, the secondhand garment troubles the boundaries between different owners and characters, presenting a dividual model of the person.

One spectacular example of this process is provided in Rachel Ferguson's middlebrow novel *Alas, Poor Lady* (1937). Ferguson was a suffragette, actress, and dancing instructor who wrote for *Punch* under her first name. She was the author of nine novels; *Alas,* which chronicles the diverging fortunes of five upper-middle-class sisters, was originally published by Jonathan Cape. Ferguson's novel, long out of print, is now available through the auspices of London's Persephone Books, and this work can be productively read alongside Woolf's *The Years* (1937) (as well as *The Pargiters* [1977]) as it traces, with an exacting and merciless eye, what happens to the sisters who marry and to those who do not and must make their own way.

In one passage, the narrator muses on the fact that, as adults, the two poorest sisters must wear their well-off siblings' cast-offs:

> neither of the sisters got as far as the discovery that the wearing of other people's frocks and coats . . . robs of personality: that with the putting of them on an actual dimming of individuality can set in. The governess. The spinster. The Aunt Sallies of life and standbys of British serialized humour. Submerged in other people's garments. (*Alas,* 391)

This process of "submersion" points to the role of clothing, in this case used garments, in constructing personality, individuality, and indeed selfhood. While Ferguson's characters have little agency because of their poverty and unmarried status (they are "The governess. The spinster"), the narrator states that another person's clothing places a lens over subsequent wearers, who are no longer self-authored but become compound subjects, both themselves and made up of "other people." Garments, in Ferguson's novel, are far from inert. They "submerge" those who wear them, casting humans as less mistresses of the material world than positioned by it in ways they do not always perceive.

This process is represented in numerous other middlebrow texts, including Molly Keane's *Devoted Ladies* (1934), a novel devoted to romantic intrigues in an Anglo-Irish hunting set; in an extensive range of cartoons in *Punch* magazine; in Delafield's wildly popular (and funny) *Diary of a Provincial Lady* (1930); and in Flora Thompson's *Lark Rise* (1939), the first book in her best-selling *Lark Rise to Candleford* trilogy (1945). It also shows up in nonfiction prose of the period. In 1915, for example, the *Atlantic Monthly* printed a short piece titled "Old Clothes Sensations." The writer humorously addressed the problem of accepting used clothes from a known donor, speculating that the

> delicacy inherent in the present of a cast-off suit or frock is due perhaps to the subtle clinging of the giver's self to the serge or silk. It is a strong man who feels that he is himself in another man's old coat. If an individuality is fine enough to be worth retaining, it is likely to be fine enough to disappear utterly beneath the weight of another man's shoulders upon one's own. (139)[3]

The piece was, significantly, unsigned, published under "The Contributor's Club" heading that gathered together essays by the journal's regular writers. Although the *Atlantic Monthly* routinely published several short pieces under this title in each issue, the content of "Old Clothes Sensations" suggests several reasons why its author might have preferred to remain anonymous. The essay revealed that the writer was clothed out of the "missionary box" in childhood and confessed his or her current joy in being well-off enough to donate clothes to others (140).

Anonymity may have been most desirable because the writer, whom *Atlantic* records identify as Winifred Kirkland, openly expresses the sense that she is not master of the material world and specifically of garments. As the essay put it, "Clothes acquire so much personality from their first wearer,—adjust themselves to the swell of the chest, the quirk of the elbow, the hitch in the hip-joint,—that the first wearer always wears them, no matter how many times they may be given away" (140). Positing the power of used garments to distribute an original wearer, "Old Clothes Sensations" suggests that the first owner of a coat, gown, or other item so permeates his purchase that no subsequent wearer can feel him or herself in that article of clothing.

Rachel Ferguson's and Winifred Kirkland's publications and careers have little else in common, but reading across their work, one finds repeated representations of the "dimming of individuality" that Ferguson lamented. What is most surprising, however, is that middlebrow texts generally treat this situation *lightly*, more in line with Kirkland's tone than with Ferguson's, perhaps because so many middle-class readers relied on secondhand attire during the economic changes that characterized the interwar years. During a period when *The Lady* and other periodicals published articles with titles like "Every Woman Her Own Chimney Sweep" (June 1920), few readers could afford to adopt Ferguson's attitude, and while the middlebrow cannot be collapsed with the middle class, it is clear that a certain register of fiction chose to make light of, or accept, what could not be changed.

Like Ferguson's exceptionally angry and sorrowful middlebrow treatment of secondhand garments, high modernist representations of cast-offs generally take on a tragic or militant hue. James Joyce, Jean Rhys, and Virginia Woolf figure selling, buying, and wearing used clothing as endangering individuality. One can see this by dipping into Joyce's *Dubliners* (1914), *A Portrait of the Artist as a Young Man* (1916), and *Ulysses* (1922), into Jean Rhys's *After Leaving Mr. Mackenzie* (1930) and "A Solid House" (1987), or into Woolf's *Three Guineas* (1938). For example, in Joyce's "Ivy Day in the Committee Room" (1914), Mr. Henchy disparages Tierney, the politician for whom he is canvassing, because the latter won't pay him. Henchy speculates, "'I suppose he forgets the time his little old father kept the hand-me-down shop in Mary's Lane. . . . The men used to go in on Sunday morning before the houses were open to buy a waistcoat or a trousers—moya! But Tricky Dicky's little old father always had a tricky little black bottle up in a corner.'"[4] Here, one sees the stain that the secondhand trade leaves on the Tierney family; Henchy speaks as though the work were a kind of genetic marker, passed down from father to son. Equally important, Henchy suggests that the weekly process of buying garments in which to attend mass served as a pretense for early morning drinking, aligning secondhand clothing with immoral behavior as well as poverty. What was, in fact, an economically necessary practice is framed as an abject form of material interdependence that thwarts individual improvement and taints the generation to follow.

In the second chapter of her polemic *Three Guineas,* Woolf similarly casts secondhand clothing as a threat to individual independence and identity. This chapter responds to a "letter" that requests, in part, donations of used clothing to be sold at "bargain prices" to "women whose professions require that they should have presentable day and evening dresses which they can ill afford to buy" (159). Woolf asks why the representative of professional women is so poor "that she must beg for cast-off clothing for a bazaar" (41), a query that launches the author into an exploration of the continued economic disparities between professional men and women as well as into the difficulty women had in entering the professions generally. While the need for secondhand clothing recedes into the background of her analysis, it seems clear that Woolf regarded consumption of genuinely *new* clothing as a norm for all but the working class. Her selection of the cast-off as a telling detail locates *Three Guineas* at a particular historical moment when Woolf, Joyce, and many others assumed that most people ought to be able to purchase new garments. If, as Woolf reflects elsewhere, "a cast-off dress here and there are the perquisites of the private servant" (50), the cast-off is emphatically *not* desirable for the daughters of educated men, representing as it does a form of material dependence that compromises the "weapon of independent opinion" (40). *Three Guineas* positions women's relative poverty—the fact that they can "ill afford to buy" new clothes—as a threat to individual thinking and action; like Ferguson, Woolf figures used clothing as constructing an interrelationship that compromises those who must put on the dresses, and even stockings, that have been molded to another body beforehand.

A focus on secondhand garments brings to light points of contact among authors who wrote for different audiences in different styles. Object-centered study has this general effect: by making a thing, and not an author or movement, the center of attention, a scholar has to follow where *it* leads, not where one has necessarily trained or even where one has expertise. This reconfiguration of scholarly approach has challenges, but it also has benefits, such as denaturalizing expectations that might not be otherwise evident. For example, as a feminist scholar, I had never thought to challenge Woolf's assumption that a professional woman ought not to have to depend on secondhand clothing to complete a wardrobe. Even though I have *worn* plenty of secondhand clothing (sometimes by choice

THE NEW POOR.

"Good morning, Madam. I deal in cast-off clothing."

"Oh, how lucky! Do you think you have anything that would suit my husband?"

FIGURE 2.1. Bert Thomas, "The New Poor," *Punch*, January 21, 1920, 45.

and sometimes not) and regarded it with less distaste than Woolf evidently did, I viewed the request articulated in the second letter as an outrage. After finding cartoons like Bert Thomas's "The New Poor," which was published in *Punch* on January 21, 1920, I came to see that professional women *and men* often resorted to secondhand clothing during the economic depression between the wars. (See fig. 2.1.) In Thomas's sketch, the man at the door has come to purchase cast-off clothing from the type of household that would have sold such garments in the past. The woman responds, however, with an undisguised eagerness: "'Oh, how lucky! Do you think you have anything that would suit my husband?'" (45). Although the dealer's face registers some surprise, the cartoon suggests that the declassing of many people had shifted previous patterns of consumption and that *Punch* readers would recognize the situation depicted.

This insight does not dismantle the powerful arguments of *Three Guineas*, but it does recalibrate how one understands Woolf's text when reading it within a wider field. In other words, reading *Three Guineas* alongside *Alas, Poor Lady* demonstrates that texts aimed at vastly different audiences shared the sensibility that wearing secondhand clothes was a feminist issue *and* that the women who were forced to don such attire must find the experience distasteful. At the same time, putting such texts in dialogue with "Old Clothes Sensations" and "The New Poor" reveals that many *men and women* had to resort to secondhand attire due to economic necessity. It also reveals that a sense of humor about the experience could leaven the process significantly: there might not be a choice of attire, but there was a choice of affect. The important point here is not that reading different registers side-by-side reveals that any one stratum speaks in unison about cultural phenomena. Rather, studies of an object encourage scholars to look at different registers and therein to detect general patterns as well as when individual authors become outliers.

Method and Theory: Resources and Challenges in Following Things

Approaching modernist authors and their contemporaries through material culture and object theory is enabled by (more or less) recent technical advances and critical developments. First, it will doubtless be obvious that this type of work would not have been possible before the age of the internet, digital archives, and search tools. I write about texts like "Old Clothes

Sensations" or, to take another example, "Milly's Old Lavender Gown," which was published in *The Windsor* magazine in 1899, only because a search of Google Books located them. Similarly, many *Punch* cartoons fell into my lap through the auspices of the Internet Archive, and those lucky enough to have access to the magazine's own digital portal would have doubtless found more.[5] While the results thrown up by Google Books and other online archives are patchy (for example, other issues of *The Windsor* had not been digitized when I conducted my original search) and full of false leads, they streamline the process of locating texts on or about specific objects. Anyone who has painstakingly culled periodicals in an archive knows how long one can leaf through the pages before finding a relevant piece: while digital libraries will perhaps never bring about the end of the physical archive, they speed the process of locating representations of specific items and cast the net further than a single scholar might.

My point is, perhaps, all too evident, but it is worth pausing to think about the difference between research questions that start with an *author* and those that start with an *object*. If a scholar wants to write about Jean Rhys and clothing, for example, a campus library still supplies most of what one needs: her fiction, her letters, and access to books and articles written about Rhys. If that same scholar wants to write about mackintoshes, the archive needs to be much more capacious and searchable. It must be capacious because one cannot determine what an object might have meant, and how (in the case of garments) wearers would have understood it, by looking to the production of a small group of canonical authors alone. And it must be searchable because no one reader can peruse all the periodicals, novels, memoirs, and films—to say nothing of the volumes of letters, fashion theory and history, and advertisements—published in the modern period alone.

Second, publishers like Persephone Books are also crucial to object studies, excavating as they have writers whom few scholars would have encountered previously. Rachel Ferguson, Dorothy Whipple, Amber Reeves, and many others are newly available to readers. Equally important, Persephone has also republished neglected work by Virginia Woolf (*Flush* [1933]) and Katherine Mansfield (*The Montana Stories* [2001]), thus positioning writers securely in the modernist canon alongside names that are lesser-known and encouraging comparisons. As Urmila Seshagiri writes, the publisher has a "potentially transformative significance within both modernist and feminist studies" as its republication of neglected female (and a few male) writers works "to write neglected authors into modern literary history, approach canonical authors anew, and further our understanding of modernist cultural production."[6] Persephone Books, and similar publishers such as Virago and the Feminist Press, has helped books that scholars might never encounter rise above the firmament, making it possible for an object-studies approach to range across middlebrow as well as modernist texts. Although their increasingly large catalogue requires voracious reading with a low "hit rate"—catalogue descriptions are brief and often address authors' biographies as extensively as the text they nominally describe—that reading is undoubtedly pleasurable.

While internet archives and new publishers support an object-studies approach, tracing a thing offers challenges that one does not usually encounter when working on individual authors: how does one know when one is done, for example? With an ever-expanding archive, when has one found "enough"? Every scholar has had the experience of finding a journal article or book she would have cited after sending work off to the press, but object studies presents additional obstacles. Next week, for example, a library might digitize additional issues of *The Windsor,* and these issues could contain material that would bolster—or contradict—my claims. In working to trace garments across a variety of (very different) authors and texts, object studies brings together cultural and literary studies and raises acute methodological problems of scope and range. This is a version of a general challenge raised by the new modernist studies, which has—as Douglas Mao and Rebecca Walkowitz noted in 2008—been characterized by expansion.[7] One can, in some cases, limit the impact of spatial expansion, which has broadened the field to include authors and texts from outside traditional modernist centers (New York, London, Paris, and Berlin), by focusing on objects that have particular (and even peculiar) local uses and meanings. What Mao and Walkowitz call the "vertical reconfiguration"[8] of modernist studies is, however, a more disruptive challenge, as it requires scholars to take in cultural registers formerly regarded as "outside" of modernism. While I have explained the crucial need to examine such registers (and the tools that help one do so) above, determining whether one has responsibly accomplished this task remains difficult.

A second challenge of object studies is the access to archives, where examples of historical items survive but are not always available to researchers. And, as I discovered in my own work, when objects are accessible, they can be difficult to read. For instance, the Messel Dress Collection at the Brighton Museum and Art Gallery contains rare examples of dresses worn by six generations of women in the same family. I studied the collection while I was tracing the work of Sarah Fullerton Monteith Young, a court dressmaker who produced the gowns worn by Virginia and Vanessa Stephen when they made their society debut. Little information survives about Young,[9] and the Messel archive thus provides a rare opportunity to visualize the kinds of garments worn by two of the major female artists of the twentieth century and to think about the ways evening gowns position women.

One gown has remained a source of particular fascination since I first viewed it in 2013: a purple silk velvet evening gown with an eighteenth-century man's waistcoat inserted into the bodice. (See fig. 2.2.) While the Messel collection has an excellent catalogue that provides detailed accounts (cut, materials, condition, and other information) of most items, this dress had no documentation with it. What to make of the insertion of a male garment so prominently into an evening dress? The catalogue for a 2005 exhibition of the Messel Family Dress Collection indicates that Maud Messel was often "directly responsible" for the unusual fabrics and trimmings of her gowns, noting that one bill from Young "reveals that a morning gown was made up with 'her [Maud's] own embroidered muslin.'"[10] This knowledge, however, only raises more questions. Was the man's waistcoat something Messel located in an attic, and thus a keepsake from an ancestor, or was it a garment she purchased with an eye to later reuse?[11] And more important, did she see integrating a man's garment into her evening gown as transgressive and witty, or simply a fashionable use of fine embroidery and materials? Dress historians have characterized Maud Messel as practicing a "sanitized aesthetic style,"[12] so it seems unlikely that her use of the waistcoat was a foray into gender-bending play. At the same time, the experience of wearing such a garment might well have invited questions about historical change, and in particular about the way that gender and sex are constructed through specific sartorial forms. Men wore embroidered waistcoats once: what might men and women wear in the future?

These types of questions demonstrate the challenge of reading objects proper as well as of putting them into conversation with representations of those same objects in literary texts. In the case of the latter—think here of Jean Rhys's short story "Illusion" (1927) in which the narrator describes evening gowns and imagines them possessing affect and opinion—garments

FIGURE 2.2. Evening dress made by Sarah Fullerton Monteith Young circa 1907 (CT004015). Courtesy of the Royal Pavilion & Museums, Brighton & Hove.

and those who wear them often speak. Objects in archives, however, remain silent, and in this case, there is no record of Maud Messel's feelings about, or experiences in, her dress. Scholars can identify the material it is made of as well as the dressmaker, and we can place it in dialogue with the other garments in the collection to highlight Messel's general style.[13] The individual item with its unusual, and perhaps transgressive, insertion resists a fuller reading.

*　*　*

While object studies confronts these challenges and others, theorists like Jane Bennett underline the promise of the field, observing that "a touch of anthropomorphism . . . can catalyze a sensibility that finds a world filled not with ontologically distinct categories of beings (subjects and objects) but with variously composed materialities that form confederations."[14] Messel's dress works as such a confederation, linking up *two* wearers (one of whom appears to have spilled wine on the waistcoat) of different sexes who lived at different historical moments. More abstractly, it links up Messel with Virginia and Vanessa Stephen via the medium of Sarah (or "Sally," as Stephen called her[15]) Fullerton Monteith Young, serving as a reminder of the types of attire and the experience of consumption and wear they and other women had in common. It provides a tactile node, linking up different women and providing texture to study of an object that is literal but also figurative and represented in a range of cultural registers.

Object studies provides a new perspective not only on things but also on our literary archive: if a coat or pair of boots exercises as much agency as a literary character in a particular text, or if a woman leaves behind a wardrobe that documents her life as well as any book might, there seems little reason to privilege certain subjects or objects when we tell the story of the early twentieth century. Moreover, this approach helps one see, in the words of the art theorist Alfred Gell, that "as social persons, we are present, not just in our singular bodies, but in everything in our surroundings which bears witness to our existence, our attributes, and our agency."[16] Such observations might inspire new kinds of readings as well as a new politics: what are you wearing, driving, or carrying, and how is it working with you? How do the things around us make us? And finally, how do they challenge assumptions about individuality that threaten our profession, our cities, our countries, and the planet? These are the icebergs on whose tip such theorists perch.

Notes

1. See Humble's *Feminine Middlebrow Novel*; Hammill's *Women, Celebrity, and Literary Culture*; and Scholes's *Paradoxy of Modernism*.

2. As Hammill writes, middlebrow writers were not cynical about popularity but regarded wide audiences and fame as "reward[s] for genuine achievement" (*Women, Celebrity, and Literary Culture*, 15). Such a belief was anathema to modernist writers, or at least to the views they expressed in public.

3. "Old Clothes Sensations" was published anonymously but was written by Winifred Kirkland, who later republished the essay in *The Joys of Being a Woman* (1918). This collection includes essays on world travel and includes such details as Kirkland's purchase of clothing in Paris, which helps to mitigate her familiarity with secondhand clothes.

4. Joyce, *Dubliners*, 123.

5. My university library elected not to subscribe to the *Punch* archive after a trial period because the costs of an institutional subscription were not merited by the number of users during the trial. I mention this example because it points toward the larger issue of access.

6. Seshagiri, "Making It New," 242, 248. Seshagiri provides an extensive account of the press's list, book design, and connection both to modernism and contemporary literary culture with a special emphasis on two books about suffrage.

7. Mao and Walkowitz, "New Modernist Studies," 737.

8. Ibid., 738.

9. De la Haye, Taylor, and Thompson, *Family of Fashion*, 56–57.

10. Ibid., 64.

11. Maud Messel also owned a dress that had a "false waistcoat front in brocade." This dress, made by the court dressmaker Madame Ross, has been read as evidence of Messel's "aesthetic touch." See Taylor, "Wardrobe," 127, 126.

12. Ibid., 129.

13. See De la Haye, Taylor, and Thompson, *Family of Fashion,* 60–64.

14. Bennett, *Vibrant Matter*, 99.

15. Virginia Stephen refers to "Mrs. [Sally] Young" in *The Letters of Virginia Woolf,* vol. 1 (San Diego: Harvest/HBJ, 1975), where she describes having purchased new dresses that "deserve to be shown" (42).

16. Gell, *Art and Agency*, 103.

Works Cited

Anon. [Winifred Kirkland]. "Old Clothes Sensations." *Atlantic Monthly* 116 (1915): 139–41.

Bennett, Jane. *Vibrant Matter: A Political Ecology of Things.* Durham, NC: Duke University Press, 2010.

Delafield, E. M. *Diary of a Provincial Lady.* 1930. Chicago: Academy Chicago, 2002.

De la Haye, Amy, Lou Taylor, and Eleanor Thompson. *A Family of Fashion: The Messels: Six Generations of Dress.* London: Philip Wilson, 2005.

Ferguson, Rachel. *Alas, Poor Lady.* 1937. London: Persephone Books, 2006.

G. E. E. "Every Woman Her Own Chimney Sweep." *The Lady,* June 24, 1920.

Gell, Alfred. *Art and Agency: An Anthropological Theory.* Oxford: Clarendon, 1998.

Hammill, Faye. *Women, Celebrity, and Literary Culture Between the Wars.* Austin: University of Texas Press, 2007.

Humble, Nicola. *The Feminine Middlebrow Novel, 1920s to 1950s: Class, Domesticity, and Bohemianism.* New York: Oxford University Press, 2001.

Joyce, James. *Dubliners.* 1914. Edited by Robert Scholes and A. Walton Litz. New York: Penguin, 1976.

———. *A Portrait of the Artist as a Young Man.* 1916. New York: Penguin, 1993.

———. *Ulysses.* 1922. New York: Vintage, 1990.

Keane, Molly. *Devoted Ladies.* 1934. London: Virago, 1984.

Mao, Douglas, and Rebecca L. Walkowitz. "The New Modernist Studies." *PMLA* 123, no. 3 (2008): 737–48.

Pilkington, Elizabeth C. "Milly's Old Lavender Gown." *The Windsor* 10, no. 4 (1899): 419–24.

Rhys, Jean. *After Leaving Mr. Mackenzie*. 1930. New York: W. W. Norton, 1997.

———. "A Solid House." In *The Collected Short Stories*. New York: W. W. Norton, 1987.

Scholes, Robert. *Paradoxy of Modernism*. New Haven: Yale University Press, 2006.

Seshagiri, Urmila. "Making It New: Persephone Books and the Modernist Project." *Modern Fiction Studies* 59, no. 2 (2013): 241–87.

Taylor, Lou. "The Wardrobe of Mrs. Leonard Messel, 1895–1920." In *The Englishness of English Dress*, edited by Christopher Breward, Becky Conekin, and Caroline Cox, 113–32. Oxford: Berg, 2002.

Thompson, Flora. *Lark Rise to Candleford*. London: Oxford University Press, 1957.

Woolf, Virginia. *Three Guineas*. 1938. Orlando: Harvest, 1966.

3

The Haunting of Mary Hutchinson

JANE GARRITY

Be a writer, and accept all the necessary simplifications: only remember that you have got to write with your own temperament—your taste for fine underclothes and choice living.

(Clive Bell, 1916)

Your pretty article is as pretty as one of your gowns, flounced and garlanded.

(George Moore, 1923)

Not a blue-stocking, but delightfully feminine, she lent chic to a ribbon or glove by the way she wore it. In eighteenth-century Paris she would have made an ideal patroness for the Encyclopaedists and painters.

(Raymond Mortimer, 1977)

What is notable about the Clive Bell and George Moore epigraphs above, written to the erudite and witty early twentieth-century author Mary Hutchinson (née Barnes) (1889–1977), is how they underscore a close relationship between her sartorial preoccupations and her writing—unproblematically seeing the two as analogous vehicles for the articulation of a uniquely feminine style. Hutchinson's writing is "as pretty" as one of her dresses, but what does "pretty . . . flounced and garlanded" mean from a literary perspective? Is Moore linking configurations of a feminine aesthetic of self-fashioning to prevailing forms of modernist representation? He never suggests that, and one has no sense that either Moore or Bell is upholding Hutchinson's use of femininity as a governing literary metaphor in order to challenge conventional gender roles or argue that fashion

FIGURE 3.1. Black-and-white photograph of Mary Hutchinson (photographer unknown). Courtesy of the Jeremy Hutchinson Estate.

has been unjustly trivialized. And yet, both men do appear to admire her engagement with fashion and regard it as emblematic of her being. As British theater critic James Agate, another contemporary, writes to her: "As for the clothes . . . in a hundred years' time, whatever the fashion then, any woman will realize that you were marvelously dressed."[1]

While Virginia Woolf may not have agreed with that assessment, at times ridiculing Hutchinson for her gaudiness, she simultaneously admired her exceptional fashion sense. (See fig. 3.1.) In a 1933 letter to Quentin Bell, Woolf writes: "Mary is to me ravishing; in chalk white with a yellow turban, like an Arab horse, or a pierrot."[2] For Hutchinson, fashion was an aesthetic field and she was a preeminent experimenter. The view that Hutchinson was regarded as a paragon of style is epitomized by French artist Jacques-Émile Blanche, who observed that Hutchinson "seemed to lead feminine taste" in the 1920s.[3]

The problem with such assessments is that they lead to a conflation of Hutchinson's work with a conservative concept of femininity, metaphorically transposing an idea about the culture's fascination with the artificiality of the modern woman (obsessed with grooming, adornment, and self-presentation) onto her writing. We see this most vividly in Raymond Mortimer's obituary for Hutchinson (excerpted above), published in the London *Times* in 1977 after her death at age eighty-nine. The obituary mentions that Hutchinson "revealed a gifted pen" in her only book, *Fugitive Pieces* (1927), but Mortimer focuses not on this collection but instead on the degree to which Hutchinson was regarded as a "delightfully feminine" arbiter of taste.[4] Like many other critics, Mortimer's tribute draws attention to Hutchinson's lifelong friendships with famous (primarily male) writers and highlights both her "spontaneously avant-garde taste" in art and dress as well as her integral cultural role as an artistic helpmate.[5] Cumulatively, such depictions foreground a model of femininity that aligns Hutchinson with the irrationality and fickleness of modern fashion—frantically paced and subject to relentless change in search of novelty.[6] Woolf captures this image of the fashionable woman as the quintessential parrot, endlessly parodying the new, when she refers to Hutchinson as "a little popinjay of fashion."[7]

Such assessments have arguably contributed to the pervasive assumption that Hutchinson—to borrow David Bradshaw's language—was not "a writer of substance" and they have been instrumental in facilitating her obscurity.[8] The topos of the feminine—particularly the feminization of fashion—has repeatedly served a very specific function in the evaluation of Hutchinson's work: it has operated as a source of praise ("your pretty article") and has simultaneously functioned as a pejorative and dismissive reminder of why her writing is peripheral to more substantive accounts of modernity. This essay seeks to counter that view by demonstrating how Hutchinson's complex articulation of early twentieth-century femininity in *Fugitive Pieces* has been unjustly trivialized because of its association with the realm of fashion. Hutchinson urges us to rethink the naturalization of modern femininity as spectacle by repeatedly drawing attention to its constructed nature; in *Fugitive Pieces* she critiques public culture's insistence that women satisfy "all the perversities of refinement" even as she celebrates the "certain glamour" of feminine self-fashioning.[9]

Ghost Images

Compared to a writer like Woolf, what we know about Mary Hutchinson's biography is extremely sparse in some spots while robust in others, inviting us to speculate about the persistent and troubling gaps. We know that she was a Bloomsbury-affiliated writer and socialite, a cousin of the Stracheys who had, like Duncan Grant, spent her childhood in India. From 1914 to 1927 she was the lover of Clive Bell, even though she had married the liberal barrister St. John ("Jack") Hutchinson in 1910.[10] Hutchinson and her husband had two children, Barbara and Jeremy, but before the birth of her second child in 1915, she had already become involved with Bell. Various sources concur that Hutchinson's sexuality was complicated. Hermione Lee refers to Hutchinson as bisexual, while David Garnett characterizes her as "rather repressed."[11] In contrast, Carole Seymour-Jones refers to Hutchinson as "flirty" and promiscuous.[12] Woolf developed a passionate friendship with her, affectionately calling her "Weasel" and flirtatiously writing, "I like Weasels to kiss: but . . . they kiss to bite: and then to kiss," but we have few letters from Hutchinson to Woolf that would help to clarify the terms of their relationship.[13] Letters from Aldous and Maria Huxley document a fascinating ménage a trois with Hutchinson, but this "secret and steamy" liaison is not widely known.[14] Bloomsbury gossiped about a rumored affair between Hutchinson and T. S. Eliot, and, despite the actual sexual content of that relationship, we know that she was a loyal confidante and trusted friend to both Vivienne and Tom.[15] D. H.

Lawrence's belief that "Mary is one of the few women left on earth who really listens to a man," is perhaps borne out by Eliot's repeated requests that she provide literary counsel.[16] Katherine Mansfield dismissed her as excessively "artful with those she wants to please," while Lytton Strachey believed that they shared "an extraordinary sympathy" because of their common ancestry.[17]

Critics must grapple to piece together empirical evidence that is at times contradictory. Richard Shone surmises that it was mainly through Clive Bell's influence that Hutchinson's taste in painting developed, whereas Donald Stanford argues that Hutchinson "belonged more properly to high society" and "had a genuine taste for the arts."[18] Vanessa Bell concurs, commenting in a 1916 letter to Lytton Strachey that Hutchinson's "exquisiteness" is "made for salons" and "ought really to be seen by the polite world" rather than Bloomsbury.[19] Several years later, Dora Carrington dismisses Hutchinson's engagement with high society as a sign of Francophilic affectation, complaining in a 1920 letter to Gerald Brenan that "Clive Bell and Mrs. Hutchinson aren't my style. Too elegant and 18 cent. French; for that's what they try to be."[20]

Vanessa Bell's biographer Frances Spalding speculates that Bloomsbury imposed a more fashionable image on Hutchinson than was perhaps true, citing as evidence Hutchinson's refusal of invitations from leading hostesses such as Sibyl Colefax and Lady Cunard even though she herself held and attended numerous parties.[21] As Clive Bell's lover, Hutchinson was a frequent visitor to Lady Ottoline Morrell's retreat, Garsington Manor, where in 1916 the three would sit on the lawn alongside Lytton Strachey and two of the "Slade cropheads, Barbara Hiles and Faith Bagenal . . . discussing life and art."[22] This is just one example of Hutchinson's immersion in the world of Bloomsbury. We know that Hutchinson maintained cordial relationships within the circle and experienced "early moments of confessional intimacy with" Vanessa Bell, who happily decorated rooms for her in successive London homes and entertained her as Clive Bell's companion.[23] Roger Fry invited Hutchinson to become a founding member of the Omega Club in 1917, a social group that met at the Omega Workshops once a week to socialize "without any formalities."[24] Hutchinson was both a patron of the workshops and a supporter of the Contemporary Arts Society, collecting paintings by British artists Mark Gertler and Duncan Grant, as well as French artists Henri Marchand, André Derain, and Henri Matisse.

The letters to Hutchinson from her contemporaries document their esteem for her, but why did she fall into obscurity while others—including the numerous important literary and artistic figures such as Strachey, Eliot, and Huxley, who were her friends—have remained in view? An author herself, Hutchinson published numerous short essays and stories in periodicals as well as a book with the Hogarth Press, but today relatively little is known about her work.[25] The question is: why? In order to begin to answer this difficult query it is useful to think about Rebecca Solnit's analysis of Woolf's genius, because it can help us to frame the conversation about Hutchinson's obscurity and its relation to the category of artistic stature.

In her 2009 essay titled "Woolf's Darkness: Embracing the Inexplicable," Solnit proposes that Woolf's genius resides in her rejection of "the pretenses of authoritative knowledge" and in her espousal of "the language of nuance and ambiguity and speculation."[26] This perceptive assessment of Woolf as the celebrant of the "the unknown, the unseeable, [and] the obscure" is compelling, but less persuasive is Solnit's corollary that the attempt to secure and stabilize knowledge is always a form of literary aggression (86). She maintains that academic scholarship's attempt to nail things down, "to classify and contain" a work of art, is akin to trying "to turn the flight across the sky into the roast upon the plate" (100). While no academic would want to be accused of killing the spirit of a creative work through restrictive interpretation, I would argue that our pleasure in the ineffable presupposes a certain familiarity with that work's conditions of emergence or existence. In short, it is easy to uphold Woolf as an author whose work escapes categorization and confinement precisely because we have so much evidence of her life-long engagement with the concepts of multiplicity, open-endedness, and uncertainty. Solnit jokes that "museums love artists the way that taxidermists love deer," but this witty image of curated ossification belies another truth: that there is great utility and liberty in the act of classification and circumscription (100). By this I mean to suggest that the deep knowledge associated with Woolf's voluminous archive has liberated us from the hunt for facts and has allowed us to search instead for ambiguities and contradictions. By contrast, for marginalized women modernists, such as Hutchinson, who suffer from a dearth of interpretation, obscurity functions not as a value but as an impediment.

The critic's ability to take pleasure in "the language of nuance and ambiguity" (Solnit, 88–89) is dependent upon certain undeniable material realities, such as, well-trained eyes that can decipher an author's illegible handwriting; the existence and accessibility of a catalogued and well-documented archive; the ready availability (in print or on demand) of a writer's books and essays (88–89). If an author is a lost subject of history, then the categories of classification and circumscription read less as signs of the restrictiveness of containment than as evidence of the burden of obscurity. Ambiguity, absence, and neglect are only utopian in a world of archival surfeit. Although Solnit does not acknowledge this, her argument depends upon a certain repression—a forgetfulness of the fact that what any critic needs is a stable basis of knowledge and an available critical vocabulary from which to animate the past and make it visible. Solnit ignores the fact that authoritative knowledge does not necessarily foreclose interpretation, but often facilitates it.

Revisionary Readings: The Hutchinson Papers

I want here to test this cultural hypothesis by focusing upon Hutchinson while privileging what Michel Foucault famously called subjugated knowledge—that body of knowledge that the official register represses within its own institutions. Hutchinson was a woman who is today arguably best known for two things: she was Clive Bell's lover who was supposedly never welcomed into the "inner circle" of Bloomsbury; and she was the subject of Vanessa Bell's dazzling color portrait reminiscent of Matisse that allegedly captures both Hutchinson's "outward coldness" and the artist's strained relations with her husband's "mistress" (this is the pejorative term that is repeatedly invoked throughout the literature to characterize Hutchinson's status).[27] Although Hutchinson was the subject of works by other artists—Henry Tonks exhibited a pastel of her in a red jacket in the summer exhibition of the New English Art Club in 1913, Duncan Grant painted her portrait between 1915 and 1917, and Matisse did two charcoal drawings of her in 1936—it is this striking pink and chartreuse Bell portrait of Hutchinson in 1915, with the "green diagonal" indicating a shadow that "slithers" across her subject's cheek, that resonates with those who are familiar with the Mary-Clive affair (Spalding, 146).[28] Is the painting really just an autobiographical testament to Vanessa Bell's rivalry with Hutchinson, as Bell's biographer suggests when she contends that "Vanessa could not disguise her feelings toward Mary when she came to paint her portrait" (ibid.)? Richard Shone concurs, arguing that the "unflattering" portrait conveys Bell's hostility and "controlled impatience" with the affair.[29]

But what if we consider a different representation of Hutchinson, the one allegedly captured in a little-known 1922 Bell painting titled *The Party* that was featured in a *Vogue* article that same year?[30] (See fig. 3.2.) Although no critic has verified that the figure on the far left is Hutchinson, it looks very much like her, and the woman's elegant off-the-shoulder gown, as well as the depiction of a party setting, are congruent with what we know about Hutchinson's life as a socialite. If we entertain the hypothesis that this is indeed Hutchinson, the painting gives rise to several questions: is that a woman's hand resting on her shoulder, or is that hand actually suspended above her green dress? Do those fingers belong to Hutchinson herself, or to someone else? Why does this painting contain such ambiguity regarding the ownership of fingers?[31] Moreover, why is the imposing central female figure standing in such close proximity to Hutchinson, and what does that woman's extremely revealing décolleté suggest about the colloquy between the two women? If Bell is here alluding to Hutchinson's bisexuality through the confusion of fingers and the proximity of female bodies, then this is arguably a more complex representation of Bell's "feelings" toward her husband's "mistress" than has hitherto been acknowledged.

Because the source material that we have about Hutchinson is so fragmented and discontinuous, it is difficult to counter the veracity of conflicting statements about her life. In order to attempt this, I want to focus upon the Hutchinson archive at the Harry Ransom Center at the University of Texas at Austin because there one encounters a much more complicated and nuanced account of the author than is available at first glance. Hutchinson can be read as a disciplinary object that exemplifies the argument that visibility depends upon archival plentitude. And yet, as we shall see, the dialectics of visibility and invisibility still involve a constant negotiation between what can be seen and what remains in the shadows.

The Hutchinson Papers comprise 22.5 boxes of materials that include correspondence, typescript manuscripts, and both articles and biographical sketches of several members of the Bloomsbury group. Incoming correspondence makes up the bulk of these papers with well over 2,500 personal letters, postcards, notes, and telegrams sent to Hutchinson over a period of sixty years. By far the largest contributor to this section is Clive Bell with

FIGURE 3.2. "The Party" (1922) by Vanessa Bell. Courtesy of Barbara and Howard Ginsberg. Copyright Estate of Vanessa Bell, courtesy of Henrietta Garnett.

nearly 1,400 letters. Other large accumulations of letters are present from Samuel Beckett, Vanessa Bell, Dora Carrington, T. S. and Vivienne Eliot, Aldous and Maria Huxley, Lytton Strachey, and Virginia Woolf. The letters to her are particularly revealing in their estimate of her not only as a perceptive reader and witty stylist but also as a loyal friend and confidante as well. The papers also include Hutchinson's unpublished biographical sketches of Aldous Huxley, Desmond MacCarthy, George Moore, Lytton Strachey, T. S. Eliot, and Virginia Woolf, as well as five vertical files of newspaper clippings saved by Hutchinson that include several periodical articles but, frustratingly, no early drafts or reviews of her work.

However, by far the most frustrating aspect of this archive is the fact that only an infinitesimal fraction of the correspondence is *outgoing*—that is, from Hutchinson to her contemporaries. There is one folder of letters from Hutchinson to Samuel Beckett (dating from 1963 to 1973), and two folders (comprising 114 letters and 28 postcards and telegrams) of letters from Hutchinson to Lytton Strachey that date from 1915 to 1931. The Hutchinson-Strachey correspondence is important not only for revealing Hutchinson's intimacy with Strachey but also for being the only known substantial two-way correspondence (the archive includes over 100 letters sent by Strachey). Notable is Strachey's admiration for Hutchinson's arch wit and "delicious style," and Hutchinson's candid disclosures regarding her commitment to writing and her "dream of composing" an "immortal work" of art.[32] It is puzzling why so much of the correspondence *to* Hutchinson survives while so very little *from* her has surfaced, but numerous correspondents lament the infrequency of Hutchinson's letters and complain about the difficulty of deciphering her illegible handwriting.[33]

Despite this conundrum, the Hutchinson Papers enable us to fill in some of the gaps of what Avery Gordon calls "ghostly things," those affective and material traces of what is absent, excluded, repressed, or invisible. While Gordon writes from a sociological perspective and focuses upon literal disappearances and losses enforced by the conditions of modernity, her desire to find a method of knowledge that can conjure and narrate that which has been "marginalized, trivialized, denied, [and] disqualified" is, I believe, a useful paradigm for thinking about the category of the obscure in relation to female modernists such as Hutchinson.[34] Gordon's interest in the elements that the objective register attempts to minimize, and her preoccupation with "the relationship between what *assembles and joins* and what is gaping, detouring, and haunting," provides us with useful tools for talking about a writer such as Hutchinson—who does indeed "haunt" the borders of Bloomsbury without ever coming fully into sharp focus.[35]

The Harry Ransom Center archive is of great import because it can help to teach us, albeit through haphazard imaginative design, what official frameworks minimize or occlude. To take just the one example of Vanessa Bell's oft-cited jealousy: the archive contains several intimate letters from Bell to Hutchinson that reveal a range of concerns such as her problems with servants, her worry that Quentin may have influenza, and her fear

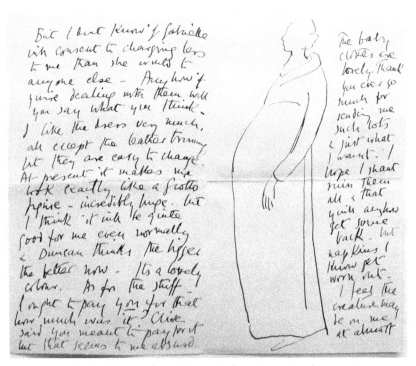

FIGURE 3.3. Undated Letter from Vanessa Bell to Mary Hutchinson. Harry Ransom Center, The University of Texas at Austin. Copyright Estate of Vanessa Bell, courtesy of Henrietta Garnett.

she "should never be able to paint any more" because of pressing domestic demands.[36] Alongside such disclosures, Bell makes several references to her "disreputable" clothes and also her delight in a leather trimmed maternity dress that Hutchinson purchased for her while she was pregnant with Angelica: "I like the dress very much. . . . At present it makes me look exactly like a Giotto—incredibly huge, but I think it will be quite good for me even normally. . . . It's a lovely color. . . . How much was it? Clive said you meant to pay for it but that seems to me absurd."[37] Embedded in this letter is Bell's full-page sketch of her pregnant body and a note thanking Hutchinson for sending such "lovely" baby clothes to Charleston. (See fig. 3.3.) What these details reveal is a much more complicated and nuanced understanding of Bell's relationship to Hutchinson, one that coheres with David Garnett's own observation that Bell in fact welcomed Hutchinson's affair with Clive because it gave a reassuring balance to her own amatory arrangement with Duncan Grant.[38] Similarly, the argument

FIGURE 3.4. Black-and-white photograph of Mary Hutchinson (photographer unknown). Harry Ransom Center, The University of Texas at Austin. Courtesy of the Jeremy Hutchinson Estate.

that Hutchinson was always ostracized from Bloomsbury's inner circle is contradicted by another letter in which Bell reassuringly writes: "I don't see why not agreeing with Bloomsbury should necessarily make you outside of it—for doesn't it contain people who do not agree very fundamentally?"[39] Here we see Bell's loyalty to the most fundamental Bloomsbury ethos: friendship.

Yet while the archive has the power to shed light on the intricacies of subjectivity and transform prevalent modes of inquiry, it also has the power to produce mystery—as is evidenced by this arresting black-and-white photograph. (See fig. 3.4.) I discovered this stunning image of Hutchinson in Clare Ratliff's article on her friendship and correspondence with Strachey.[40] The picture is undated, and the article offers no information about its origin or context beyond the fact that it is a part of the photography collection at the Harry Ransom Center. I was startled because I never saw any mention of this photograph when I was doing research on the Hutchinson Papers. What I ultimately learned from one of the archivists is that while it would in theory have been possible to stumble across this photograph—it was highly unlikely. One would have needed to know that a "Literary File" (alphabetized according to author) exists at the very bottom of the Photography Collections page, but this "Literary File" is not mentioned or linked on Hutchinson's inventory of papers.[41] When the librarian retrieved the photograph for me he found the name "S.A. Vigano" stamped in purple on its verso, but no information at the Harry Ransom Center and no online search for that name pulled up anything conclusive. The photography curator confirmed that no additional photographs of Hutchinson exist in their collection. This is a compelling example of what Gordon calls the "unvisibility of the hypervisible"—that is to say, "ghost images" that have a high degree of visibility but nonetheless still render certain things oblique or invisible.[42]

A Lady of Fashion

Ghost images can encourage us to investigate how things that are obscure or appear to be absent can be rendered present—brought into material being. In the case of the Hutchinson photograph, the setting conjures images the viewer may have seen of lounge chairs at Garsington Manor, and that is indeed the estate where Hutchinson and Clive Bell were weekend visitors. Hutchinson's pose invokes her semi-reclining position in Boris Anrep's mosaic, *The Awakening of the Muses,* which opened at the National Gallery in 1933. Hutchinson was the model for Erato, the muse of lyric (especially erotic) poetry.[43] There she reclines at the feet of Bacchus, portrayed by Clive Bell, even though their affair had ended by 1927.[44] The pose also recalls another mosaic by Anrep, the 1922 reclining image of a fashionable woman on the phone titled *Daily Incidents in the Life of a Lady of Fashion.*[45] While Hutchinson was not the model for this mosaic, Fry's observation that this work was a milestone because it captured a "completely modern theme, the daily life of a lady of fashion in 1922," speaks to Hutchinson's own role as a purveyor of fashion and patron of the arts during this period.[46] We know that Hutchinson contributed to the National Gallery's mosaics fund and commissioned a tabletop from Anrep. Is the reclining photograph in conversation with the Garsington lounge chairs and Anrep's mosaics? There is no concrete evidence to suggest this reading, but the ghostliness of the photograph bears the trace of these material objects, drawing us to infer and speculate about the echoes and murmurs of that which has been lost. The photograph is also a paradigmatic example of why recovery work is not about segregated knowledge—that is, recovering an individual—but is an interdisciplinary enterprise that requires an ensemble of cultural imaginings.

Yet, while the photograph draws us affectively and carries with it the hope of reanimating the depth and density of Hutchinson's life, the imaginary possibilities of conjuring are constrained by what we do know. To many she was considered a paragon of style; she bought her clothes from Poiret, was well known for her elegant soirees, and was a source of both admiration and envy. Hutchinson's exquisite self-fashioning provoked Woolf, who was always anxious about dress, to seek her out for wardrobe advice.[47] But this was not an uncomplicated relationship. Woolf records in her diary in 1922: "[Mary] dined with me, alone. . . . I opened the door, & there she was with her white Pierrot face, black satin, orange shawl, laced shoes—the whole outfit merely to dine with me. . . . She is an impulsive generous woman . . . but subterraneously I think, floored over by her society varnish."[48] This disparaging assessment is complicated by many other diary entries that capture Woolf's admiration for Hutchinson's high fashion wardrobe[49] and convey the "teasingly affectionate, semi-erotic friendship" that developed between the women in the mid-1920s, but what is important to note here is Hutchinson's sartorial extravagance—which was renowned.[50] Indeed, Hutchinson was one of the first women in London to own Charles James's stylish "Taxi dress," a simple garment that wound around the body from left to right, fastening with clasps at the right hip; this wrap-around dress was a revolutionary idea at a time when shapeless, tubular flapper shapes prevailed. James dubbed his frock the "Taxi dress" because it was constructed so simply that it could be put on (or removed) in a cab.[51] In a 1933 letter to Vita Sackville-West, Woolf describes the James dress as "symmetrical, diabolical and geometrically perfect," capturing both the designer's and Hutchinson's own sartorial excess.[52]

Mary Hutchinson's reputation for self-fashioning influenced her literary output—she was a regular contributor in the 1920s to *Vogue* magazine, when it was under the editorship of Dorothy Todd, and to the *Nation and Athenaeum* after Leonard Woolf was appointed literary editor. I will return in the final section of this essay to Hutchinson's publications in *Vogue,* but here I want to highlight Leonard Woolf's interest in her as a contributor to his political weekly. In a 1923 letter on the *Nation and Athenaeum* letterhead, he invited Hutchinson to write a 1,200-word article entitled "A

Letter from a Lady in Paris"—observing that her perspective would be "real literature, and yet deal with Paris fashions in such a way that people who take an interest in fashions, and people who take an interest in literature, will both read it with delight."[53] He also suggests that she might sign her letter "Penelope," although he gives no reason for that possible alias.

Hutchinson accepted Woolf's commission but chose the pseudonym of Polly Flinders, publishing six articles and two book reviews under that alias on a variety of topics ranging from fashion shows, shopping, the ballet, and urban life between 1923 and 1926.[54] One of Clive Bell's endearments for Hutchinson was "Polly," and this pseudonym is arguably an allusion to the nineteenth-century nursery rhyme that was popular in England: "Little Polly Flinders / Sat among the cinders, / Warming her pretty little toes. / Mother came and caught her, / And whipped her little daughter / For spoiling her nice new clothes." This is clearly a cautionary tale, warning little girls that they need to keep their clothes clean because no fairy godmother is going to clean them up, but it is also an apt pseudonym for Hutchinson, who would gaze in wonder as the gowns of her stepmother, Edith Helen Barnes, were unpacked at the family home in London during her brief visits from India.[55] Hutchinson writes: "Thus were sown the seeds of a love of dress and of unattainable freshness and finish, which was to bear fruit later in the salons of Poiret, Nicole Groult . . . Charles James. . . . And thus perhaps too were sown the seeds of a love of disguise and myth."[56] Hutchinson's love of disguise is realized in her pseudonym, which self-consciously plays with her reputation for elaborate body dressing. A striking photograph of her by Maurice Beck and Helen Macgregor captures this idea of concealment. The slightly blurry portrait appeared in *Vogue* in late October 1924 with this caption: "So this is 'Polly Flinders.' It is not easy to imagine that airy and fantastic pen wielded by so grave a person. But here she is, the witty lady of fashion . . . who has sometimes been described as 'the modern Millamant.'"[57] (See fig. 3.5.) This is an allusion to the charming and ironic heroine of William Congreve's Restoration comedy, *The Way of the World* (1700), and it is a fitting comparison to Hutchinson who had a dual reputation for compassion and biting wit. Vivienne Eliot perhaps uttered the best epithet that captures this tension when she characterized Hutchinson as a "civilized rebel."[58]

Maurice Beck and Macgregor

POLLY FLINDERS

So this is "Polly Flinders." It is not easy to
imagine that airy and fantastic pen wielded
by so grave a person. But here she is, the
witty lady of fashion with the cynical glance
and the touch of sentiment, who has sometimes
been described as "the modern Millamant"

FIGURE 3.5. Maurice Beck and Helen Macgregor, photograph of Mary Hutchinson, *Vogue* (London, Late October 1924). Vogue © The Condé Nast Publications Ltd.

Fugitive Pieces

We can see Hutchinson's preoccupation with charm, rebellion, and fashion in her book, *Fugitive Pieces,* published by the Hogarth Press in June 1927. How did Hogarth come to publish this collection of five stories and thirteen essays in large part about fashion? The Harry Ransom Center archive contains letters and postcards from Virginia Woolf to Hutchinson that were not reproduced in the original collected *Letters of Virginia Woolf* that shed light on this question.[59] Despite the dynamic of repulsion and attraction that largely characterized Woolf's relation to Hutchinson, she was drawn to her for more than her "exquisiteness of dress" and in 1924 encouraged her to "write us a book upon dress. What we have in mind is a book with a practical bearing—it might be for those who have little to spend—but treated in a whimsical and imaginative way, with . . . perhaps black and white drawings."[60] This intriguing practical guide to fashion featuring visual images never materialized, but Woolf did speculate about what form such a book might take: "Should it be prefaced by an account of a great dress show—of the Clients—mannequins—and frocks—and the buying of a frock?"[61]

What Hogarth eventually published in June 1927 was a collection that contained what Woolf called "some serious and well informed articles upon *Dress*" even though she also expressed disparagement for the writing.[62] The press originally printed 1,000 copies, but 509 were pulped, and today this is an exceedingly rare book (only nineteen library copies are extant).[63] What is notable about the copy that is held in the Victoria University Library at the University of Toronto is how visually unexceptional it is for a Hogarth edition. (See fig. 3.6.) In contrast to the bright paper wrappers featuring colorful splotches of color designed by Vanessa Bell for which the press became known, this cover is inordinately plain and monochromatic.[64] Howard Woolmer's description of the first edition of *Fugitive Pieces,* published June 1927, offers a variation on this theme: "Red cloth printed in gilt. Pale blue dust wrapper printed in black," but it does not solve the mystery as to why the volume housed in Victoria is so radically spare.[65] It also does not explain why a press that was in the vanguard of publishing new writers and fresh ideas would not have marketed a book largely about fashion and high culture in a more conspicuously appealing way.

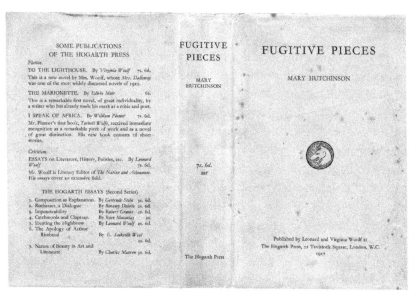

FIGURE 3.6. *Fugitive Pieces*, published by the Hogarth Press, June 1927. Copyright Estate of Vanessa Bell, courtesy of Henrietta Garnett. Used by permission of Victoria University Library (Toronto).

At the same time, we can read the book's spare look as an index of its appeal to seriousness—that is to say, as a disavowal of fashion's persistent association with triviality, irrationality, and changeability. The cover of *Fugitive Pieces* is consistent with the bland, monochromatic cover of the other Hogarth Press book about sartorial practice—J. C. Flugel's psychosexual study, *The Psychology of Clothes*, published just three years later in 1930. Both books are concerned with how minds and bodies are fashioned by garments, and both in different ways examine how the dressed body is an expression of corporeal discipline that dictates regulatory gender roles in culture.[66] As Hutchinson puts it in her essay, "Femininities": "Our clothes have not time to help us, and so it is sometimes difficult to see what we are really like—we tend to resemble one another and never to resemble ourselves" (*FP*, 136). Yet despite this critique of dress as signs of homogeneity and inauthenticity, fashion was a generative matrix for Hutchinson and was for her a source of tremendous pleasure. Her seeming disavowal of fashion's relevance is counterbalanced by a robust embrace of the proliferating possibilities of the fashion cycle for women—what she calls the instantiation of "excitements" and "possibilities" of "disguises and transformations" for "the feminine spectator" (144).

I will say more about how the topic of fashion was imbued with a charge of the new for Hutchinson in a moment, but here I want to underscore the degree to which she regarded dress and adornment as important markers of modernity even as she recognized the limits (and potential dangers) of the mechanics of self-fashioning. Echoing Woolf's concerns about the cultural disparagement of dress in *A Room of One's Own* (1929)—"'Speaking crudely, football and sport are 'important'; the worship of fashion, the buying of clothes 'trivial'"[67]—Hutchinson writes: "Perhaps no one has . . . very carefully examined a few hours in a lady's day" such as "her visit to a dress show" (*FP*, 140). *Fugitive Pieces* examines, in part, women's preoccupations with dress, accessories, and cosmetics, demonstrating how the symbolic and affective meanings attached to women's relationship to their possessions illuminate broader questions about their relationship to commercialized consumption and the fantasy world of cultural objects. As Hutchinson writes: "Indeed, to a perspicacious eye, what a revelation can a woman be!" (144).

The *Times Literary Supplement* published an ad for *Fugitive Pieces* that drew attention to Hutchinson's modernist celebrity—"Mrs. Hutchinson has hitherto written under the pseudonym of 'Polly Flinders' and her work has been widely appreciated"—but a muted review published there one month later contradicts this assertion.[68] This *Times Literary Supplement* review, the only one of *Fugitive Pieces* that has surfaced, contains some measured praise but ultimately regards Hutchinson as an "amateur" who writes about "shopping, Paris fashions, [and] 'femininities'"—in other words, trivial topics that generate initial "pleasure and entertainment" but do not warrant a second reading.[69] This male reviewer denounces Hutchinson's narrative style as slight—"restlessly emphasizing with an eloquence that is breathless and often a little arch"—an observation that conflates her prose with presumptions about femininity (469). Ultimately, her themes are regarded as a "defect" because of their association with the capriciousness and peculiarities of women: "'Spritely' would be a pale word to use of these articles" (ibid.). The reviewer even singles out the book's final words for censure, finding the parenthetical "(To be continued)" that appears on the last page as a sign of Hutchinson's inability to sufficiently develop an idea—"it remains hanging in the air . . . before it has got anywhere at all" (ibid.).

Those ghostly words, "to be continued," merge the visible and the invisible in ways that remind us of the unsettled relationship between what we know and do not know about Hutchinson's writing. Despite the tantalizing final page, Hogarth published nothing further, and *Fugitive Pieces* was Hutchinson's only book. Separate from *Fugitive Pieces*, she published one short story in the *Egoist* in 1917, at least one additional article in the *Nation and Athenaeum* in 1928 under her own name (a review of a book titled *The Technique of the Love Affair*), an article on George Moore in the *London Mercury* in 1936, an introduction to *The Life of Henry Tonks* in 1939, and a brief reminiscence of childhood titled "Kaleidoscope of Childhood" in 1960.[70] Because there is no comprehensive bibliography of her work, we have no idea if this list is exhaustive. There is no authoritative biography and no collection of her extant letters. Instead, what we have is a tiny output of scholarly research: one dissertation by Clare Ratliff on Hutchinson's correspondence with T. S. Eliot and Aldous Huxley (completed in 1991); one article derived from this research (published in 1998); and three additional articles (two by David Bradshaw, published in the *Charleston Magazine* in the 1990s, and one by Nancy Hargrove, published in the *Yeats Eliot Review* in 2011).[71] Contemporary responses have been similarly dismissive. Ratliff argues that "*Fugitive Pieces* has its moments, but ultimately is more valuable as socio-historical data [than as literature]."[72] Bradshaw is similarly disdainful, calling the collection "slight" and damning it with faint praise: "[the book is] attractively quirky and not unreadable."[73] These assessments confuse the allegedly "slight" topic of fashion with Hutchinson's treatment of it, and it is arguably this dismissive misogynistic perception that has contributed to the book's invisibility.

In reality, *Fugitive Pieces* is a very complex and nuanced depiction of modernist concerns that highlights female experience of the everyday and reminds us of Rita Felski's attempts to unravel the complexities of modernity's relationship to femininity. Hutchinson is not a cultural historian, nor is feminism an articulated organizing metaphor in her book, but she does repeatedly put femininity and modernity into conversation, and she does implicitly ask (anticipating Felski's query by almost seventy years): "what if feminine phenomena . . . were given a central importance in the analysis of the culture of modernity?"[74] Hutchinson's female characters are, for the most part, from the upper classes and repeatedly encounter the reorientation of gender roles; a hermeneutics of suspicion in heterosexual relationships; the culture's obsessive attention to clothing and physical appearance; the porous nature of time—particularly in relation to domestic objects; the place of the family in the British class system; the enduring role of empire in a world where a bygone English society is already rapidly fading; and both the assault and allure of mass culture in early twentieth-century England—to name but a few recurring topics. The book is divided into two sections: the shorter "Shuttlecocks," consisting of five short stories; and "Weathercocks," a group of thirteen essays on a diverse range of cultural topics (such as Parisian fashion, the ballet, shopping, and modern art). The two section titles appear extraneous at first glance, but the content in each underscores their titular relevance. The term "shuttlecocks" is an allusion to the small plastic object that is struck by rackets in badminton and essentially means to bandy to and fro—an apt term that characterizes the tumultuous nature of human relationships in the five short stories that comprise that section.

The first story in the "Shuttlecocks" section, "Tea," captures this dynamic through the back and forth machinations of a wealthy childlike woman named Anne, who contemplates notions of "solitary and glorious independence" that seem to her as "impossible as flying to the moon" (*FP*, 14, 20). Anne struggles in her choice of suitors, debating between an uninteresting and nameless young man who shares her family's upper-class values—yachting, golf, and shooting—and her "inexplicable attraction" to a seemingly altruistic and shabby middle-aged elder who makes her feel "powerful," loans her books, and promises to "spread the world before [her]" (20, 17, 18). When this man compliments her looks by comparing her to a Venetian painting—Tintoretto's *Susanna and the Elders* (1555–56)—Anne feels elated but is unfamiliar with the artwork. As a result, she has no idea that the painting's allusion to lustful elderly men sneaking a view of a naked Susanna as she prepares to bathe situates her as the sumptuous object of a predatory male gaze. As the story unfolds, we learn that the older man's pedagogical ambitions are not altruistic, but coercive—he wants to "possess" her and "teach [her] everything" while restraining her in a "golden cage" (22)—and in the end Anne realizes that she has been "completely taken in" by his encouragement of her "absurd fancies," and she "come[s] back to [her] senses with a sort of jerk" (19). Hutchinson dramatizes the stark "incongruity" between Anne's private "imaginary world," which mistakenly reads male attention as a conduit to freedom from domestic constraint, and her cushy confinement—full of aristocratic pleasures but devoid of any actual autonomy (20).

In the story's final pages, we learn that Anne has reluctantly accepted the proposal from her upper-class peer, a gesture that has less to do with her rejection of the shabby suitor than it does with the story's depiction of the illusory nature of her intoxicating "sense of power" (19). Hutchinson shows us the impossibility of Anne's "ludicrous situation" (24), caught between a tantalizingly unconventional but controlling admirer who (as her friends put it) wants to turn her into "a slave" (25), and a mundane but suitable man who would secure her class position and enable her to retain her family's cultural status—she would sacrifice her "ideas of independence" (20) but would travel in a "two-seater Rolls" (25). Ultimately, "Tea" can be read as a feminist critique of female gender conformity and the dangers of male seduction—fluent in the rhetoric of independence but insidiously working against that emancipatory ideal. "Tea" contains many of the thematic elements that we see repeated in the "Weathercocks" editorials: the constraining nature of class; the heavy price that women pay for material comfort; the coerciveness of male attention that frames itself in the language of liberation; and perhaps most important, the ideologically contested relation between dress and makeup to the construction of female identity.

Polly Flinders in *Vogue*

The chapters that comprise the lengthier "Weathercocks" section were originally published in *Vogue* and in the *Nation and Athenaeum* under Hutchinson's pen name, Polly Flinders, between 1923 and 1926, but in *Fugitive Pieces* the essays are not attributed to either publication—nor are any specific dates or any bibliographical information listed. Archival research, however, reveals that six of the *Fugitive Pieces* articles were published in *Vogue*, and seven were published in the *Nation and Athenaeum*.[75] This section will focus on the *Vogue* articles, which were published during the period when Bloomsbury flourished in its pages, and Hutchinson's home was featured there three times. The most sumptuous display of Hutchinson's home as an exemplary space of domestic modernity appears in the article titled "The Work of Some Modern Decorative Art" (1926), where photographs of her drawing room and study highlight decorative schemes by Vanessa Bell and Duncan Grant.[76] (See fig. 3.7.) The article proclaims that "the time has come to domesticate modern art," and Hutchinson's home is clearly in the vanguard of this movement.[77] The seven *Vogue*

The untidiest child would not mind putting its toys away in a cupboard as attractive as this designed by Allan Walton, painted bright blue, with a gay "nursery sea" design in pinks and browns. From Herriron

(Below) These lovely curtains by Marion Dorn are printed on white roman satin, and, completely filling the end wall of a large and lofty bedroom, form a striking decoration. The pelmet is green and the semi-classical design of the curtains is carried out in soft greens and pinks

(Right) The doors in Mrs. St. John Hutchinson's drawing-room are painted stone grey, the design being etched out in white. The Vanessa Bell panel over the books is in browns and blues and the vertical panel by Duncan Grant in purple browns. The delicate overdoor decoration shows a classical feeling befitting the period of the house

Another white and gold chair by Marion Dorn designed for the same room as that opposite

FIGURE 3.7. Hutchinson's drawing room, *Vogue* [London] (Late August 1926). Vogue © The Condé Nast Publications Ltd.

articles that she published capitalize on this notion of domestic modernity by highlighting the concerns of women.[78] In her first *Vogue* essay, "A Quoi Revent Les Jeunes Filles?" (1923), Hutchinson playfully addresses the social construction of gender and at the end encourages women not to "dream of being . . . a perfect mistress to a Byron"; instead, she urges them to focus on their own desire—it is "better to be heroines and dress ourselves up, thereby discovering our tastes and our talents" (*FP,* 130).

This plea for self-actualization through dress is echoed in an article that Hutchinson published the following year titled "Femininities" (1924) that addresses the frantic tempo of fashion—its relentless changeability—and offers a radical and perhaps counterintuitive suggestion: one can actually slow down this accelerated pace of modernity through dress. Hutchinson posits that women can accomplish this by returning to the pleasure of an old garment, purposefully resurrected, because those clothes not only retain the "shape" of the wearer but "preserve[s]" the very identity of a person in ways that "swift-changing fashions" never can (*FP,* 134, 135). In "Femininities," Marie Laurencin is upheld as the exemplar of this *"démodé"* modernity because her paintings of women are "modern, as modern as anything can be" while simultaneously capturing a temporal anomaly—an aspect of "feminine character [that] is out of place" because it recalls an outmoded past (136–37). There is a melancholic character to Laurencin's portraits—"brushed with an unexpected sadness" (137)—that is similarly captured in the "modern Millamant" portrait of Polly Flinders that appeared in *Vogue* in 1924. The *Vogue* blurb claims that Hutchinson's look conveys a "cynical glance" with "the touch of sentiment," and perhaps if one is persuaded by this plausible reading then it is also a tribute to the melancholy Marie Laurencin cover of *Vogue* that ran one year prior. (See fig. 3.8.)

Both portraits feature fashionable women with downcast gazes that avoid the viewer and arguably convey a similar skepticism about the internal dynamic of the fashion cycle: aware of fashion's transitoriness and its insistence on a conformity that perpetually advertises itself as a vehicle for personal expression. Elsewhere Hutchinson refers to Laurencin as a "true artist" who is "the enemy of 'chic'" because she "knows the value of the ugly" (168)—a characterization that situates Laurencin in opposition to the dominant view that beauty is the defining feature of feminine culture. The gaze of both portraits, in short, seems to convey the perceptual shock produced by the awareness—to borrow from Charles Baudelaire—that

VOGUE

FIGURE 3.8. Marie Laurencin / Vogue © The Condé Nast Publications Ltd.

modernity is characterized by the simultaneity of the fleeting and the eternal. Hutchinson herself cites Baudelaire elsewhere in an essay that meditates upon this tension between permanence and innovation, seeing women as the bearer of these temporal modes through dress: "we shall be in new and ravishing clothes . . . changeable as we know ourselves to be, ever ready for new issues . . . or to read Baudelaire" (196, 198).[79]

Several of the *Vogue* articles play with this tension between the past and the present, drawing attention to the plight of the modern woman: caught between her awareness of the proximity of the historical past (with both its comforts and constraints) and inhabiting a moment defined by the relentless dynamic of innovation characterized by aesthetic modernism and industrial modernization. Two of the Polly Flinders *Vogue* articles that were not republished in *Fugitive Pieces* highlight this unease: one, "A Plea for Renaissance" (1925), juxtaposes lines from T. S. Eliot's "Prufrock" (1915) alongside the discussion of a recent, uninspired production of John Dryden's Restoration comedy, *The Assignation: Or, Love in a Nunnery* (1672), incorporating references to Jean-Antoine Watteau and Duncan Grant.[80] Ultimately, Hutchinson seeks to provoke readers by inviting them to imagine the possibility of a re-staging of Dryden's satire with post-impressionist scenery by Grant. This, in her view, would be a genuine theatrical "renaissance"—a modernist "birth" rather than the "recurring funerals" that are produced by uninspired theater companies "in the name of culture."[81]

The other *Vogue* article that was not republished in *Fugitive Pieces*, "Pianos" (1924), similarly re-envisions history by inviting readers to contemplate an object—the piano—from a modernist perspective. Here Hutchinson moves from a discussion of Robert de Montesquiou's memoir (where he recounts how his grandmother used to read aloud to him as a sibling would silently practice scales) into a meditation on where our own thoughts and fingers go when someone reads Charles Dickens or Walt Whitman aloud to us: "Here indeed is a question Mr. Joyce might answer, and a page, if not a book, for him to write."[82] Through this visualization of contemporaneity, Hutchinson reimagines the past from the vantage point of her modernist present and again expresses an enthusiasm for the generative possibilities of artistic experimentation (in this case Joyce, rather than Grant). While both "A Plea for Renaissance" and "Pianos" appear to have little overtly to do with fashion, their construction and examination of the past through a backward glance that is informed by a modernist sensibility speaks directly to the dynamic of the fashion system and is precisely how Hutchinson understands the allure and the limits of contemporary fashion.

One of the last two *Vogue* essays that was published in *Fugitive Pieces,* "The River at Maidenhead" (1925), underscores this tension regarding the historical peculiarity of the fashion system—both forward- and backward-looking at once. The essay is overtly a meditation on the contiguity of past and present and the inseparability of materiality and culture—specifically, how certain affective objects have the capacity to reawaken one's intimate relationship to the past and dramatically change one's relationship to the present. Situating herself as a passenger in a car as it winds its way through the English countryside, Hutchinson writes: "wisely, when motoring, we have discarded parasols" because this antiquated relic of the "Victorian age" would be "out of place" in modernity (154). The essay purports to discard the parasol but nonetheless repeatedly crosses the boundaries between the past and the present as the speaker moves from car to boat and her mind meanders, visualizing the "ancient pleasures" of "cows, buttercups and beeches" while thinking about Thomas Hardy's *Tess of the d'Ubervilles* (1891) (ibid.). Alongside this rural idyll, the speaker simultaneously observes a panorama of "modern life" (156–57): fashionable young women in "coloured frocks . . . preparing a mannequin parade" on the lawn as a "jazz band" plays and "couples ceaselessly dance" (155, 156).

Hutchinson's gaze momentarily invokes the period's nostalgic longing for a return to rural England, but her meditation on nature is quickly superseded by her confrontation with modernity: "the new world is before me" (155). This new world is characterized not only by the refinement of modern dress—the mannequins' "dazzling elegance and freshness"—but also by a profound reorientation of perspective: "The 'Impressionist movement' seems to have got into our blood, and we are drunk with the appearances of things" (155, 157). For Hutchinson, this intoxicating re-visioning of "things" entails the embrace of a multi-perspectival, "Post-Impressionist" point of view, which in turn coincides with the rejection of customary practices regarding dress.

Thus, "The River at Maidenhead" first invokes a stock image of antiquated fashion—an "immortal couple: he in his white flannels, she with her paper Japanese sunshade" situated in an English punt moving along the Thames—then morphs into a more contemporary visual image that links modernity to more provocative sexual and racial imagery (*FP,* 156).

Hutchinson conjures an image of two couples sitting in a "new electric canoe" that seems to "move by magic," guided by a "sort of Charon" figure (in Greek mythology, the ferryman of Hades who carries souls of the newly deceased across the river) who recalls a "sultan carry[ing] his harem" across the Bosphorus (158). This orientalized Charon sits in the stern of this boat that has a gramophone affixed to its prow, from which blasts the "siren's song" of lyrics from "Hard Hearted Hannah, the Vamp of Savannah" (158, 159).[83]

Here Hutchinson invokes the humor and satire of the African-American blues to paint an ambivalent portrait of modernity—Hannah is an icy "cold refrigerating . . . vamp" who compulsively delights in the torture of men—and cumulatively these images can be read as a sign of the paradoxical nature of modern culture: both enticing and terrifying in its rapid evolution (159). One leaves behind the safe and predictable world of English particularity (cows and buttercups) and sails into the dangerous and implicitly racialized space of American jazz, sexuality, and the proximity of death. Into this perilous and vulnerable wider context Hutchinson evokes references to the "shifting finery" of dress, pitting its changeability—the inevitable "ebb and flow"—against abstract "immemorial forms" that recall Baudelaire's celebration of ephemeral beauty (157). Ultimately these two spheres cultivate an ardent watchfulness in the reader, who seeks to make sense of fashion's aspirations in modernity.

Cumulatively, the *Vogue* articles convey ambivalence toward the category of fashion, for its rapid change and insistence upon novelty often confound one's efforts to make sense of the affective and mental life of the moment. In "The River at Maidenhead," Hutchinson regards this as the perpetual contemporary challenge, that is to say, the ongoing struggle to "detect the scaffolding" and "penetrate [the] mysteries" of "modern life" (156–57). Within this schema, the materiality of dress—the cultural object that is most proximate to the body—at times seems to facilitate this quest to excavate "the passions" while in other instances it appears to contribute to its obfuscation (157). The final essay that Hutchinson published in *Vogue,* "Fireworks" (1926), seeks to make sense of these material practices by focusing upon the topic of fashionable manners and the phenomenon of the party. Anticipating Woolf, Hutchinson regards the party as a transformative experience, an intensification of life: "Like tropical plants all should extravagantly flower [there]" (149). Hosts are required to provide the "scaffolding"—champagne, disguises, music, brightly colored paper crackers—while guests are expected to sartorially "puff themselves out," he in "his white tie" and she in "her best frock" (151). The social force of dress at a party cannot be underestimated; it functions as a kind of "distorting mirror" through which the "mirage" of one's appearance can "become real" (ibid.).

Fashion's relevance here stems not from facilitating the meeting of an "unknown admirer," but rather, from the cultivation of self-discovery— the revelation of putting on a "best frock" for a party and encountering there among the guests "an unknown emotion" (ibid.). Interestingly, Hutchinson frames this revelatory possibility in conventionally English terms: "voyages of discovery . . . [to] America" (ibid.). Within this conquest of new worlds, fancy dress plays an instrumental role by enabling one to circulate and probe the broader question of one's relationship to modernity—holding out the possibility of an escape from the habitual arrangement of daily life. Hutchinson calls this incipient sensation the "premonition that . . . lies in wait . . . [of] something fantastic and enchanting, the memory of which will not fade . . . the rumour of America" (151–52). Here the imaginative appropriation of space at the party illustrates the tenacity of the familiar English trope of conquest, reminding us that Hutchinson's engagement with modern style is inseparable from the historicizing discourses that inform its representation.

Notes

1. James Agate to Mary Hutchinson, June 3, 1940. Harry Ransom Center, University of Texas at Austin (HRC). Hereafter cited as HRC.

2. Woolf, *Letters of Virginia Woolf, Volume V*, 207.

3. Blanche, *More Portraits of a Lifetime*, 39. I am very grateful to Nicholas Hutchinson for his permission to reproduce the two photographs of his grandmother, Mary Hutchinson.

4. Raymond Mortimer, "Mrs. St. John Hutchinson," 18.

5. Ibid.

6. In contrast to this view, Hutchinson's brother James recalls that while she was the "most feminine of women," Mary was extremely intelligent—"it would be difficult to talk above her head"—and possessed the "most discerning artistic sense" (87, 89). See James Strachey Barnes, *Half a Life*, 87, 89.

7. Lee, *Virginia Woolf*, 378.

8. Bradshaw, "'Those Extraordinary Parakeets,' Part One," 5.

9. Hutchinson, *Fugitive Pieces*, 118–19. Hereafter cited parenthetically in the text as *FP*, followed by page number.

10. No authoritative biography of Hutchinson exists, but scattered references to her life can be found in various sources that at times offer contradictory evidence regarding dates and details. We know that Hutchinson was born in Quetta, India, on March 29, 1889; she was the eldest of two children of Sir Hugh Barnes and Winifred Strachey, the fourth child of John Strachey—Hutchinson's grandfather was a younger brother of Lytton Strachey's father. Her father was an eminent figure within the Indian colonial government, and when her mother died (when Hutchinson was only two), she was raised in Italy by her maternal grandparents. After their death, she returned to England and was boarded at Effingham School in Surrey. All of these elements—a colonial childhood, her cosmopolitan upbringing, her upper-class status and early marriage—play a role in her fiction and essays. Hutchinson published one autobiographical essay that documents her itinerant childhood. See "Kaleidoscope of Childhood," 121–27. For a snapshot of Hutchinson's biography, see Spalding, *Vanessa Bell*, 145. For additional references to Hutchinson's life, see Bradshaw, "'Those Extraordinary Parakeets,' Part One," 5–12; Bradshaw, "'Those Extraordinary Parakeets,' Part Two," 5–11; Crawford, *Young Eliot*; Hargrove, "Remarkable Relationship"; Mathis, "'double eye of love,'" 337–44; Ratliff, "A Bloomsbury Friendship," 14–41; Stanford, "The First Mrs. Eliot," 89–110.

11. Lee, *Virginia Woolf*, 378; Garnett, *Flowers of the Forest*, 48.

12. Seymour-Jones, *Painted Shadow*, 293, 267.

13. Woolf, *Letters of Virginia Woolf, Volume VI*, 527. Lee cites some excerpts from Mary's "seductive letters" to Woolf—such as her passionate exclamation, "I pine for you"—but she concludes that "if this was a love-affair it was probably one sided" because "Virginia always wrote of Mary with a hostile edge" (378). This is not entirely true, as is evidenced by this 1924 diary excerpt in which Woolf reflects upon her relationship with Hutchinson and contemplates the meaning of female friendship: "Mary in black with lotus leaves round her neck. If one could be friendly with women, what a pleasure—the relationship so secret & private compared with relations with men. Why not write about it? Truthfully?" See *Diary of Virginia Woolf, Volume II*, 320. Is the language of secrecy and privacy here a euphemism for sapphic amorosity? That certainly seems possible. For an examination of Woolf's techniques of rhetorical seduction, see Mathis, "'double eye of love.'"

14. Hargrove, "Remarkable Relationship," 6. The unpublished letters from the Huxleys are in the Hutchinson collection of the Harry Ransom Humanities Research Center at the University of Texas at Austin. In addition to the Hargrove article, see also Nicholas Murray, *Aldous Huxley*. Murray documents the

"extraordinary *ménage à trois*" of Aldous, Maria, and Hutchinson during the 1920s and argues that both of the "Huxleys seem to have existed in a permanent state of sexual desire for Mary" during this period (175).

15. Seymour-Jones, *Painted Shadow,* 252. For an examination of Hutchinson's relationship to Tom and Vivienne Eliot, see Seymour-Jones, especially chapter 11. For a focus on Vivienne's relationship to Hutchinson, see Stanford, "The First Mrs. Eliot." For an analysis of Tom's relationship to Hutchinson see Crawford, Hargrove, and Stanford. Seymour-Jones reads the intense friendship that developed between Vivienne and Hutchinson as a presage to Hutchinson's subsequent erotic relationships with Maria Huxley and Vita Sackville-West (256–57).

16. Sagar and Boulton, *Letters of D. H. Lawrence, Volume VII,* 227. We know that Hutchinson and Eliot were intensely close and read one another's work in draft. Robert Crawford documents this intimacy and also touches upon the erotic content of Vivienne's relationship with Hutchinson. See Crawford, *Young Eliot,* 267–70, 326.

17. O'Sullivan and Scott, *Collected Letters of Katherine Mansfield,* 126. Letter from Lytton Strachey to Mary Hutchinson, February 22, 1928, HRC. Ratliff notes that Hutchinson and Strachey were first cousins once removed, but she argues that their relationship was more like that of siblings. See Ratliff, "A Bloomsbury Friendship," 24.

18. Shone, "Matisse in England," 479–84. Stanford, "The First Mrs. Eliot," 93. Shone dates Hutchinson's involvement with Bell "since about 1913" (484), whereas Stanford dates its inception at 1915. Hargrove, in "Remarkable Relationship" (5), claims the affair began in 1914. Such small discrepancies reappear throughout the criticism, suggesting the need for an authoritative biography on Hutchinson. Mark Hussey is writing a biography of Clive Bell (to be published by Bloomsbury) that should shed some light on Hutchinson's life as it relates to Bell. Hutchinson herself claims that her "love of the arts" was fostered both by her grandfather and the sensuous sights, smells, and colors of her childhood in Florence. See Hutchinson, "Kaleidoscope of Childhood," 123. In her dissertation, Clare Ratliff refers to a January 2, 1929, letter from Clive Bell to Hutchinson in which he asks "if she realized how much she had helped form his taste and ideas" about art even though he did not work out his aesthetic theories in his correspondence. See "Correspondence of Mary Hutchinson," 81.

19. Marler, *Selected Letters of Vanessa Bell,* 195. Ratliff refers to a letter from Clive Bell to Hutchinson (January 2, 1929), in which he asks "if she realized how much she had helped form his taste and ideas." See Ratliff, "A Bloomsbury Friendship," 81.

20. Chisholm, *Carrington's Letters,* 140. Carrington goes on to detail her duress in having to host Clive and Hutchinson: "I felt my solidity made them dislike me.

Then I had to make their beds, and empty chamber pots because our poor cook Mrs Legg can't do everything and that made me hate them, because in order they should talk so elegantly, I couldn't for a whole weekend do any painting and yet they scorned my useful grimy hands" (140–41).

21. Spalding, *Vanessa Bell*, 146.

22. Darroch, *Ottoline*, 162–63.

23. Shone, *Art of Bloomsbury*, 103.

24. Roger Fry to Mary Hutchinson, February 14, 1917, HRC. The letter is typed on Omega Workshops letterhead, a bold rectangular design with reclining figures attributed to Wyndham Lewis.

25. Clare Ratliff maintains that Hutchinson's 1927 Hogarth publication, *Fugitive Pieces*, was "well received," but she cites no evidence of this, and I have unearthed only one review of this work (by Orlo Williams). See her "A Bloomsbury Friendship," 17. Ratliff makes note of the few works published by Hutchinson separately from *Fugitive Pieces*: a short story, "War" (1917) published under the pseudonym, Polly Flinders, in the *Egoist*; an article, "George Moore—Another View" (1936) published under her own name in the *London Mercury*; and a short story, "The Noon's Repose" (1956) also published under her own name in *London Magazine*. Ratliff observes that of these three works, "War" was included in *Fugitive Pieces*, but the title was changed to "Near the Barracks." Ratliff also maintains that "Paris Fashions" (1923), an article that was published in *Nation and Athenaeum*, was the only other essay published separately from *Fugitive Pieces*, but this is not the case. I discuss Hutchinson's *Nation and Athenaeum* essays in the body of the text. Ratliff also neglects to cite Hutchinson's introduction to the artist, Henry Tonks, published in *The Life of Henry Tonks* by Joseph Hone in 1939.

26. Solnit, "Woolf's Darkness," 88–89. Hereafter cited in the text.

27. Spalding, *Vanessa Bell*, 196–97, 146. Spalding argues that Vanessa Bell's painting "triumphantly" satirizes her attitude toward Hutchinson (146). For a reference to Hutchinson as Clive Bell's "mistress," see Lee, *Virginia Woolf*, 326. For a reproduction of the Vanessa Bell portrait, see plate 35 in Shone, *Art of Bloomsbury*, 104.

28. For reference to the Tonks pastel (as well as an earlier watercolor of Hutchinson), see Bradshaw, "'Those Extraordinary Parakeets,' Part One," 7. A black-and-white reproduction of Grant's "Portrait of Mary Hutchinson" is illustrated in the Gallery Edward Harvane catalogue, *Ottoline* 40. Grant's use of chartreuse and pinks is clearly in conversation with the hues that dominate Bell's own palette. For reference to the two Matisse portraits, see Shone, *Art of Bloomsbury*, 480–81. Shone reproduces the two portraits, one of which Matisse retained (whereabouts unknown). Hutchinson sat for Matisse in his studio at 132 Boulevard Montparnasse and she and her husband paid 8,000 francs for the charcoal drawing. In June 2018, Sotheby's sold Matisse's "Portrait of Mary Hutchinson" for £3,130,00.

29. Shone, *Art of Bloomsbury*, 102, 103.

30. I am very grateful to Regina Marler, for bringing this painting to my attention, and to Christopher Reed, for clarifying the correct title of the painting and telling me about the *Vogue* article: "Preparing for the Grand Style," 59, no. 11 (Early June 1922): 62–63. (The illustration of *The Party* is on p. 63.) Marler recalls that Quentin Bell allegedly discovered the painting, still rolled up, in the Monk's House attic, and then Barbara and Howard Ginsberg purchased it from Caroline Cuthbert at the Anthony d'Offay Gallery in London in the 1980s. The painting somehow picked up the title, *Mrs. Dalloway's Party*, along the way—perhaps as a selling point suggested by d'Offay. Marler confirms that the painting is signed VB 1922 in pencil on the verso. Diane Gillespie refers to the painting by its earlier working title, *Mrs. Dalloway's Party*, but points out that it predates both *Mrs. Dalloway* (1925) and the seven short stories written between 1922 and 1927 that were published by Stella McNicol as *Mrs. Dalloway's Party* in 1973. See Gillespie, "Virginia Woolf, Vanessa Bell and Painting," 129. Gillespie does not speculate on the possible identity of the figures and instead talks about the painting in terms of its formal qualities and color.

31. I am grateful to the Virginia Woolf listserv for responding to queries about the painting (October 19, 2018), in particular, Christine Froula, Diane Gillespie, Manuela Palacios, and Angela Runciman. I am also grateful to Howard and Barbara Ginsberg, and especially to Henrietta Garnett, for their permission to reproduce *The Party*.

32. Lytton Strachey to Mary Hutchinson, July 23, 1916; Hutchinson to Strachey, January 1, 1917, as quoted by Ratliff, "A Bloomsbury Friendship," 30–31.

33. Ratliff, "A Bloomsbury Friendship," 20. A characteristic response is from Mark Gertler, who laments in a July 18, 1919, letter written from the Garsington Manor, "How difficult your writing is to read!" Gertler to Mary Hutchinson, undated letter, Box 13, Folder 7–8, HRC. We know that the Harry Ransom Center purchased the Hutchinson collection from Frank Hollings on June 11, 1968. He sent the center a rather effusive catalogue description, in which he went on at length about the depth and breadth of correspondence *to* Hutchinson, but did not leave any clues as to where her own letters might be. An international search via a database called "Archives Hub" turned up two additional archives related to Hutchinson: her correspondence with art historian Kenneth Clark (held at the Tate), and her letters to the actor Michael Redgrave (at the Victoria and Albert Museum). In addition, several letters from Mary Hutchinson to Virginia Woolf and Vanessa Bell (some originals and some duplicates) are archived at The Keep, the archive at the University of Sussex Special Collections. I have recently learned that St. John Hutchinson's papers will also be archived at *The Keep*.

34. Gordon, *Ghostly Matters*, xvii.

35. Ibid., 27.

36. Vanessa Bell to Mary Hutchinson, undated letter. (The first page written by Vanessa Bell says Charleston Firle, Friday.) Several letters from Clive Bell to Hutchinson also address intimate domestic concerns, particularly the deleterious effects of reproduction on women. In an undated one-page letter written on "46, Gordon Square, Bloomsbury" stationery, Clive Bell recounts Vanessa Bell's outrage over the fact that Hutchinson's doctor "didn't give her a breast pump and tell her to pump away her superfluous milk. She seems to think the man ought to be hanged. She says you can get one in Chichester. For God's sake send for it. Please do!" Clive Bell to Mary Hutchinson, undated letter, HRC. In another undated letter to Mary, he laments the cultural prescription that idealizes maternal devotion: "Babies have been the ruin of half the women I know. And it's all superstition too, superstition and sentimentality." Clive Bell to Mary Hutchinson, undated letter, HRC. Yet Clive Bell's seemingly progressive views on gender are undermined by his colonialist ideas about race. In the same letter, he continues: "Everyone knows it would be the death of people like you and Vanessa to try and do the work of peasants but in the matter of babies you're expected to be a match for the blackest savage in Togoland." Togoland was a German protectorate in West Africa from 1884 to 1914, and then in 1916 was split into two territories, French Togoland and British Togoland. In 1922, British Togoland was formally placed under British rule.

37. Vanessa Bell to Mary Hutchinson, undated letter, HRC. (The first page written by Vanessa Bell says Charleston Firle Dec.13 12/13/ 1918?, with the date written in pencil by a librarian on a separate slip.)

38. Garnett's point of view is summarized by Michael Holroyd in *Lytton Strachey*, 322.

39. Vanessa Bell to Mary Hutchinson, undated letter. HRC. (The first page at the top says "Charleston Sunday," written by Vanessa Bell, but does not provide a year.)

40. This article is not indexed in the list of items for Hutchinson's bibliography on the HRC page, even though Clare Ratliff's dissertation is listed.

41. For a link to the HRC "Literary File" see http://norman.hrc.utexas.edu/fasearch/lf.hp.html.

42. Gordon, *Ghostly Matters*, 17.

43. For a reproduction of *The Awakening of the Muses*, see Lois Oliver, *Boris Anrep: The National Gallery Mosaics*, 36–37. Hutchinson is the model for the figure to the left of Bacchus, who is in the center of the frame next to Apollo.

44. For a discussion of Anrep's conflation of ancient figures with their modern Bloomsbury counterparts (such as Virginia Woolf as the model for Clio, the muse of history), see Benjamin Harvey, "Virginia Woolf, Art Galleries and Museums," in *The Edinburgh Companion to Virginia Woolf and the Arts*, 140–59.

45. Oliver, *Boris Anrep*, 12

46. Fry, "Modern Mosaic and Mr. Boris Anrep," 277. The model for the *Daily Incidents in the Life of a Lady of Fashion* mosaic series was Lesley Jowitt, the wife of eminent lawyer and British politician William Jowitt. They commissioned a mosaic floor for their Mayfair home at 35 Upper Brook Street. The series included Lesley Jowitt telephoning from the bed dressed in pajamas, applying lipstick, at her dressing table, and shaking cocktails. Fry reproduces these mosaics in "Modern Mosaic and Mr. Boris Anrep," plates B–F. For a color reproduction of the telephone image, see plate 3 in Oliver, *Boris Anrep*, 12.

47. In a 1921 letter to Roger Fry, Woolf writes: "Mary Hutchinson has a dressmaker who would make me look like other people." Woolf, *Letters of Virginia Woolf, Volume II*, 485.

48. Woolf, *Diary of Virginia Woolf, Volume II*, 182.

49. Woolf, *Letters of Virginia Woolf, Volume V*, 207.

50. Lee, *Virginia Woolf*, 383.

51. Jan Glier Reeder, "The Personal and Professional Life of Charles James," 22. For a reproduction of James's drawing for a taxi dress, conceived in 1929, see Harold Koda, "Spirals and Wraps," in *Charles James*, 23. In the same volume see also page 65 for two additional views of the taxi dress in ink. According to Koda, although the taxi dress was difficult to manufacture because one side of the top and the spiral wrap skirt were made without seams, it was the first garment to be sold in department stores' accessories departments in sealed cellophane packages (65).

52. Woolf, *Letters of Virginia Woolf, Volume V*, 158. Woolf goes on to write: "So geometrical is Charlie James that if a stitch is crooked, Vita, the whole dress is torn to shreds: which Mary bears without wincing" (158).

53. Leonard Woolf to Mary Hutchinson, May 9, 1923, HRC.

54. The articles published in the *Nation and Athenaeum* are "Paris Fashions," 33, no. 15 (July 14, 1923): 484–85; "Streets to Shop In," 34, no. 13 (December 29, 1923): 488; "Thoughts Suggested by Madame Groult's Show of Models," 36, no. 12 (December 20, 1924): 440–41; "The Ballet Season," 37, no. 18 (August 1, 1925): 543–44; "La Rentree," 38, no. 1 (October 3, 1925): 15–16; "The Gamekeeper," 40, no. 5 (November 1926): 180–81. The book review was titled "Omnibus for Weekenders," 35, no. 18 (August 2, 1924): 567–68.

55. Bradshaw, "'Those Extraordinary Parakeets,' Part One," 6.

56. Hutchinson, "Kaleidoscope of Childhood," 126.

57. See *Vogue* magazine (London) 8, no. 64 (Late October 1924): 58. David Bradshaw speculates that Clive Bell wrote the *Vogue* vignette. See Bradshaw, "'Those Extraordinary Parakeets,' Part Two," 7. Maurice Beck and Helen Macgregor were the chief photographers for British *Vogue*. Hutchinson's article, "La

Belle France" (Late October 1924), a travelogue, appears in the same issue of *Vogue* on the adjacent page (59).

58. Valerie Eliot and Hugh Haughton, *Letters of T. S. Eliot*, 320.

59. Only some of these letters have been published in Appendix B of *The Letters of Virginia Woolf, Volume VI*. Stuart Clark estimates that approximately 225 uncollected letters have been published in the "Virginia Woolf Bulletin," but that about 400 in total are extant and uncollected. For a discussion of the significance of the unpublished letters, see Mathis, "'double eye of love,'" 340.

60. Woolf, *Diary of Virginia Woolf, Volume IV*, 164. Woolf, *Letters of Virginia Woolf, Volume VI*, 505. The editors' note to this letter (1472a) stipulates that "Mary rejected this idea" (505n1) but provides no evidence for this.

61. Lee, *Virginia Woolf,* 462. Lee cites the letter from Mary Hutchinson to Virginia Woolf (dated May 26, 1924), located in the Monk's House Papers, University of Sussex, on 823n132. Woolf's enthusiasm for Hutchinson's fashion sense was intertwined with expressions of flirtatious intimacy, as is evidenced in this 1924 letter: "Mary!!!!! . . . Don't you smell me? I am like a civet. . . . Yes: you've entirely altered my life, and given a new channel for vanity to flow in . . . you have removed an inhibition, ruined a home, intoxicated a heart, and made me for life your slave, suppliant, servant, debtor . . . you've admitted me to the great company of *real* [sic] women—the desire of my heart." See Woolf, *Letters of Virginia Woolf, Volume VI*, 505.

62. Woolf, *Letters of Virigina Woolf, Volume VI*, 503. In her diary, Woolf dismisses Hutchinson's book—"Mary's stories, I fear, are bad"—but it is unclear from this quote if Woolf is talking about the short stories that comprise the first section of *Fugitive Pieces* or if she is characterizing the entire work. See Woolf, *Diary of Virginia Woolf, Volume III*, 52. For a reference to Hutchinson's "furious" irritation with the delay that accompanied her book's publication, see Woolf, *Letters of Virginia Woolf, Volume III*, 371. Woolf recounts that "Mary is said to be in a rage because we dont bring her book out at once. As she wont correct the proofs, and perpetually adds and scratches out, we put the blame on her" (368). For Woolf's mocking reference to a dinner party that she was attending with Clive Bell "'to celebrate the success of Fugitive pieces,'" see p. 390. Woolf's irritation seems largely to stem from the fact that Hutchinson's book ate into the press's profits because it did not sell well. See Woolf, *Diary of Virginia Woolf, Volume III*, 150, 162.

63. Woolmer, *A Checklist*, 60. For a reference to the number of copies pulped see the Woolmer addenda for book number 122 (*Fugitive Pieces*).

64. Vanessa Bell was a frequent collaborator at the Hogarth Press, creating abstract, geometrical, and pictorial cover designs for all of Woolf's works except for *The Voyage Out* (1915). Did she decline an offer to design the cover for *Fugitive Pieces*? We do not know. According to J. H. Willis, Bell designed twenty dust

jackets and supplied seven additional designs for various Hogarth Press series and editions. Although Hogarth displayed a variety of styles by various artists on its dust jackets, Willis argues that it was "the Postimpressionist, Charleston style of Vanessa Bell that spoke most eloquently and pervasively for the press." Willis, *Leonard and Virginia Woolf as Publishers*, 385. For further discussion of Bell's artistic importance to Hogarth, see pp. 31–33, 75–76, 113, and 381.

65. Woolmer, *A Checklist*, 60.

66. R. S. Koppen discusses the gendered implications of Flugel's historiography. Koppen perceives the main line of division in his work as that between female sartorial emancipation and "The Great Masculine Renunciation," the willing subordination on the part of bourgeois men of individual sartorial distinction. Koppen, *Virginia Woolf, Fashion and Literary Modernity*, 123–25.

67. Woolf, *A Room of One's Own*, 73.

68. For the ad, see *Times Literary Supplement* no. 1323, June 9, 1927, 405.

69. Williams, review of *Fugitive Pieces*, 469.

70. For an incomplete but useful account of Hutchinson's publications separate from *Fugitive Pieces*, see Ratliff, "A Bloomsbury Friendship," 17n8.

71. See Ratliff, "Correspondence of Mary Hutchinson"; Bradshaw, "'Those Extraordinary Parakeets,' Part One,'" 5–12; Bradshaw, "'Those Extraordinary Parakeets,' Part Two,'" 5–11; Hargrove, "Remarkable Relationship," 5–15; Ratliff, "A Bloomsbury Friendship," 14–41.

72. Ratliff, "A Bloomsbury Friendship," 238.

73. Bradshaw, "'Those Extraordinary Parakeets,' Part Two," 8.

74. Felski, *The Gender of Modernity*, 10.

75. Hutchinson published two articles in *Vogue* that were not republished in *Fugitive Pieces*. They are Polly Flinders, "Pianos," *Vogue* (London) 63, no. 2 (Late January 1924): 47; and Polly Flinders, "A Plea for Renaissance," *Vogue* (London) 65, no. 8 (Late April 1925): 65. I discuss both of these articles later in the essay. In addition, two of these essays appeared in American *Vogue*, also under Polly Flinders: "La Belle France," *Vogue* (New York) 65, no. 8 (April 15, 1925): 144, 146; and "Marie Laurencin, Artist," *Vogue* (New York) 65, no. 9 (May 1, 1925): 130, 132.

76. Another photograph of Hutchinson's drawing room was featured in *Vogue*, 63, no. 8 (Late April 1924), in an article titled "Good Interiors" that sought to highlight the happy juxtaposition of "antique furniture with modern paintings" with an illustration of a "decorative ornamental" canvas by Duncan Grant above a "row of Chinese jars" (85). The last *Vogue* article to feature Hutchinson's home was "Dining-Rooms of To-Day," *Vogue* (London) 70, no. 5 (September 7, 1927). This article featured a photograph of Hutchinson's dining room table, decorated with an abstract modernist design, and it referred to her as a student of "modern decoration" (55).

77. *Vogue* (London), "The Work of Some Modern Decorative Art," 68.

78. The six *Vogue* (London) essays published under the pseudonym of Polly Flinders in chronological order are "A Quoi Revent Les Jeunes Filles?," *Vogue* (London) 62, no. 12 (Late December 1923): 51; "Pianos," *Vogue* (London) 63, no. 2 (Late January 1924): 47; "Femininities," *Vogue* (London) 64, no. 3 (Early August 1924): 43; "La Belle France," *Vogue* (New York) 65, no. 8 (April 15, 1925): 144, 146; "A Plea for Renaissance," *Vogue* (London) 65, no. 8 (Late April 1925): 65; "The River at Maidenhead," *Vogue* (London) 66, no. 2 (Late July 1925): 39, 80; "Fireworks," *Vogue* (London) 67, no. 1 (Early January 1926): 49.

79. Ilya Parkins provides us with an extremely helpful and compelling understanding of how the female body functions as a bearer of these two temporal modes (past and present) in the work of Walter Benjamin, where fashion makes visible his theory of the dialectical image. Parkins, *Poiret, Dior and Schiaparelli*, 139–44.

80. See Hutchinson, "A Plea for Renaissance," 65, and "Pianos," 47. As in "A Plea for Renaissance," Hutchinson's "Pianos" re-envisions history by inviting readers to contemplate an object—in this case, the piano—from a modernist perspective. In "Pianos" she moves from a discussion of Robert de Montesquiou's memoir, in which he recalls how his grandmother used to read aloud to him while a sibling would silently practice scales, into a meditation on where our own thoughts and fingers go when someone reads Dickens or Whitman aloud to us: "Here indeed is a question Mr. Joyce might answer, and a page, if not a book, for him to write" (47).

81. Hutchinson, "A Plea for Renaissance," 65.

82. Hutchinson, "Pianos," 47.

83. Hutchinson does not attribute the lyrics to anyone, but we know that "Hard-Hearted Hannah" was composed by Jack Yellen, Bob Bigelow, and Charles Bates and published in 1924. The song was popularized by vocalists Margaret Young and Lucille Nelson, among America's first wave of jazz and blues recording artists in the 1920s.

Works Cited

Agate, James. Letter to Mary Hutchinson, June 3, 1940. Harry Ransom Center (HRC), University of Texas at Austin.

Bell, Clive. Letter to Mary Hutchinson, undated letter. Box 3.6, dated August–December 1916. HRC.

Blanche, Jacques-Émile. *More Portraits of a Lifetime*. Translated by Walter Clement. London: J. M. Dent and Sons, 1939.

Bradshaw, David. "'Those Extraordinary Parakeets,' Part One: Clive Bell and Mary Hutchinson." *Charleston Magazine* 16 (1997): 5–12.

———. "'Those Extraordinary Parakeets,' Part Two: Clive Bell and Mary Hutchinson." *Charleston Magazine* 17 (1998): 5–11.

Chisholm, Anne, ed. *Carrington's Letters: Dora Carrington*, London: Chatto and Windus, 2017.

Crawford, Robert. *Young Eliot: From St. Louis to "The Waste Land."* London: Jonathan Cape, 2015.

Darroch, Sandra Jobson. *Ottoline: The Life of Lady Ottoline Morrell.* New York: Coward, McCann and Geoghegan, 1975.

Eliot, Valerie, and Hugh Haughton, eds. *The Letters of T. S. Eliot, Volume 1: 1898–1922.* New Haven: Yale University Press, 2011.

Felski, Rita. *The Gender of Modernity.* Cambridge, MA: Harvard University Press, 1995.

Fry, Roger. "Modern Mosaic and Mr. Boris Anrep." *Burlington Magazine for Connoisseurs* 42, no. 243 (1923): 272–73, 276–78.

Gallery Edward Harvane. *Ottoline: An Exhibition of Works by Those Artists Who Gathered about the Personality of Lady Ottoline Morrell*: October 27–November 27, 1971.

Garnett, David. *The Flowers of the Forest.* New York: Harcourt Brace, 1955.

Gertler, Mark. Letter to Mary Hutchinson, undated letter. Box 13.7, dated July 18, 1918. HRC.

Gillespie, Diane. "Virginia Woolf, Vanessa Bell and Painting." In *The Edinburgh Companion to Virginia Woolf and the Arts*, edited by Maggie Humm, 121–39. Edinburgh: Edinburgh University Press, 2010.

Gordon, Avery F. *Ghostly Matters: Haunting and the Sociological Imagination.* Minneapolis: University of Minnesota Press, 2008.

Hargrove, Nancy. "The Remarkable Relationship of T. S. Eliot and Mary Hutchinson." *Yeats Eliot Review* 28, no. 3–4 (Fall 2011): 3–15.

Harvey, Benjamin. "Virginia Woolf, Art Galleries and Museums." In *The Edinburgh Companion to Virginia Woolf and the Arts*, edited by Maggie Humm, 140–59. Edinburgh: Edinburgh University Press, 2010.

Holroyd, Michael. *Lytton Strachey: The New Biography.* New York: W. W. Norton, 1994.

Hutchinson, Mary. [Polly Flinders.] "A Quoi Revent Les Jeunes Filles?" *Vogue* (London) 62, no. 12 (Late December 1923).

———. [Polly Flinders.] "The Ballet Season." *Nation and Athenaeum* 37, no. 18 (August 1, 1925).

———. [Polly Flinders.] "Femininities." *Vogue* (London) 64, no. 3 (Early August 1924).

———. [Polly Flinders.] Editorial, "Fireworks: On Giving and Going to Parties, Showing What Character, Conversation and Contact Are to be Aimed at by Guest and Host." *Vogue* (London) 67, no. 1 (Early January 1926).

———. *Fugitive Pieces*. London: Hogarth, 1927.

———. [Polly Flinders.] "The Gamekeeper." *Nation and Athenaeum* 40, no. 5 (November 1926).

———. "George Moore—Another View." *London Mercury* 33 (January 1936): 334–36.

———. Introduction to *The Life of Henry Tonks*. By Joseph Hone. London: Heinemann, 1939.

———. "Kaleidoscope of Childhood." *X: A Quarterly Review* 1, no. 2 (1960).

———. [Polly Flinders.] "La Belle France." *Vogue* (London) 64, no. 8 (Late October 1924).

———. [Polly Flinders.] "La Belle France." *Vogue* (New York) 65, no. 8 (April 15, 1925).

———. [Polly Flinders.] "La Rentree." *Nation and Athenaeum* 38, no. 1 (October 3, 1925).

———. "Marie Laurencin, Artist." *Vogue* (New York) 65, no. 9 (May 1, 1925).

———. "The Noon's Repose." *London Magazine* 3, no. 11 (November 1956).

———. [Polly Flinders.] "Omnibus for Weekenders." *Nation and Athenaeum* 35, no. 18 (August 2, 1924).

———. [Polly Flinders.] "Paris Fashions." *Nation and Athenaeum* 33, no. 15 (July 14, 1923).

———. [Polly Flinders.] "Pianos." *Vogue* (London) 63, no. 2 (Late January 1924).

———. "Playing the Game." Review of *The Technique of the Love Affair*, by a Gentlewoman. *Nation and Athenaeum* (November 17, 1928): 261.

———. [Polly Flinders.] "A Plea for Renaissance." *Vogue* (London) 65, no. 8 (Late April 1925).

———. [Polly Flinders.] "The River at Maidenhead." *Vogue* (London) 66, no. 2 (Late July 1925).

———. [Polly Flinders.] "Streets to Shop In." *Nation and Athenaeum* 34, no. 13 (December 29, 1923).

———. [Polly Flinders.] "Thoughts Suggested by Madame Groult's Show of Models." *Nation and Athenaeum* 36, no. 12 (December 20, 1924).

———. [Polly Flinders.] "War." *Egoist* 6, no. 11 (December 1917).

Koda, Harold. "Spirals and Wraps." In *Charles James: Beyond Fashion,* edited by Harold Koda and Jan Glier Reeder, 59–89. New Haven: Yale University Press, 2014.

Koppen, R. S. *Virginia Woolf, Fashion and Literary Modernity*. Edinburgh: Edinburgh University Press, 2009.

Lee, Hermione. *Virginia Woolf.* New York: Alfred A. Knopf, 1997.

Marler, Regina. *Selected Letters of Vanessa Bell*. New York: Pantheon Books, 1993.

Mathis, Mary. "'The double eye of love': Virginia Woolf and Mary Hutchinson."

In *Virginia Woolf: Themes and Variations: Selected Papers from the Second Annual Conference on Virginia Woolf,* edited by Mark Hussey and Vara Neverow-Turk, 337–44. New York: Pace University Press, 1993.

Moore, George. Letter to Mary Hutchinson, letter dated July 20, envelope dated July 21, 1923. HRC.

Mortimer, Raymond ("R. M."). "Mrs. St. John Hutchinson: Wit and Taste in Bloomsbury Circle." *The Times,* April 21, 1977.

Murray, Nicholas. *Aldous Huxley: A Biography.* New York: St. Martin's, 2002.

Oliver, Lois. *Boris Anrep: The National Gallery Mosaics.* London: National Gallery, 2004.

O'Sullivan, Vincent, and Margaret Scott, eds. *The Collected Letters of Katherine Mansfield, Vol. 4: 1920–1921.* Oxford: Clarendon, 1996.

Parkins, Ilya. *Poiret, Dior and Schiaparelli: Fashion, Femininity and Modernity.* London and New York: Berg, 2012.

Ratliff, Clare. "A Bloomsbury Friendship: The Correspondence of Mary Hutchinson and Lytton Strachey." *Library Chronicle of the University of Texas at Austin* 48 (1989): 14–41.

———. "The Correspondence of Mary Hutchinson: A New Look at Bloomsbury, Eliot and Huxley." PhD diss., University of Texas at Austin, 1991.

Reeder, Jan Glier. "The Personal and Professional Life of Charles James." In *Charles James: Beyond Fashion,* edited by Harold Koda and Jan Glier Reeder, 16–51. New Haven: Yale University Press, 2014.

Sagar, Keith, and James T. Boulton, eds. *The Letters of D. H. Lawrence, Volume VII: November 1928–February 1930.* Cambridge: Cambridge University Press, 1993.

Seymour-Jones, Carole. *Painted Shadow: The Life of Vivienne Eliot.* New York: Doubleday, 2002.

Shone, Richard. *The Art of Bloomsbury: Roger Fry, Vanessa Bell, and Duncan Grant.* Princeton: Princeton University Press, 1999.

———. "Matisse in England and Two English Sitters." *Burlington Magazine* 135, no. 1084 (July 1993).

Solnit, Rebecca. "Woolf's Darkness: Embracing the Inexplicable." In *Men Explain Things to Me.* Chicago: Haymarket Books, 2014.

Spalding, Frances. *Vanessa Bell.* New Haven and New York: Ticknor and Fields, 1983.

Stanford, Donald E. "The First Mrs. Eliot." *Library Chronicle of the University of Texas at Austin* 40 (Fall 1987): 89–110.

Strachey Barnes, James. *Half a Life.* New York: Coward McCann, 1934.

Vogue (London). "Dining-Rooms of To-Day." 70, no. 5 (September 7, 1927).

Vogue (London). "Good Interiors." 63, no. 8 (Late April 1924).

Vogue (London). "Preparing for the Grand Style." 59, no. 11 (Early June 1922).

Vogue (London). "The Work of Some Modern Decorative Art." 68, no. 4 (Late August 1926).

Williams, Orlo. "Fugitive Pieces," review of *Fugitive Pieces* by Mary Hutchinson. *Times Literary Supplement*, July 7, 1927, 469. *Times Literary Supplement Historical Archive.*

Willis, J. H., Jr. *Leonard and Virginia Woolf as Publishers: The Hogarth Press, 1917–41.* Charlottesville: University of Virginia Press, 1992.

Woolf, Leonard. Letter to Mary Hutchinson, May 9, 1923. HRC.

Woolf, Virginia. *The Diary of Virginia Woolf, Volume I: 1915–1919.* Edited by Anne Olivier Bell. London: Hogarth, 1977.

———. *The Diary of Virginia Woolf, Volume II: 1920–1924.* Edited by Anne Olivier Bell. London: Hogarth, 1978.

———. *The Diary of Virginia Woolf, Volume III: 1925–1930.* Edited by Anne Olivier Bell. London: Hogarth, 1980.

———. *The Diary of Virginia Woolf, Volume IV: 1931–1935.* Edited by Anne Olivier Bell. London: Hogarth, 1982.

———. *The Question of Things Happening: The Letters of Virginia Woolf, Volume II: 1912–1922.* Edited by Nigel Nicolson. London: Hogarth, 1976.

———. *A Change of Perspective: The Letters of Virginia Woolf, Volume III: 1923–1928.* Edited by Nigel Nicolson. London: Hogarth, 1977.

———. *The Sickle Side of the Moon: The Letters of Virginia Woolf, Volume V: 1932–1935.* Edited by Nigel Nicolson. London: Hogarth, 1979.

———. *Leave the Letters Till We're Dead: The Letters of Virginia Woolf, Volume VI: 1936–1941.* Edited by Nigel Nicolson. London: Hogarth, 1980.

———. *A Room of One's Own.* Edited by Susan Gubar. New York: Harcourt, 2005.

Woolmer, J. Howard. *A Checklist of The Hogarth Press, 1917–1938.* Andes, NY: Woolmer Brotherson, 1976.

4

Peggy Guggenheim's and Bryher's Investment

How Financial Speculation Created a Female Modernist Tradition

JULIE VANDIVERE

How is it that, given the poverty of most modernist women writers, we have a female modernist tradition? The persistence of their presence is unlikely, since, traditionally, fame has relied on financial support, and, as Kathleen D. McCarthy points out in her work on patronage, women have never received the money they needed. It is not just a matter of living expenses; modernist women artists were able, at times, to cobble together enough money to pay the rent and buy some space to create. However, once they produced work, they did not have the financial connections to exhibit and sell it.

In contrast, modernist men historically found patrons who not only underwrote their living expenses but also provided the avenues to disseminate their work. As McCarthy outlines, these patrons "exhibited [the artist's] holdings, opened their galleries to the public or joined in schemes to foster artists' professional careers."[1] It is this dissemination that is as important to an artist's reputation as a roof is to her sustenance. Women can paint or write as their limited work time allows, but the canvases will pile up in studios and the typed pages accrue on shelves as the female artist or writer struggles to find a patron to underwrite their exhibition or support their publication. The problem of disseminating one's art becomes even worse when the work is simply not marketable to most buyers, a characteristic that is one of the hallmarks of the modernist period and distinguishes the work of modernists like H.D., Dorothy Richardson, or Mina Loy.

While critics like Paul Delaney have charted the ways female patrons paid for the unsalable art and literature of the male modernists, scholars have not paid attention to how modernist women survived and were able to produce work that became part of the canon. Delaney outlines the almost unimaginable generosity of the female patrons who did not expect an immediate return on their money but who sought company and community, hoping to "gain entry into literary circles and bask in the reflected glory of the writers they assisted."[2] These wealthy women were willing to make long-term investments in the hope that there might be a future, rather than an immediate, return.[3] More important, Delaney establishes that these patrons did far more than finance the artists. They also funded the pipelines to canonicity, creating venues to educate a small and elite public about the worth of the unaesthetic, convincing buyers that the worth of the object resides precisely in its lack of marketability. Thus, because they controlled both the artists and the path to the canon, these patrons significantly shaped the modernist movement.[4]

If patrons created the male modernist canon, are they also partially responsible for the female one? Where did the money come from? What did the patron ask in return from the female modernist, and, most important, how were modernist ventures that were created by women shaped by the patrons' expectations? Examining the patronage of two wealthy women, Peggy Guggenheim, the well-known American collector, and Bryher, the less well-known English writer, reveals how women patrons shaped modernism produced by women.

Most modernist scholars are aware of the tremendous financial cost of underwriting a writer's life. A more important critical angle that provides insight into the existence of a modernist female canon shows us how these patrons created scaffolding for the canon itself. As Lawrence Rainey demonstrates in *Institutions of Modernism*, these patrons bought access to a market that did not function on sales based on popularity or, in most of the cases, even literary merit.[5] Focusing on T. S. Eliot and James Joyce, among others, Rainey outlines how the success of these writers was based not on merit but on investors who were willing to manipulate the market.

For example, Rainey points out how *Ulysses* (1922) sold out before its release, purchased and collected by "dealers and speculators in the rare book trade who bought the overwhelming majority of copies of the first edition" because they were predicting the book would be banned for obscenity and eventually become sensational, rare, and thus valuable.[6]

Similarly, *The Dial* awarded its own prestigious award to *The Waste Land* (1922) before ever seeing even a single line of the poem because the poem was already slated to appear in the magazine, and if it were advertised as the winner of the prestigious award, circulation would increase. The editors were banking on a success similar to that risked by the book buyers: if the speculation paid off, not only would *The Dial* sell better but also that edition would become a collector's item, valued as the first purveyor of a collectible object, the prizewinning poem. Thus, neither *Ulysses* nor *The Waste Land* succeeded in popularity because of readers' opinions or even the judgment of experts; both were unseen commodities in a game of financial gain, made famous by the investment in an object whose value was constructed and then manipulated by the market.

In a market that depended on financial speculation, who would be willing to invest and speculate on women, a commodity that had no value whatsoever? Perhaps it is no coincidence that the two women modernists who managed to find a foothold in the modernist canon were two of the wealthiest: Gertrude Stein lived off the fortunes made from her family's streetcar production industry, and Virginia Woolf inherited family money, first a small sum from her father and then a larger sum from her aunt. These inheritances allowed both to participate for years in the time-consuming art of revision, a gift denied almost every other lesser-known modernist woman writer. While Stein would struggle to get her work published, a quest that would eventually succeed (as I will discuss later in the essay), Woolf did not wait around for others to publish her work but ran the press herself, and engaged with her husband, Leonard Woolf, in turning the crank and selling the books. There were also, of course, great numbers of successful women writers who did not participate in modernist experimentation but who made their livings by producing middlebrow literature. Many, like Dorothy L. Sayers, E. H. Young, Rosamond Lehmann, Storm Jameson, Vera Brittain, Winifred Owens, and Kay Boyle, wrote to pay the bills, turning out popular literature that studies of modernism often disparage as thin and uninteresting.

And yet, there is a third category of women, those who were not born into wealth but were still able to produce art that we now associate with high modernism. Dorothy Richardson, Emily Coleman, Mina Loy, and Djuna Barnes were all able to solicit enough funding to find the space and time to write and revise, minimize and expand, thereby creating that esoteric form that we associate with high modernism. More, they were all able to find the pipeline to publish, even though none of their work ever attracted a broad reading public. Perhaps it is no surprise, then, that what distinguishes these writers is that, like the male modernists who succeeded, they had a patron. What might be surprising, however, is that they all had the same patrons. All were friends with Peggy Guggenheim and/or Bryher and received financial support from one or both of them.

In a moment, I will discuss these two patrons in greater depth, but before I do, it is important to note that there were a number of other heiresses who moved through modernism and had an interest in women writers; they all, however, were primarily interested in funding social circles and handing out occasional gifts. Most famous among them was Natalie Barney, who used part of the 3.5 million dollars she inherited in 1909 to create the Académie des Femmes. The venue hosted women writers and artists from around the world for over sixty years—including Radclyffe Hall, Edna St. Vincent Millay, Caresse Crosby, Colette, Djuna Barnes, Gertrude Stein, and Mina Loy among others.[7] Barney also occasionally gave small amounts of money to artists, providing, for example, 1,600 francs to Barnes for an abortion.[8] Most other wealthy women, like Nancy Cunard, Margaret Anderson, Jane Heap, and even Gertrude Stein, followed Barney's model and funded small requests, while organizing salons, suppers, parties, and reading events to help women artists create friendships and find inspiration. Nevertheless, whatever inspiration the writers might have found in the soirees hosted by these wealthy women, they did little to create the financial support offered to the male writers.

While Guggenheim and Bryher distinguished themselves from these other women by offering more substantial gifts that allowed writers and artists space, means, and time to create, these two women could not have been more different: Bryher's wealth was roughly six times that of Guggenheim's; Bryher supported mostly women, while Guggenheim gave far less to women than she did to men; and Bryher gave anonymously and often without strings, while Guggenheim wanted to be recognized for her charity. The differences between the two investors reveal a tremendous amount about how money makes a canon and how the financial engine behind the dissemination of art influences the sort of art that gets made and shapes the market in which it circulates. Furthermore, I argue that, in the case of Guggenheim and Bryher, the source of the money predicted the canons they created; each followed a path of literary and artistic investment that replicated the financial investments from which they derived their fortunes.

Bryher's wealth was not only greater than Guggenheim's, but it was larger than that of any other heiress who helped foster either male or female modernist writers. Indeed, her family's wealth dwarfed that of every other family in England,[9] so much so that the 37 million pounds her father left behind at his death in 1933 was twice as much money as was owned that year by the next wealthiest individual and constituted roughly 30 percent of the wealth left by all adults who died in Great Britain that year. Moreover, that amount was but a fraction of the money he was known to have, and as Ben Fenton reveals, "it is also a mystery as to what happened to it."[10] Only a small portion, £120,000, went to his daughter, while he willed 36 million to his son.[11] The missing money, in conjunction with Bryher's lack of bitterness about her brother's lion's share of the inheritance, certainly allows for speculation that, in addition to her £120,000, Bryher received the money that disappeared. She never spoke of nor initiated any investigation into the missing funds. And she never lacked for money or complained about any conceivable expense. While Bryher inherited £120,000 (roughly 6 million dollars) in 1932, Guggenheim received $950,000 when her mother died in 1937.[12] Although a million dollars was still almost unimaginable in a world where the average yearly wage was just over a thousand dollars, it was still roughly a mere fifth of Bryher's wealth.

Although both women used their money almost exclusively to support the arts, they did so very differently, and the difference corresponds to the ways each of their family's wealth was acquired. Guggenheim secured her money from her family's conservative and material investments and invested in physical objects created by reliable and predictable producers: she bought paintings made by men. Her investment in women writers occupied a position of secondary importance. Bryher, whose fortune came from her father's speculation in high risk, non-tangible ventures, invested in the previously untested demographic of women writers and in writing, a medium that, unlike the tangible art Guggenheim invested in, relies on transmission and reproduction.

While Guggenheim created physical galleries of discrete pieces of mostly visual art produced by men and gave grudgingly, sparingly, and sporadically to women, Bryher created avenues for women to publish.

Her galleries relied on neither the visual and tangible object nor on the potential value of a scarce object in a rigged system of speculation (as is the case with W. B. Yeats and Joyce). Rather, Bryher invested in an unknown commodity, women. And she invested in a medium where a singular object held no worth (writing), imagining that at some future point, probably long after her death, the writers might be known, and the first editions might then be of worth. In a sense, she created invisible galleries for unknown writers, speculating that their work would someday enjoy a fame she would never see.

Peggy Guggenheim's style of acquisition is very similar to that of the Guggenheim family. They are known for making their fortune from mining, but that broad brush ignores important specifics, for they were not interested in precious metals and they were not even primarily interested in the mining itself. Instead, the Guggenheims concentrated on relatively worthless metals, tin and silver, and focused almost entirely on smelting, the process whereby you extract the metal under intense heat from the rock. In fact, they eventually sold their mines but kept their smelting facilities, including a caveat in the sales contract that the new owners could only smelt the ore in a Guggenheim facility, a brilliant move that allowed them to turn a profit on the sale, collect a revenue from the ongoing operation of the mine, and control the output of the metals. In short, they risked almost no exposure while retaining control of the mine, because without the smelting, the mine was worthless.[13]

The distinction between mining and smelting is an important one—one that provides a model for the way Guggenheim invested in the arts. The Guggenheims were not so much interested in speculating or discovery as they were in taking an object, a near-worthless piece of ore, submitting it to a process, deriving what was valuable, and then making a profit from the resulting object. In a similar way, Guggenheim would eventually grow her investment in modern art, not by risky speculation or discovery, but from paying little for a tangible and undervalued object and submitting it to an intense process whereby it was changed into something of worth.

Peggy Guggenheim did not set out to find groundbreaking art on her own but relied on male experts to guide her purchases: Marcel Duchamp, Samuel Beckett, and Max Ernst. It was Beckett who talked her out of buying the masters, arguing that her investment dollars would go much further if she collected modern artists, and that she would be able to pick up the work of lesser-known artists at bargain-basement prices. In 1938, Guggenheim asked her influential art adviser, Howard Putzel, for a wish list of what would be a great collection of modern art, and then, while others were fleeing the Nazis, she headed into dangerous areas, committed to buying a piece of art every day at the cheapest possible price, driving her car to the small houses of as many impoverished artists as possible to buy their work, regardless of whether she liked it.

From her autobiography, it is clear that Guggenheim's motivation did not derive from personal aesthetic appreciation; rather, she was motivated by a good deal, explaining that she was "in the market for anything I could lay my hands on" and that some of it was "very cheap."[14] With the remarkable lack of self-awareness for which she was infamous, Guggenheim recounts her bargains with callous delight, bragging that artists rushed between transfers or bothered her before she got out of bed in the morning because they were so desperate to save their art from the Nazi advance. Constantin Brancusi was so unhappy with the discounted price Guggenheim insisted on that he felt cheated and cried as he turned *Bird in Space* (1928) over to her.[15]

Since Guggenheim treated art as an investment, consulting experts and looking for a bargain, it is no surprise that the vast majority of works she bought were produced by men, the most reliable and predictable of demographics. Her frenzied cut-rate purchases during the 1930s is the Who's Who of canonical male artists: Pablo Picasso, Georges Braque, Salvador Dali, Marcel Duchamp, Giorgio de Chirico, Jackson Pollock, Joan Miro, Max Ernst. More, following the pattern of family investment, she had no interest in mass reproduction—shunning photography, prints, texts, anything that could be mechanically replicated and circulated—but instead bought single, discrete, concrete objects—paintings and sculptures. Like the metals on which her family made its fortune, her art could be presented for sale or held in storage until the market was right.

Perhaps the most valuable lesson Guggenheim learned from her family business was how to transform something of the purchase into a desired and precious object; she created her valuable collection primarily by performing what is the art connoisseur's equivalent of smelting. She would take an undervalued piece of art that she had acquired for little outlay and then purchase galleries and mount exhibitions to turn the work into valuable masterpieces by manipulating the availability of the artist's work.

Not only would she decide what to promote and whom to ignore but also often bought the gallery's art herself, sometimes anonymously, thereby inflating sales and giving an artificial impression of the art's desirability and worth. These galleries almost invariably lost money—in the short term. But the short-term loss was simply a further investment in the long-term value of the art in which she had invested. She created wealth and fame by using the galleries as her family had used the smelting industry: to turn the valueless into the valuable while maintaining control. She could ease the work she had bought for pennies on or off the market as she maintained a balance of value through limited accessibility, keeping an eye to the long-term value of her collection.

How then did Guggenheim's investment in women writers and artists compare to her investment in male visual artists? Her commitment as a patron to women followed a very different pattern. Neither literature nor women artists could be manipulated in the same ways; as the financial machinations that surround Joyce's and Eliot's work proves, the financial profitability of a literature that holds no attraction to the mass market is even more difficult to manipulate than modern art. And women had never historically been worth the investment. In terms of Guggenheim's investment strategy, women producing literature had two strikes against them, while men and their canvases had a proven history of future profitability. Yet Guggenheim did invest relatively small amounts in women artists and writers, both in outright purchases and in ongoing efforts, and even that small investment looms much larger than almost any other attempt to promote women artists and writers.

Most famously, in 1943, in Guggenheim's New York The Art of This Century Gallery, she mounted the first-ever exhibit that was exclusively for women visual artists. The press from the time indicates the challenge it was to orchestrate and execute a woman's exhibit. The art critic from *Time Magazine* refused to cover the show at all, arguing that it would be a waste of time because "there had never been a first-rate woman artist and that women should stick to having babies."[16] Only three works in the entire show sold, and Guggenheim did not follow her strategy for investing that she had used for male artists; she did not purchase a single piece, either anonymously or in her own name. However, despite the bad press and unprofitability, she did mount a second show two years later.

When asked why she had persisted, Guggenheim declared with an uncharacteristically feminist explanation that she was tired of women existing only in art as muses, models, and mistresses, and besides she had "no husband to lose anymore, so it wasn't as dangerous."[17] Guggenheim, however, never provided the sort of unprejudiced support for female artists that she had for men. Although her show was the first to showcase women, her selection was based on affection and affiliation. All the artists were either the wives of male artists she was friends with or women she was closely affiliated with but who were not primarily visual artists: her daughter, Pegeen Vail; the writer, Mina Loy; and the stripper, Gypsy Rose Lee.

Her investment in women artists who were not painters followed the same capricious route, and, like her patronage of male artists, was driven by the suggestions of a male lover. In 1923, Laurence Vail initially talked her into giving money to women, arguing that, since she had no talent of her own, she should give money to women who did.[18] With the exception of Djuna Barnes, whom I will discuss below, she never gave consistently and never without strings attached. Her generosity is seen in the number of "things" or one-time financial gifts she gave women who were attempting to break into the arts. That said, the sheer number of famous women to whom Guggenheim gave something is impressive: she gifted $500 to Margaret Anderson for the *Little Review*, an expensive camera to the young and ambitious Berenice Abbott, $500 and the use of a cottage to Emma Goldman to write her memoirs, and a vacation home to Emily Coleman and Antonia White to pursue their writings. She also helped Mina Loy set up shop to sell Loy's artistic lampshades. Without exception, however, these exchanges were riddled with conflict since Guggenheim expected both gratitude and to receive something commensurate in return. Abbott, for example, was required to create a series of portraits of Guggenheim's children, while Coleman was roped into secretarial tasks. If the benefactress did not offer equivalency or was not sufficiently grateful, as was the case with Emma Goldman, who did not acknowledge her debt to Guggenheim in her memoirs, Guggenheim would snub her altogether. Many other women, including Mary Butts and Isadora Duncan, asked in vain for even the smallest financial contributions.[19]

Peggy Guggenheim gave money differently to women than to men because male artists produced prestige and, eventually, more wealth, while women produced the potential of intimate emotional labor. She used every tool in her shrewd calculations to play out the investments in male artists, building cultural and financial capital. Women, in contrast, could offer neither culture nor financial compounded interest, and so Guggenheim always insisted on an immediate quid pro quo return. Her demands, especially since the exchange involved trading goods for affection, rarely turned out as Guggenheim might have hoped, and Guggenheim was invariably left feeling the victim.

Guggenheim's request for emotional connection with women in exchange for artistic support is illustrated most painfully in her relationship with the two women to whom she gave the most: Mina Loy and Djuna Barnes. The relationship with Loy demonstrates again how Guggenheim's approach to art and galleries mirrors her family's concentration on converting valueless mass into commodities. Loy came to Guggenheim's attention because she had produced a collection of sculptures from found objects: illuminated spheres that had been made from globes and old maps, lamps made from antique bottles and hand-fashioned shades. Guggenheim promised Loy capital and instructed her to find more trash, convert it into art, and to open a shop to sell the art. However, Guggenheim backed out of the initial investment and never showed up to do the extensive renovation the shop required or any of the actual selling. Instead, she sent Loy critical letters, urging her to speed up the opening and offering to use her connections to make sure the wares sold. Whether it was because of or in spite of Guggenheim's connections, the store was a success, and Loy sold out of every piece she had. Only when the art was successful did Guggenheim make good on her promise and invest the initial amount.

Guggenheim's financial shrewdness later took a different turn when the heiress offered to expand Loy's market and take it to sell in the galleries of New York. While Guggenheim did place a few pieces in a gallery, her willingness to minimize female talent in a way that she would never diminish a man's manifested itself, and despite Loy's explicit instructions that Guggenheim sell only to galleries and boutiques, Guggenheim dumped the whole lot into department stores and sent Loy a check for $500 to account for the wholesale price.[20] Like the family mining business, Guggenheim had little outlay and little exposure until the venture proved successful. Only then did she enter into the business, leverage it for commercial gain, and use what she could in order to make a profit.

While Guggenheim's relationship with Loy seems almost entirely motivated by an exchange of quick service and labor, and was, like most of her other relationships with women, subject to Guggenheim's emotional whims that could leave the artist completely cut off from future patronage, one woman, Djuna Barnes, seemed able to offer Guggenheim something that would convince the heiress to consistently support her. For Barnes, Guggenheim broke her rule about refusing long-term support, and, over the course of forty years, invested roughly $72,000, a significant amount of money—which does not compare with the sum Harriet Shaw Weaver gave to Joyce but does compete with the amounts gifted to other modernists like Yeats or Ezra Pound. Guggenheim began the stipend in the mid to late 1920s with a monthly $40 and gradually increased it to $125, maintaining her commitment with an endowment in her will that the payments would continue until Barnes's death.[21]

Guggenheim's generosity, however, does not so much demonstrate that she made an exception to her rule about supporting women but rather shows that Guggenheim's bequest was based on manipulating an emotional bond, using the money to control Barnes with an almost sadistic pleasure. For example, in 1950, Barnes took a horrible tumble that severely damaged her back and broke her ribs. The destitute and ill Barnes struggled to recover and pay the accruing medical bills and wrote to Guggenheim of her condition. Guggenheim never offered to help Barnes with the hospital bills nor did she increase her stipend. Instead, she cheerfully suggested that a trip together through Europe would be nice, and if Barnes could get clearance from her doctor to travel from America to Europe with her injuries, Guggenheim would love to have the company. Barnes, having no other option, took her up on the offer and traveled with Guggenheim while ill. The trip, of course, neither improved her injuries nor her debts.[22] Guggenheim had no eye or interest in supporting Barnes in any practical manner, like paying the bills or acquiring a nurse. Instead, Guggenheim used her money to coax Barnes into unwilling servitude.

Ultimately, however, sporadic and bitterly won support is better than no support at all—at least for modernist literary production—for without Guggenheim there would be, for example, no writing from Barnes, or, without Guggenheim, Goldman would not have had the funds or place to write her memoirs. One need only look at the list of petitioners to whom Guggenheim refused patronage to see the difference her money made. Emily Coleman, Antonia White, and Mary Butts all struggled to find their narrative voices and came to Guggenheim seeking ongoing financial support to free them up to write. She refused, and none of the three were able to find the time to create either an esoteric form associated with high modernism or a body of work significant enough to gain major writer status. But Barnes did. Although she may have felt that she produced nothing significant after *Nightwood* (1936), she continued to write, and more important, to rewrite, revising some of her poems as many as five hundred times, a luxury given to her by Guggenheim's money. Such revisions enabled her to produce the highly polished form on display in *The Antiphon* (1958), as well as in the poems she continued to produce during the last thirty-five years of her life.[23]

Surveying the clauses and complications of Guggenheim's giving, her contribution to the creation of a female modernism seems a sort of over-spray; she gave money primarily to male artists, was friends with female writers and artists, and some of the dispersion of money ended up landing in places that benefited women writers and artists. This impact on modernist women writers and artists is light when compared to Bryher's contribution. The two women were contemporaries (Guggenheim was born in 1898, four years after Bryher) and ran in close circles, occasionally meeting at gatherings in Paris as patrons of the art scene. The parallels as patrons, however, quickly diverge, for not only, as I mentioned above, did Bryher have more money to give, but also—in keeping with the difference between the ways the two families acquired their wealth—Bryher's mode of patronage was fundamentally different from Guggenheim's.

In contrast to the Guggenheim family's conservative portfolio that focused on the smelting of metals, Bryher's father, John Ellerman, made his fortune by dint of nerve and imagination, creating new ways to generate wealth that had not existed before he thought of them. While a small portion of Ellerman's money came from concrete objects like mining and brewing, the vast bulk of it came from "risk capital," a sort of investing (for which he is considered one of the founders) that relies on acquiring and using information in order to generate vast amounts of wealth.[24] Rising from the working class, Ellerman trained as an accountant and developed the ability to consider large amounts of abstract material. He could then evaluate the relative weight of assets and liabilities on a spreadsheet, basing revenue on changing currents of various kinds of circulation. The amount and source of Bryher's wealth was derived from an innovative mindset that entailed not only investing money but also investing it in non-tangible, almost illusory commodities—the flow of commerce for example, rather than the objects of commerce themselves.

John Ellerman's contemporaries marveled at his ability to see potential money where others did not.[25] As he expanded his financial empire, he did not rely, as did the Guggenheims, on turning a marginally worthless object into something valuable, but on accumulating data and imagining potential value. While such investments are common in the twenty-first century, they were not in the nineteenth century, and his knowledge of numbers allowed him to create a base of income from investment trusts that funded his expansion in other markets.[26] Those markets, unlike the Guggenheims,' rarely relied on concrete objects but instead were derived from transmission; his shipping line became the largest in the world and he eventually became the largest investor in British newspapers.[27]

Bryher's patronage followed her father's high-risk pattern and was rooted in a fundamental belief in the inherent power of currency—words, maps, and financial figures that traverse and accrue value through transport. Bryher was deeply inspired by her father and felt that she could have run his shipping and transport business better than anyone else, lamenting in most of her writing that she had been held back because she was born a girl. She took her money and imagination, then, to a new terrain and invested carefully and wisely in women writers. Unlike Guggenheim, who believed in the power of the discrete, Bryher trusted the ephemeral and the non-tangible, and believed that there are markets for things that cannot, like a painting or sculpture, be stored. She trusted that literature, like the currency and transport of her father's markets, could grow to greater worth, and that, sometimes, what no one had ever imagined as valuable could be worth a fortune.

H.D., of course, was the most famous benefactor of Bryher's ongoing patronage, receiving a very large annuity that, in 1940, was determined to be £2,450 a year.[28] But H.D. was not the only recipient of such persistent support: a £275 annuity trust for Edith Sitwell, a $200 annuity for Marianne Moore,[29] and a £100 (and rising eventually to £120) annuity for Dorothy Richardson. Bryher reportedly apportioned a full third of her income to providing financial support for others, so her resources not only helped the individuals she provided with long-term support but also she gave gifts, both large and small, to many individuals.[30] All evidence indicates she gave enthusiastically, exuberantly, and often anonymously. Unlike Guggenheim, who always asked women artists and writers for some token of exchange, Bryher released many (although not all) of the funds with no apparent strings attached. Drawn to projects through which women were trying to forge a profession or cultivate an art, she readily provided money for her favorite women-owned tea shop, Sylvia Beach's Shakespeare and Co., Harriet Shaw Weaver's journal *The Egoist*, and Berenice Abbott's darkroom. She also provided money simply to help those who were enfeebled or threatened, providing an apartment for the aging Elsa von Freytag-Loringhoven and helping a hundred Jewish intellectuals, many of them women, escape Nazi Germany.

Of equal, if not greater, importance is the way Bryher used part of the remaining two-thirds of her wealth to create forums for the artists to publish in. Compiling the list of women writers who found a publishing outlet through Bryher quickly reveals that she is the engine behind the fame of virtually every female modernist other than those associated primarily with Virginia Woolf. Her first venture was to publish Marianne Moore's poems via Harriet Shaw Weaver's Egoist Press.[31] She then went on to bigger ventures as she and her husband, Robert McAlmon, created Contact Editions, whose daring editorial statement read:

> Contact Editions are not concerned with what the "public" wants. There are commercial publishers who know the public and its tastes. If books seem to us to have something of individuality, intelligence, talent, a live sense of literature, and a quality which has the odour and timbre of authenticity, we publish them. We admit that eccentricities exist.[32]

The Bryher/McAlmon venture made experimental publishing possible—both because it promoted radical form and because it focused on writers who would not otherwise be published, specifically women. During the seven years of its existence from 1922 to 1929, it published some work by writers like Ernest Hemingway or William Carlos Williams, but its real impact was in publishing works by women writers that have since become central to present day definitions of modernism, including Gertrude Stein's *The Making of Americans* (1925), Mina Loy's *Lunar Baedecker* (1923), H.D.'s *Palimpsest* (1926), Djuna Barnes *The Ladies Almanack* (1928), as well as other works by women, including Mary Butts's *Ashe of Rings* (1925), Bryher's *Two Selves* (1923), and Gertrude Beasley's *My First Thirty Years* (1930).

When the press folded, along with Bryher's and McAlmon's marriage, Bryher immediately created other venues for women writers. *Close Up*, the film journal coedited and coproduced with her second husband, Kenneth

Macpherson, provided a platform for women writers such as H.D., Dorothy Richardson, Gertrude Stein, Marianne Moore, Elizabeth Coxhead, and Trude Weiss, but it also gave voice to essays, like Richardson's *The Film Gone Male* (1932), that align the advent of talking movies with male dominance. The longest lasting of these publishing ventures was *Life and Letters Today*, which ran from 1934 to 1950 and published, in addition to those who had been published in previous journals like H.D., Richardson, Butts, and Moore, new talents like Elizabeth Bishop, May Sarton, and Muriel Rukeyser, thus broadening the canon and historically extending its reach. In all, Bryher created publication avenues for more than twenty modernist women, most of whom continue to be read today.

One could make a facile connection aligning Bryher's lesbianism with her commitment to women, specifically to H.D., arguing, as does Rainey, that Bryher invested in H.D. out of an emotional connection and created a coterie that was strong on adulation but of relatively little artistic merit.[33] Rainey's assessment of H.D.'s poetic ability has been roundly discredited because, among other reasons, he offers no evidence that her craft is lacking. Rather, he discredits H.D.'s poetry solely because of her relationship with her patron, a link he does not draw between the business manipulations that went on with Eliot's and Joyce's work. Only in his reading of H.D., the sole woman he considers in his study, does he suggest a patron's investment should be read as a negative influence; a patron's investment in unseen works of Joyce and Eliot is a worthwhile intellectual and financial venture, but the same investment in a woman (by a woman) is a matter of misguided affection.

Examining Bryher's investment in H.D. and the many other women writers and artists she supported demonstrates the opposite of Rainey's charge. The lesbian "coterie" does not create some sort of favoritism that is unique only to women but rather elevates women to a realm where they are even considered. Or, to phrase it another way, in a culture that relies on the commodification of women—heterosexuality depends on women's exchange value—Bryher's lesbianism permitted her to see herself and the women in whom she invested as not entirely dependent on nor defined by the demands of the immediate social and financial market. Her investment in these women writers required, like her father's risky investments, a profound imagination to speculate on that which did not yet have value in the market and to trust that her eye would see value where others did not. Consequently, Bryher's vision of the worth of the person creates a different dynamic for the artist. As she explained to Marianne Moore when Moore asked why Bryher invested in her despite not liking Moore's poetry, "I don't like what you write," B[ryher] said, "but I like you."[34]

This perspective meant that Bryher, unlike Guggenheim, trusted the artist and never questioned how the money would be spent. Once she gave the impoverished Edith Sitwell £500 outright and did not offer a word of complaint when Sitwell used it to buy two Ascot hats and a fur coat. Nor is there any evidence that it bothered her when, after spending £3,000 to buy Sitwell a house in Bath, Sitwell found the house inadequate and asked Bryher to buy the house out from under her at the original price, an investment that appears poor if one is investing in property but well placed if the investment is, as it was for Bryher, in people.[35] Storm Jameson called her "quickly generous," a characterization only enhanced by the fact that she did not track how the trusted artists would spend the money.[36]

Such generosity might seem unusual or irresponsible, but if we shift the perspective a bit and return to our idea of male artists and patronage, we have to remember that a great portion of Harriet Shaw Weaver's support of Joyce was spent on his daily alcohol purchases, and yet his patron never asked and culture never critiques the budgeting. Weaver's investment was in Joyce's genius. So it was with Bryher. Whether the artist spent the money on hats or wine, Bryher did not attempt to control the investment.

As a means of relinquishing control, Bryher thus, in contrast to Guggenheim, distanced herself from the money she gave. Sometimes she used a blind, as was the case with Sitwell, who served as a conduit for Bryher's anonymous donations. She also set up trusts for those artists she supported in the long term and then endowed control over the trust to the artist as the account would predictably and consistently disperse the interest to the owner of the account. Dorothy Richardson's thank you letter to Bryher, for example, pinpoints how money creates the alchemy that allows an artist to turn the mundane into art. In 1933, after the annuity for Richardson had been established by Bryher, Richardson wrote:

> I understand that on the top of all you have done for me during the last ten years, you now ensure me an annual income of 120 pounds, tax-free. A cut and dried statement, this, of a business proposition, easy to set down. But there are no plain terms in which to state what you are really giving me. An easier mind. Sounder sleep. Steadier

nerves. Yes. But these don't convey the changed look of everything, from inkpot to hawthorn. To be able to look ahead and make plans. You are really astonishing, Bryher, you know. Properly speaking, you should be unable to imagine, in the concrete, the actual way you do imagine, circumstances of which you have no experience. The older I get the more certain I am that the exercise of imagination on behalf of anyone but oneself is the rarest faculty in existence.[37]

Worth quoting at length, Richardson's letter to Bryher explains the complex ways that the sort of support Bryher gives provides a unique opportunity for women writers. Most obviously, creating a stipend that functioned as an investment elevated Richardson beyond charity and gave her a sense of dignity, validating her role as an artist and her work as a potentially valuable investment. Moreover, the investment changed the sense of time, as Richardson could imagine a trajectory of her work, an extended and complex project. It also shifted her sense of place, as Richardson, emerging out of a financial duress that enveloped both her and the objects that surrounded her, could look at the most mundane things around her, the inkpot and the hawthorne, seeing them anew. The objects, like she, were no longer defined in terms of immediate use and exchange but now could exist as entities that would be viewed in leisure from different angles, liberated into a process to be revised and re-envisioned.

This gift of revising and re-envisioning is what these first serious patrons of women's art and literature gave to modernism. The few writers supported by Guggenheim and the many endowed by Bryher were provided the time to develop a form that levied their writing into a realm of aesthetics associated with high modernism. Guggenheim, with her funding of male painters, remains well known; Bryher, with her greater investment in women, persists in almost complete obscurity. Guggenheim was always interested in self-promotion; her galleries bore her name, and she saw the output of her artists as her property that both belonged to her and needed to wear her mark. Additionally, the nature of the art she collected guaranteed her legacy since physical objects within the legal confines of gifting and selling maintain the trace of their genealogy, always testifying that it was Guggenheim who collected them. Bryher, in contrast, remains obscure. No biography has been written about her, and few of her materials have been collected. Perhaps, however, that has to do with her motives for and methods of speculation. Bryher invested in words and writing, art forms that are not so easily captured and whose genealogy of production is not so easily traced.

But it is not just the mediums that differ, for Bryher's investment was not in herself. It was not, as was Guggenheim's, in the impulse to create a collection and a gallery that would function as a sort of art mausoleum to her taste and foresight. Bryher's motivation was much more akin to that of Harriet Shaw Weaver or other patrons who were interested in the talent of individual artists. As she said simply to Sylvia Beach, "I . . . tried always to do what [I] could for the real artists, and especially for the woman artist."[38] Investing in artists, Bryher underwrote a particular point of view on the period, one that, for the first time, included women.

While Bryher may have given anonymously and promoted writers without showcasing her own hand in the creation of their art, we are remiss to let Bryher's own self-effacement obscure the important role she played in the creation of a modernist aesthetic. Bryher invested in the possibility of dissemination that would create future worth. Marianne Moore understood this dissemination as she struggled to thank Bryher for the difference the heiress had made in Moore's artistic ambitions. In a letter to Bryher, Moore had come to the conclusion that "one's debts of gratitude must need be paid to someone other than the one from whom one receives."[39] Perhaps it is in this ripple effect then, like waves expanding ever outward, that we can best see Bryher's influence. While culture cannot readily evoke Bryher's name or the influence she wrought, the effect of her bold and unique speculation created generations of female artists and writers.

Notes

1. McCarthy, *Women's Culture*, 23.
2. Delaney, "Who Paid for Modernism?," 346.
3. Ibid., 340.
4. Delaney describes the specifics of the sizable bankroll that subsidized modernist men: Lady Gregory underwrote "the greater part" of W. B. Yeats's working life, Margaret Cravens and Olivia Shakespeare funded Ezra Pound, and, in the most extreme case, Harriet Shaw Weaver spent most of her fortune on James Joyce, supporting him with £23,000 over eighteen years (335).
5. Rainey, *Institutions of Modernism*, 44.

6. Ibid., 44.

7. Andrew Field, *Djuna*, 123.

8. Anton Gill, *Peggy Guggenheim*, 156.

9. At his death, the *Dictionary of Business Biography* noted that Bryher's father left £16,223,977 in cash, not including large holdings in shipping and other interests. Jeremy and Shaw, *Dictionary of Business Biography*, 2: 322.

10. Ben Fenton, "Was this the richest (and most secretive) British tycoon ever?" *Telegraph*, May 22, 2006, http://www.telegraph.co.uk/news/uknews/1519047/Was-this-the-richest-and-most-secretive-British-tycoon-ever.html.

11. Barbara Guest, *Herself Defined*, 212.

12. Gill, *Peggy Guggenheim*, 12.

13. Dearborn, *Peggy Guggenheim*, 17–18.

14. Guggenheim, *Out of This Century*, 217, 221.

15. Ibid., 211–14.

16. Gill, *Peggy Guggenheim*, 158

17. Ibid., 159.

18. Burke, *Becoming Modern*, 334.

19. Dearborn, *Peggy Guggenheim*, 58.

20. Ibid. 47–48.

21. Herring, *Djuna*, 252.

22. Field, *Djuna*, 221.

23. Herring, *Djuna*, 308.

24. Whalley, *Creating Risk Capital*, 23.

25. Taylor, *Ellermans*, 44.

26. Beresford and Rubinstein, *Richest of the Rich*, 124.

27. Rubinstein, *Men of Property*, 45.

28. Guest, *Herself Defined*, 264.

29. Leavell, *Holding on Upside Down*, 274.

30. Fitch, *Sylvia Beach*, 397.

31. Marianne Moore, of course, resented that Bryher had taken the publication project on herself.

32. McAlmon, *McAlmon*, 185.

33. Rainey, *Institutions of Modernism*, 146–51.

34. Leavell, *Holding on Upside Down*, 186.

35. Richard Greene, *Edith Sitwell*, 29.

36. Maslen, *Storm Jameson*, 52.

37. Richardson, *Windows on Modernism*, 245.

38. Fitch, *Sylvia Beach*, 400.

39. Leavell, *Holding on Upside Down*, 276.

Works Cited

Beresford, Philip, and W. D. Rubinstein. *The Richest of the Rich: The Wealthiest 250 People in Britain Since 1066.* Petersfield, UK: Harriman House, 2007.

Burke, Carolyn. *Becoming Modern: The Life of Mina Loy.* New York: Farrar, Straus and Giroux, 1996.

Dearborn, Mary V. *Peggy Guggenheim: Mistress of Modernism.* London: Virago, 2005.

Delaney, Paul. "Who Paid for Modernism?" In *The New Economic Criticism: Studies at the Intersection of Literature and Economics,* edited by Martha Woodmansee and Mark Osteen, 335–51. London: Routledge, 1999.

Fenton, Ben. "Was this the richest (and most secretive) British tycoon ever?" *Telegraph,* May 22, 2006. http://www.telegraph.co.uk/news/uknews/1519047/Was-this-the-richest-and-most-secretive-British-tycoon-ever.html.

Field, Andrew. *Djuna: The Formidable Miss Barnes.* Austin: University of Texas Press, 1985.

Fitch, Noel Riley. *Sylvia Beach and the Lost Generation: A History of Literary Paris in the Twenties and Thirties.* London: Penguin Books, 1988.

Gill, Anton. *Peggy Guggenheim: The Life of an Art Addict.* London: HarperCollins, 2002.

Greene, Richard. *Edith Sitwell: Avant Garde Poet, English Genius.* London: Virago, 2011.

Guest, Barbara. *Herself Defined: The Poet H.D. and Her World.* London: HarperCollins, 1985.

Guggenheim, Peggy. *Out of This Century: Confessions of an Art Addict.* London: Andre Deutsch, 2005.

Herring, Phillip F. *Djuna: The Life and Work of Djuna Barnes.* London: Viking, 1995.

Jeremy, David J., and Christine Shaw, eds. *Dictionary of Business Biography: A Biographical Dictionary of Business Leaders Active in Britain in the Period 1860–1980.* Vol. 2. London: Butterworths, 1986.

Leavell, Linda. *Holding on Upside Down: The Life and Work of Marianne Moore.* New York: Farrar, Straus and Giroux, 2013.

Maslen, Elizabeth. *Life in the Writings of Storm Jameson: A Biography.* Evanston, IL: Northwestern University Press, 2014.

McAlmon, Robert. *McAlmon and the Lost Generation: A Self-Portrait.* Edited by Robert E. Knoll. Lincoln: University of Nebraska Press, 1962.

McCarthy, Kathleen D. *Women's Culture: American Philanthropy and Art, 1830–1930.* Chicago: University of Chicago Press, 1991.

Rainey, Lawrence S. *Institutions of Modernism: Literary Elites and Public Culture.* New Haven, CT: Yale University Press, 1998.

Richardson, Dorothy Miller. *Windows on Modernism: Selected Letters of Dorothy Richardson.* Edited by Gloria G. Fromm. Athens: University of Georgia Press, 1995.

Rubinstein, W. D. *Men of Property: The Very Wealthy in Britain Since the Industrial Revolution.* London: Social Affairs Unit, 2006.

Taylor, James Arnold. *Ellermans: A Wealth of Shipping.* London: Wilton House Gentry, 1976.

Whalley, Ian. *Creating Risk Capital: A Royalty Fund Solution to the Ownership and Financing of Enterprise.* Petersfield, UK: Harriman House, 2011.

5

Bringing Women Together, in Theory

ALLISON PEASE

What are the ideas that level the playing field between major and minor female authors, enabling us to bring more women modernist writers into our conversations about the period? Since the publication of Shari Benstock's *Women of the Left Bank: Paris, 1900–1940* (1986), Bonnie Kime Scott's *The Gender of Modernism* (1990), and Sandra Gilbert and Susan Gubar's three-volume *No Man's Land* (1989–1994), feminist criticism has enacted a "recovery project" that has brought to scholarly attention dozens of women writers from the modernist period. Articles and books have been published, and courses have been taught, that include writers such as H.D., Willa Cather, May Sinclair, Dorothy Richardson, Amy Lowell, Mina Loy, Mary Butts, Djuna Barnes, Nella Larsen, and others whose writing was previously not central to conceptions of modernism or feminism. And yet conference panels are still routinely organized around major figures, and books get published more easily if major figures are included among chapters on so-called minor figures. What has long been marginal to modernism is not necessarily less so in the second decade of the twenty-first century. Feminist modernist studies keeps looking to theory to retrieve women from their spaces on the sidelines, but is theory what we need?

The marginalization of the literary output of so-called minor female authors is rooted in the aesthetic and social values that first constructed modernist criticism, not in the production of literary modernism itself, which we know was widely populated by women writers. The first generation of critics of modernism—F. R. Leavis, I. A. Richards, John Crowe

Ransom, and T. S. Eliot—valued a verbal self-referentiality and formalism that was based on liberal humanism. Leavis, Richards, and Eliot alongside the New Critics in the United States professionalized and institutionalized literary criticism in the universities, and this has shaped reading practices in English-speaking institutions. But it has done so based on an inherited tradition of western Enlightenment liberal humanism that is grounded on an inherent contradiction: liberal theory posited a new conception of human nature as universal at the same time that women and non-Europeans were not considered fully human.

Feminism is a by-product of liberalism but nonetheless it has had to fight against its definitional constraints. Just as the first-wave feminists of the early twentieth century did, feminist literary criticism that participated in second wave feminism of the 1960s, '70s, and '80s worked to eradicate this contradiction by trying to expand the concept of humanity, and human rights, to include women, and often, though not always, nonwhite and LGBT people. In doing so they were working within the tradition of liberal humanism and trying to build upon it. This has not, in general, been the work of the so-called high theory of twentieth-century post-structuralists, which instead has critiqued the tradition of liberal humanism by showing how its claims, accompanied as they have been by Kantian claims to the autonomy of art and objective critique, are undermined by other domains of knowing and being that decenter claims to autonomy, human or artistic.

Since the 1970s, feminist literary scholars have been split between those who "do theory" and those who do literary criticism, arguably with many not always drawing conscious boundaries between such activities. In a 1995 article Nina Baym characterized the historical divide between feminist critics and feminist theorists as follows:

> We thought that since feminist criticism was already critical of traditional literary criticism, it would be exempted from theory's general dismissal of criticism as parochial, naïve, and primitive. We also supposed that a specifically feminist theory would support rather than dismiss our work. Alas. High theory in general paid little attention to feminist criticism, leaving the job to feminist theory, which did not address the false universalism, misogyny and gender asymmetry of mainstream literary criticism so much as it anatomized the shortcomings of a specifically feminist criticism. Feminist theory applied

theory's general contempt for criticism to feminist criticism in particular: it was naïve, parochial, primitive.[1]

One of the reasons, and perhaps the primary reason, feminist theory saw feminist criticism as naïve is because feminist criticism primarily relies on an essentialist concept of woman, the very assumption that feminist theory sought to complicate.

From Luce Irigaray's *This Sex Which Is Not One* (1977) to Judith Butler's *Gender Trouble* (1990) to Linda Zerilli's *Feminism and the Abyss of Freedom* (2005), to use three important and time-spanning examples, feminist theory has made it clear that there can be no unifying property ascribed to women. In Butler's influential claim, "Gender is a complexity whose totality is permanently deferred. . . . Gender proves to be performative—that is, constituting the identity it is purported to be. In this sense gender is always a doing, though not a doing by a subject who might be said to preexist the deed."[2] Feminist (and queer) theory thus destabilizes the definition of woman while nevertheless purporting to work on that group's behalf. Both feminist theory and feminist criticism confront the structures that maintain patriarchal privilege, but feminist critics have done so within a more circumscribed realm of proving women's humanity and worth within the terms of liberal humanism, while feminist theory has engaged in dismantling many of the tenets of liberal humanism.[3]

More recently, literary critics *and* critical theorists have begun a self-assessment of their approaches to literature and have found the traditions that dominated the twentieth century lacking. Specifically, the tradition of negative critique, whether under the rubric of the "hermeneutics of suspicion" as defined by Paul Ricoeur[4] or "symptomatic reading"[5] as labeled by Sharon Marcus and Stephen Best, has trained literary critics to read texts as suspicious objects that cannot know their own purpose but must be "interrogated" or "unmasked" by critics who can reveal their hidden conflicts, ideological biases, or determination in the social nexus. Rita Felski's *The Limits of Critique* (2015) takes a long look at the literary critical establishment's entrenchment in negative critique, its predictable moves and blinders, and has suggested that "literary scholars are confusing a part of thought with the whole of thought and that in doing so we are scanting a range of intellectual and expressive possibilities" (5).

Critical theory, whether feminist, formalist, or queer, shares a common and now dominant approach of interrogating a text's blind spots, its collusion with the hegemonic. In doing so, Felski argues, readers are narrowing the possibilities of what it means to read and write about literature. Literature might, in fact, be given more credit for what it is and knows; there are other ways to engage literature than finding what it cannot be and what it does not know. By way of example, she lauds feminist literary scholars for reclaiming the work of women writers and in doing so emphasizing the affective dimensions of interpretation, a more dimensional, embodied form of reading. Equally, she praises the willingness of feminists to find in literature a form of self-creating that is not just embedded in sociological and psychological critique. To be sure, feminism's "recovery project" has brought with it enthusiasm and energy that is equated with positive discovery, and affective identification, rather than merely skeptical critique, or exposition of what a text does not know about itself.

If we want to find a way to level the playing field between major and minor female authors, there might be an obvious answer: act as if the playing field is already level. Feminist theory and feminist literary criticism may just now be converging on this point, as I will show below.

Act 1. Theoretical Anxieties: I Don't Know What I Am Talking about and Neither Do You

Before I had a focus for the project that became the book *Modernism, Feminism, and the Culture of Boredom* (2012), I spent a few years reading Edwardian and modernist popular fiction. It was fantastic. I read Elinor Glyn, Elizabeth von Arnim, Ada Leverson, Victoria Cross, Elizabeth Robins, Katherine Thurston, and others until I happened upon May Sinclair. The author of more than twenty novels and several tracts, May Sinclair is an important example to me of a writer who was once at the center of modernist production, and has the potential to be considered a central modernist but has, since the 1930s, remained stubbornly on the margins of what has been critiqued under the rubric of high modernism. I will discuss her in the section below. But first, because it demonstrates a historical progression of critical influences, I want to relate how I arrived at this project that put so-called major and minor writers together.

Before launching into reading early twentieth-century popular fiction, I published a book on high modernist works in relation to the ultimate low-brow genre, pornography. This book, *Modernism, Mass Culture, and the Aesthetics of Obscenity* (2000), focused exclusively on male-authored works. After completing that project, I was weary of male-centered narratives, and I realized that I had read very few female authors of the period. My graduate program, populated mostly by men educated in elite institutions in the middle of the twentieth century, had made few attempts in that regard. I also realized that aside from pornography, I knew nothing about the popular fiction of the period. Everything I knew about popular early twentieth-century fiction I learned from Q. D. Leavis. For readers who do not understand that as a punchline, Q. D. Leavis's *Fiction and the Reading Public* (1932) outlines the reading habits of Britain's newly literate population of forty-three million in such a way that accounts for the early critical understanding of modernism as characterized by "a great divide" between high and low culture. Describing modern readers as addicted to low- and middle-brow reading as an anaesthetizing drug habit, she explained that "the general public—Dr. Johnson's common reader—has now not even a glimpse of the living interests of modern literature, is ignorant of its growth and so prevented from developing with it, and . . . the critical minority to whose sole charge modern literature has now fallen is isolated, disowned by the general public and threatened with extinction" (35). Q. D. Leavis was a student of F. R. Leavis's before becoming his wife. Her work shows how high modernism and the critical reading habits associated with it became an entrenched legacy.

Looked at differently, however, *Fiction and the Reading Public* is a fascinating repository of early twentieth-century reading practices, and it is an important reminder of the fact that the modernist period gave birth to the very first mass reading culture in human history. Just as today you cannot move without seeing people on their phones as they mass-author the internet, so in the early twentieth century in England, everyone was for the first time a reader, a consumer of fiction. Given this, it is notable that the popular literature of the period is very little written about in our scholarship. I would argue that this is because we are even now trying to emerge from the legacy of modernist criticism.

We feminist modernist scholars struggle under the legacy of modernist snobbery and modernist doubt. The study of modernism was formed with a tight set of definitions that still make it a challenge to justify the study of so-called minor authors; equally, our training in skeptical reading can limit what we value in a text. The relationship of feminists to theory qua theory is vexed. Still scholars often posit a hope for a theory that will move women writers to the fore of critical consciousness.

How might theory help us expand the modernist canon and find room for more women authors? In her special issue on Women's Fiction in *Modern Fiction Studies* (2013), Anne Fernald describes the genesis of the project as arising from the conclusion that the new modernist studies as described by Douglas Mao and Rebecca Walkowitz in their 2008 *PMLA* article, "The New Modernist Studies," had no serious interest in women writers. Mao and Walkowitz's recapping of the new modernist studies privileged the spatial and temporal expansion of what fell under the rubric of modernism; they noted the transnational turn, the interest in technologies of media, and work on politics and matters of state. Feminism got one brief nod in relation to the expansion of periodical studies.

In response, Fernald's call for papers for her special issue pointedly asked for "new theoretical approaches to modernism emerging out of feminist theory."[6] I hear concern in this call for papers: I hear Fernald saying, "Come on feminists: how are we going to make it new so that we can finally really talk about women and modernism?" The underlying fear is that if we do not come up with the next critical theory that somehow manages to take women's literary output seriously, modernist women's writing will remain forever on the margins. Will Virginia Woolf continue to be the only modernist woman writer ever taught on a general syllabus? Many feminist modernist scholars share this concern. In "Modernist Women's Writing: Beyond the Threshold of Obsolescence" (2013), Jane Garrity laments a lack of attention to experimental modernist feminist writers under the new modernism and surveys modernist anthologies to conclude "Woolf remains the only universally canonized British woman modernist."[7]

So, how do we talk about or incorporate theoretical viewpoints in a way that levels the playing field between major and minor writers? This brings me to act 2.

Act 2. Affect Is for Everyone: The Audre Lorde Redux of Turning Differences into Strengths

Affect studies has in the past decade been offered as a generative theory that can serve as an antidote to negative critique. Starting from Eve Kosofsky Sedgwick's influential essay "Paranoid Reading and Reparative Reading, or, You're So Paranoid, You Probably Think This Essay Is About You,"[8] affect has been unleashed to perform knowledge in ways other than critical or suspicious. The vogue of any theory should make us nervous. Theories rise and fall but literature remains. No one theoretical apparatus or trend will accomplish the task of stabilizing women writers' place at the center of modernist studies. While affect is currently allowing us to talk about certain kinds of literature in innovative ways, it is also, to be sure, preventing other literatures from entering the discussion. If we want to find ways to talk about feminist modernist literatures, we cannot lean too heavily on any given theory. I will come back to this point in act 3. However, for now I am going to return to my own narrative of affect via May Sinclair.

After reading a good deal of early twentieth-century popular fiction in my quest to understand modernism outside of high modernist parameters, I read Sinclair's *The Three Sisters*, published in 1914. I was floored. The reading experience was so rich. *The Three Sisters* is an overtly feminist novel with dark wit, psychological acuity, and formal interest. Sinclair was clearly a novelist to follow. I next read Sinclair's 1919 novel, *Mary Olivier: A Life*, first published in the *Little Review* in the same edition as *Ulysses*. Wow! *Mary Olivier* is like *Portrait of the Artist*, but feminist, full of psychology and a second- and first-person interior narrative that is formally innovative.

Why wasn't Sinclair being taught alongside Woolf and Joyce, I wondered? On the back of the jacket of the *New York Review of Books* 2002 reprint of *Mary Olivier* I was excited to see Hermione Lee declare in *Gone with the Wind* fashion, "No one will be able to ignore May Sinclair again." A quick check of the Modern Language Association Bibliography indicates that Lee's enthusiasm was premature, if not misguided. From 2003 to 2015 there were 2,024 articles, chapters, or books published about Virginia Woolf and her literary output. This was only slightly eclipsed by the 2,777 articles, chapters, or books published between 2003 and 2015 on James Joyce's works. During this same period, a mere thirty-four articles or books were written about May Sinclair. The major writers have remained major, and the minor writers have remained minor.

But back in 2004 when I first discovered her, I wanted to find a way to write about May Sinclair. I read the three monographs in print at the time on her and her work. Not one of these books ever put Sinclair squarely into the context of modernism, this despite the fact that she knew and had relationships with most anyone we ever study or think about in connection to modernism, including H.D., Katherine Mansfield, Dorothy Richardson, Virginia Woolf, Arnold Bennet, H. G. Wells, among others. In fact, from about 1910 to 1920 Sinclair was considered *the* foremost British woman novelist, a mantle that was taken up by Woolf in the subsequent decade. This is where my having read all of that popular fiction became useful, because there was a common phenomenon I was able to observe in popular literature that I had first seen in Elizabeth von Arnim's 1914 novel, *The Pastor's Wife*, but that Sinclair also wrote about: boredom, specifically women's boredom. Once I saw boredom in modernism, I could not unsee it. Women's boredom is everywhere in modernism, and its representations forge a public inquiry into women's lives that simultaneously create political and affective identities for women as suppressed or would-be agents.

In order to talk about a so-called minor female author, I had to find the affective commonalities she shared with other authors of the period—including Woolf—to discover what those things might have meant during the period it was written. And let me just say that though methodologically my work is always rooted in the ideas written about and circulating in the periods I write about, I could not have written about minor female authors and their so-called female complaints in the modernist period without Lauren Berlant's 2008 book, *The Female Complaint*, which created a rich vocabulary for talking about affect as it creates and frays noninstitutionalized or minor publics of women. Notably, Berlant's book brings together disparate texts and authors, and in doing so achieves the elusive goal of leveling the playing field between major and minor authors and textual forms. So, though I am leery of overreliance on any given theory, I readily admit that affect theory enabled me to read feminist modernist texts differently and productively. Theories can open texts, and that can be useful. The question for all of us, however, is whether we are leveling playing fields, or setting up new hierarchies.

In "The Master's Tools Will Never Dismantle the Master's House," Audre Lorde offers that learning how to turn differences into strengths is one way to combat the master discourse.[9] Jack Halberstam has recently glossed this statement in his book *The Queer Art of Failure* (2011), which argues that failure and other negative affects comprise a powerful counternarrative to disciplinary and disciplined knowledge. By privileging the naïve or nonsensical, Halberstam suggests, we disclose vistas around us that allow us to approach the unknown imaginatively. Affect, neither rational nor discursive but always mediating and morphing relationships, does this. There are positive affects and negative affects; acceptable affects or unacceptable, ugly feelings.[10] Feminists know this, and it is a wonderful way to talk about modernist women writers, major and minor. But surely this is but one way, and is only temporarily fashionable. We must continue to seek ways to challenge the values that persistently register women's value as less than men's, even as we acknowledge that there is no essential or permanent category called woman. This brings me to act 3.

Act 3. Transvaluation Is Possible through Low Theory, So Now Go Do It

In *The Queer Art of Failure*, Halberstam adapts Stuart Hall's term "low theory."[11] Halberstam's use of the term is valuable to the political project of transvaluation that allows for major and minor writers to be assessed side by side. Low theory combines the long-dominant realm of negative critique that Rita Felski identifies as maintaining the conservative—read patriarchal—forces of literary study with the generative "grammar of possibility" accorded to affect and other, popular ways of knowing and being. According to Halberstam, low theory is theoretical knowledge that works on many levels at once. It is a mode of accessibility; it is assembled from eccentric texts and examples and "refuses to confirm the hierarchies of knowing that maintain the *high* in high theory."[12] Low theory will remain open to possibility and look for the non-hegemonic, even in its failure, to see what it teaches us.

Perhaps all new knowledge is created out of a refusal to accept the given world. In the case of feminist modernist studies, the given world that existed for the writers we study is already gone. So, what is it we propose to know, and how do we know it? Can knowing be confirmed by repeating empty rhetorical gestures of negative critique? Certainly not. It cannot be confirmed by any a priori theory or critical approach. The literary texts we read and the lives we research can teach us more if we do not approach them with ready-made, univocal critical frameworks, even as we need and can value those frameworks as entryways or connective tissue.

Celia Marshik's work, most recently in *At the Mercy of Their Clothes* (2016), is a positive example of low theory as literary criticism that enables transvaluation and the bringing together of communities of women heretofore not grouped in modernist criticism. Marshik does not presume that thing theory, for instance, has more to tell us about modernist literature than, say, a mackintosh coat. Her deep, attentive reading starts in literature and then heads to the archive, the place of ignored and forgotten knowledge that can help us to generate ideas, feelings, and frameworks for literary paradigms. The approach Marshik uses should be distinguished from a cultural studies approach, which concerns itself with how cultural practices and objects reflect and create systems of power. Rather, her approach brings together protagonists, objects, and affect, and assumes that each modifies and mediates the other in continuous and surprising ways.

Methodologically, Marshik starts from a place of unknowing and rather than approach the material as a sculptor with a tool to carve from raw material, she is ethnographer and historian, letting the materials speak for themselves in their strangeness first, and only then connecting what she has learned with ideas in circulation. For instance, in the chapter, "At the Mercy of the Evening Gown," she brings together material from *Punch*, *Vanity Fair*, *Gentlewoman*, *Ladies Field*, *Vogue*, *Eve*, the *Times*, *Illustrated London News*, fashion historians, thing theorists, sociologists, period encyclopedias, the 1905 biograph/mutoscope film *A Ballroom Tragedy*, a serial novel by Kathlyn Rhodes, "The Harvest of Folly," published in the *Sunday Graphic* in 1928, multiple memoirs from the early twentieth century, the work of two different *Vogue* fashion photographers, the Messel Family Dress Collection, and the Fashion Museum of Bath archives, all alongside readings of memoirs, diaries, letters, essays and fiction by Virginia Woolf, Rebecca West, Jean Rhys, Osbert Sitwell, and Aldous Huxley. Such an assemblage necessarily enacts a transvaluation of any one of the list above via the leveling of the information they express about women, clothes, class, literature, and a disappearing way of life. The story of the evening gown that Marshik weaves is not one of triumph and hegemony; it is not a familiar story. It is eerie and unnerving and invites the reader to understand modernist literature anew by refusing the well-trod moves of theory that typically lead the writer to stock conclusions.

Caroline Levine's 2015 book *Forms: Whole, Rhythm, Hierarchy, Network* advocates that we begin to think about how different forms—and Marshik's list above is certainly a diverse list of forms—when put together, might create unpredictable exchanges and politically radical possibilities. Feminist modernist studies will not advance without this kind of juxtaposition, or low theory. Women writers are still in an undervalued position; low theory uses the high and already-valued in such ways that enable us to see the low from fresh vantage points.

So, we must act as if the playing field between major and minor authors, men and women, is already level. In doing so we will reinvent what we know. One of the dangers of becoming too specialized in a field is ceasing to see it afresh. If we read in the spirit of unknowing, and approach all texts not with the tools of the modernist scholar looking to see what she already knows but instead with the spirit of the ethnographer, hoping to find the strange and unusual and to be taught by it, we *will* find new ways to talk about women writers. But we have to be unafraid if what they have to say does not connect to the dominant narratives of modernism. That may in fact be the point.

Notes

1. Baym, "Agony of Feminism," 101.

2. Butler, *Gender Trouble*, 16, 25.

3. Baym makes the point that "liberal feminism has not *failed* to define 'woman' in a consistent or rigorous manner; it has positively refused to do so. It categorically insists on assimilating women to the class 'human'" ("Agony of Feminism," 104).

4. Felski's *The Limits of Critique* assesses Paul Ricouer's term, especially on pages 30–35.

5. Best and Marcus, "Surface Reading," 1–21.

6. The published issue is *Modern Fiction Studies* 59, no. 2 (Summer 2013).

7. Garrity, "Modernist Women's Writing," 17.

8. This essay appears in Kosofsky Sedgwick's, *Touching Feeling: Affect, Pedagogy, Performativity*, 123–52.

9. Baym points out that "in this much-quoted sentence she used the master's tools quite effectively" ("Agony of Feminism," 107).

10. I reference here, of course, Sianne Ngai's *Ugly Feelings* (Harvard University Press, 2007), which organizes itself around a series of known or coined affects through which Ngai, like Berlant, is able to bring a series of disparate texts into conversation.

11. Halberstam, *Queer Art of Failure*, 1–5.

12. Ibid., 16.

Works Cited

Baym, Nina. "The Agony of Feminism: Why Feminist Theory Is Necessary After All." In *The Emperor Redressed: Critiquing Critical Theory*, edited by Dwight Eddins, 101–17. Tuscaloosa: University of Alabama Press, 1995.

Benstock, Shari. *Women of the Left Bank: Paris, 1900–1940*. Austin: University of Texas Press, 1986.

Berlant, Lauren. *The Female Complaint: The Unfinished Business of Sentimentality in American Culture*. Durham, NC: Duke University Press, 2008.

Best, Stephen, and Sharon Marcus. "Surface Reading: An Introduction." *Representations* 108, no. 1 (2009): 1–21.

Butler, Judith. *Gender Trouble: Feminism and the Subversion of Identity*. New York: Routledge, 1990.

Felski, Rita. *The Limits of Critique*. Chicago: University of Chicago Press, 2015.

Fernald, Anne. "Women's Fiction, New Modernist Studies, and Feminism." *Modern Fiction Studies* 59, no. 2 (Summer 2013): 229–40.

Garrity, Jane. "Modernist Women's Writing: Beyond the Threshold of Obsolescence." *Literature Compass* 10, no. 1 (2013): 15–29.

Gilbert, Sandra M., and Susan Gubar. *No Man's Land*. 3 vols. New Haven: Yale University Press, 1989–1994.

Halberstam, Jack (Judith). *The Queer Art of Failure*. Durham, NC: Duke University Press, 2011.

Irigaray, Luce. *This Sex Which Is Not One*. Translated by Catherine Porter and Caroline Burke. Ithaca: Cornell University Press, 1985.

Leavis, Q. D. *Fiction and the Reading Public*. London: Chatto and Windus, 1932.

Levine, Caroline. *Forms: Whole, Rhythm, Hierarchy, Network*. Princeton: Princeton University Press, 2015.

Lorde, Audre. *Sister Outsider: Essays and Speeches*. New York: Crossing Press, 1984.

Mao, Douglas, and Rebecca L. Walkowitz. "The New Modernist Studies." *PMLA* 123, no. 3 (2008): 737–48.

Marshik, Celia. *At the Mercy of Their Clothes: Modernism, the Middlebrow, and British Garment Culture*. New York: Columbia University Press, 2016.

Pease, Allison. *Modernism, Feminism, and the Culture of Boredom*. New York: Cambridge University Press, 2012.

———. *Modernism, Mass Culture, and the Aesthetics of Obscenity*. New York: Cambridge University Press, 2000.

Scott, Bonnie Kime. *The Gender of Modernism: A Critical Anthology*. Bloomington: Indiana University Press, 1990.

Sedgwick, Eve Kosofsky. "Paranoid Reading and Reparative Reading, or, You're So Paranoid, You Probably Think This Essay Is About You." In *Touching Feeling: Affect, Pedagogy, Performativity* (2003): 123–51.

Sinclair, May. *Mary Olivier: A Life*. 1919. New York Review of Books, 2002.

———. *The Three Sisters*. London: Macmillan, 1915.

Von Arnim, Elizabeth. 1914. *The Pastor's Wife*. London: J. M. Dent, 1993.

Zerilli, Linda. *Feminism and the Abyss of Freedom*. Chicago: University of Chicago Press, 2005.

6

Emma Goldman among the Avant-Garde

CATHERINE W. HOLLIS

Emma Goldman began writing her autobiography in the early morning hours of June 27, 1928, her 59th birthday. She had been putting it off for weeks, as she settled into the St. Tropez cottage that would serve as her writing retreat. The beautiful temptations of the landscape—its vineyards, pine forests, and "riot of color in flowers"—were a soothing balm for the exiled Goldman, who had not enjoyed a home of her own in over a decade: "Really if I fail to do good writing here you'll have to give me up as a cripple," she wrote to a friend.[1] Goldman employed a young American writer, Emily Holmes Coleman, to act as secretary, although Coleman arrived in St. Tropez with a broken typewriter and no skills in stenography. Perhaps this was a fair trade, given that Goldman could pay no salary, although she provided room and board.

Despite the thirty years separating them, the two women quickly grew close: Coleman was working on the manuscript of the novel that would become *The Shutter of Snow* (1930), which Goldman read and commented on, even as she struggled to begin her own book. The day before her birthday, Goldman wrote to another younger friend, American novelist Evelyn Scott: "to me one of the great delusions is the notion that writing is a joy. (It may be to some, as interjected by my impetuous secretary—damn her—but it is not to most)."[2] Despite, or because of, Coleman's presence, Goldman finally got down to work, writing in a postscript to Scott: "I actually started my book. Wrote until five o'clock this morning."[3] In the next two days, after Coleman surprised Goldman with a champagne-laden birthday party, Goldman wrote 6,000 words, making a solid beginning on her autobiography, *Living My Life* (1931).

It may sound incongruous to find firebrand anarchist Emma Goldman drinking champagne in St. Tropez, but by 1928, Goldman had earned her rest. Back in America, through her tireless work as an activist, speaker, editor, and writer, Goldman had organized, agitated, and done jail time for issues as various as workers' rights, free speech, birth control, and anti-conscription. Deported from America in 1919 under the Sedition Act, Goldman spent most of her sixth decade stateless and increasingly depressed, unsure how to continue her life's work toward the "beautiful ideal" of an egalitarian world (Goldman, *Living My Life*, 56). Since her first speaking tour in 1896, Goldman had thrived on life center-stage in the often violent conflicts of Progressive-era America. For decades, Goldman's personal life *was* her political life, as she pursued "freedom, the right to self-expression, everybody's right to beautiful, radiant things."[4] After her deportation, Goldman bitterly missed America and her role in the political and cultural vanguard there. Although her friends and supporters urged her to use this time off the front lines of political struggle to record her remarkable life for posterity, Goldman felt that she had become invisible and irrelevant in the eyes of the world. This made the prospect of spending a year or more quietly writing emotionally fraught, despite the pleasures of St. Tropez.

Goldman was particularly troubled by issues relating to her age and gender, as she notes in many of the letters written while procrastinating on the autobiography: "the world counts no years in men. But every additional year on the back of a woman increases the indifference and cynicism toward her of the world."[5] Goldman felt that "indifference" keenly, both personally and politically. While her lifelong friend and lover, Alexander "Sasha" Berkman, had been deported with Goldman, he was now ensconced in a tumultuous romantic relationship with a young woman, Emmy Eckstein. Goldman's own passionate affair with the charismatic Ben Reitman had foundered a decade earlier, while her subsequent affairs with men were brief, and did nothing to assuage her growing sense of rootlessness and insecurity. After a lifetime of advocating for free love and the healthy expression of sexuality, Goldman was angry that aging men still retained currency in the heterosexual economy, while aging women saw their "value" decrease: "If I belonged to your sex," she wrote to her

American lawyer Arthur Ross, "it would be dead easy. Look at Frank Harris. But there is no mercy for the female of the species—no matter how she looks or feels, years are [against] her."[6] From Goldman's perspective, an aging Lothario like Frank Harris—author of *My Lives and Loves* (1931)—had access to stores of emotional and physical intimacy from which Goldman now felt shut out.

In this frame of mind, Goldman turned toward her friendships with women: "the modern woman," she wrote in 1923, "wants understanding, comradeship, she wants to be treated as a human being. . . . Since she cannot always find it in the man, she turns to her own sisters."[7] The younger generation of American expatriate women Goldman met in France—Emily Coleman, Djuna Barnes, Peggy Guggenheim, Sylvia Beach, among others—seemed to Goldman to be following in her own footsteps in their rejection of traditional female roles. In their modernity and pursuit of freedom, these women were creating new modes of relationship and a more open sexuality, as if they had been called into existence by Goldman's own words. In a sense, Goldman turned toward this younger generation for proof that she was still relevant, still "the most dangerous woman in America."[8]

Goldman's relationships with this emerging generation of rebellious women were often marked by deep affection. For Emily Coleman, who gave Goldman the pseudonym "Hero" in her diary, Goldman was a venerable role model and mentor. But more than one contemporary observed the strong emotional demands Goldman placed on these quasi-maternal relationships of her later years. Ethel Mannin, a socialist novelist and close friend of Goldman in the 1930s, writes from her own experience that "Emma attached considerable importance to friendships with women in her later years, responding eagerly, out of her inner loneliness, to affection and sympathetic understanding."[9] Goldman's biographers have noted the ways in which, throughout her life, Goldman could unconsciously impose upon other people, particularly women, in pursuit of freedom and justice; ironically perhaps, she seems to have felt that since her life's work was in the service of liberty, to assist her was to serve the larger movement.[10]

This essay focuses on Goldman's intergenerational relationships with women, marked by the complex dynamics noted above, in order to trace a two-way pattern of influence. How were modernist women's communities shaped by Goldman's example and ideas, and how was Goldman in turn influenced by her relationships with modernist women? This essay argues that Goldman's anarchist feminism is a vital, if under-studied, influence on modernist women's communities. Goldman found the "modern woman" she had envisioned in the generation of expatriate American women she came to live among during her own exile from America. Goldman and her younger friends shared in the struggle to redefine traditionally gendered roles as wives and mothers, often choosing to live outside those roles altogether. Despite the generation separating them, Goldman felt that they were united by their improvised personal lives and pursuit of individual liberty. Further, through these friendships, Goldman was herself challenged to expand her definition of what counted as revolutionary in the fields of art and literature.

The first relationship this essay traces is Goldman's connection with Margaret Anderson, editor of the *Little Review*. The two women met in Chicago in 1914, when Goldman was at the height of her power and influence as an anarchist speaker: in this example, Goldman is initially the mentor-hero, and Anderson her willing pupil in a mutually beneficial— if ironically hierarchical—relationship. In April 1914, when Anderson first heard Goldman lecture in Chicago, she quickly took to the pages of the *Little Review* to enumerate Goldman's star qualities, which Anderson listed as greatness, courage, nobility, sincerity, high-mindedness, and generosity.[11] Goldman in turn admired how Anderson and Harriet Dean (Anderson's romantic partner before Jane Heap) threw off the "shackles of their middle-class homes" and became "rebels for their own liberation" (Goldman, *Living My Life,* 531).

Consequently, Anderson's the *Little Review* and Goldman's magazine *Mother Earth* began a dialogue, taking advertisements and publishing articles across platforms, linking the audiences for the *Little Review*'s artistic and literary avant-garde with *Mother Earth*'s political and social revolutionary focus. For the 1914 generation, Emma Goldman was inspiring, even if—with the bravado of youth—they did not feel that she had anything particularly new to say to them. As Anderson remarked of Goldman's vanguard ideas: "ten years ago she was preaching, under the most absurd persecution, ideas which thinking people accept as a matter of course today."[12] But Goldman fought for the ideas that Anderson could take for granted; in their differences, we see an early example of successive generations of American feminism negotiating influence and relevance. Furthermore, this encounter between Goldman and Anderson would bring the political and social avant-garde more closely in conversation with the artistic and literary avant-garde, and both women (as well as the little magazines they edited) would benefit as a result.

The essay then moves to St. Tropez in 1928 to focus on Goldman's relationships with Emily Coleman and Peggy Guggenheim. This was a more vulnerable moment for Goldman, as she faced the insecurity of aging alone, far from her friends and community in New York. "The world is indeed my country," she wrote to Arthur Ross in 1926, "but it is a damned insecure feeling not to have one particular place that I can call my own."[13] Goldman still had extensive support networks in New York, and a committee was organized, with Peggy Guggenheim as one of the donors, to raise the funds to purchase Bon Esprit, as the cottage in St. Tropez was known, for Goldman to live in while composing her autobiography. During the summer of 1928, Goldman introduced Coleman to Guggenheim, and a network of friendship was formed. Goldman brought a protective, maternal impulse to her relationships with both Coleman and Guggenheim, stepping in decisively when Guggenheim's marriage to the abusive Laurence Vail broke up later that year. For her part, Coleman kept Goldman up to date with recent developments in modernist literature, while Guggenheim financially supported Goldman's writing sabbatical, as she would go on to do for writer Djuna Barnes.

These relationships were not ideal and should not be idealized: Coleman quarreled passionately with Goldman, and Guggenheim would eventually drop Goldman. Nonetheless, through them we see Goldman, and the modernist women in her 1920s orbit, developing new forms of domesticity, work, patronage, and aging within an intergenerational woman-centered network. For Goldman, the status of modern women was an open question: "the modern woman cannot be the wife and mother in the old sense, and the new medium has not yet been devised, I mean the way of being wife, mother, friend and yet retain one's complete freedom. Will it ever?"[14] Ultimately, Goldman formulated the questions that modernist women then attempted to answer in their experimental personal lives. Goldman's influence on this younger generation of women during the last two decades of her life was profound, but under-acknowledged, both at the time and subsequently in modernist studies.

Anarchism and the Modernist Woman

In order to understand how Emma Goldman's anarchist feminism anticipates and shapes modernist women's communities, we first need to understand who Goldman was and what she represented when Margaret Anderson first encountered her. Between 1896 and 1919, the charismatic Goldman became notorious for the crowds she drew to her lectures and rallies on topics as varied as anarchism, workers' rights, and the nascent communist movement. On these tours of America, speaking on street corners and in halls, Goldman was dogged by local resistance (sometimes violent) and constant government surveillance. Goldman also spoke on the so-called sex question, a term that encompassed a variety of gendered topics including birth control, marriage, prostitution, sexuality, and the role of the "modern woman." Thus, Donna M. Kowal argues that Goldman's real infamy stems from speaking in public about women's private lives, "violating the norms of acceptable public behavior for women": in Kowal's formulation, the "intimate" threat Goldman posed to America came from the way she herself undermined social rules about women's place in the public and private spheres.[15] Similarly, Candace Falk argues that Goldman's advocacy of "women's independence" and "sexual liberation" "w[as] experienced as more threatening to the upholders of the status quo than were her anarchist ideas about retaliatory violence."[16]

By presenting her ideas in person on stage, Goldman placed not only her voice but also her body in front of mass audiences, performing the acts of rebellion she advocated in her speeches and essays. As Anderson noticed at the time: the power of Goldman's ideas came not from their originality as such but that "she says it instead of putting it into books, that she hurls it from the platform straight into the minds and hearts of the . . . people who listen to her."[17] From Goldman's earliest speeches and articles, including "Anarchy and the Sex Question" (1896) and "The New Woman" (1898), onto later talks on prostitution "The White Slave Traffic" (1910), free love "Marriage and Love" (1911), and birth control "The Social Aspects of Birth Control" (1916), Goldman fundamentally threatened the patriarchal institutions that kept women imprisoned in the private sphere.[18]

Lecturing in Yiddish, Russian, and English, Goldman spoke as a Russian-Jewish immigrant and outsider to the Anglo-Saxon patriarchal America of her time. From this position, Goldman nonetheless spoke to and for a much larger population of women just waking up to the gilded cage of traditional gender roles. Using Henrik Ibsen's Nora (from *A Doll's House* [1879]) as case in point, Goldman argued in 1911 that "the institution of marriage makes a parasite of woman, an absolute dependent. It incapacitates her for life's struggle, annihilates her social consciousness, paralyzes her imagination, and then imposes its gracious protection, which is in reality a snare, a travesty on human character."[19] By comparing marriage to prostitution, an "economic arrangement," and going on to speak freely and candidly about female sexuality and desire, about women "free and big enough to learn the mystery of sex without the sanction of State or Church," Goldman fundamentally challenged the notion of what could be said in public about women by women.[20] Yet Goldman acknowledged that the social risks of stepping outside conventional women's roles were great, both for herself and for the women listening to her: "Once she dared to be herself, to be true to her nature, to life, there is no return: the woman is thrust out from the pale and protection of society."[21] By forgoing the conventional "protections" of patriarchal relationships, and by living her life in public, Goldman lived out her message to modern women. By advocating that women pursue autonomy and pleasure, Goldman's example paved the way for the younger generation of "gender rebels" she later encountered in modernist circles.[22]

Significantly, both Goldman and the generation of women following her were strongly influenced by the tenets of individualism in circulation at the time. Goldman's anarchism, which emphasized individual freedom,[23] reflects her association with what historian Lucy Delap refers to as "vanguard" or avant-garde feminism: "avant-garde feminists felt comfortable with the term individualism, and used it in ways that complemented . . . their feminism."[24] Distinguishing between the two main schools of feminism in the late Edwardian era (1910–1917), Delap argues that the collective feminism of the suffrage movement was often at odds with the more individualistic tenets of "advanced" or "modern" feminists. We see this split in Goldman's own resistance to the suffrage movement. As an anarchist, Goldman did not believe in the state, and thus not in the act of voting, making her position clear as early as 1906 when she published "The Tragedy of Women's Emancipation" in the first issue of her journal *Mother Earth*. True emancipation, for Goldman, "begins neither in the polls nor in courts. It begins in woman's soul."[25] Speaking thus, Goldman articulates the credo of a developing trans-Atlantic "feminist avant-garde," whose belief in "self-development [is] conveyed through the idea of 'expressing one's will or 'developing personality.'"[26] The emphasis Goldman places on an "inner regeneration" as a first step toward social change rang true for the first generation of women coming of age with voting rights.

Rebels for Their Own Liberation

Given the emphasis on individuality, "personality" was an important term for avant-garde feminists, and perhaps no modernist woman could have had more personality than Margaret Anderson. "I have no place in the world—no fixed position. I don't know just what kind of thing I am. Nobody else seems to know either": neither "daughter, sister, niece, aunt, wife, mistress, or mother," *Little Review* editor Anderson locates herself in none of the familiar "human categories," categories defined exclusively through women's enmeshment in heterosexuality and middle-class patriarchal life.[27] Anderson's self-invention outside these normative roles made of her life an ongoing experiment. Thus, when she first heard Goldman speak in Chicago in April 1914, Anderson found a role model in the woman who was "the most challenging spirit in America."[28] Goldman's linkage of individual and social regeneration spoke intimately to Anderson's own struggle to liberate herself from her family and bolstered her editorial vision for her new journal. Goldman, at forty-five, offered a bold example of a woman living outside the pale for Anderson, at twenty-eight, while anarchism proved a vital energy for the *Little Review*'s admixture of art, music, poetry, and philosophy.

Goldman's crammed speaking schedule in Chicago balanced talks on modern drama with speeches on politics and the sex question. Between April 6 and 11, Goldman lectured each afternoon on a different national drama, encompassing Scandinavian, German, English, Irish, American, and Russian and including figures such as Henrik Ibsen, Gerhart Hauptmann, W. B. Yeats, J. M. Synge, and Anton Chekhov.[29] These afternoon lectures occurred at the Lexington Hotel and brought in a "fashionable feminine audience," according to Anderson. At night, Goldman lectured on political and social topics at the International Labor Hall, to a rowdier audience of anarchists, socialists, and workers, "most of whom were collarless, but who knew very emphatically what they thought of her and her ideas."[30] Anderson went to one of each type of lecture, and as she quipped in her autobiography, "I heard Emma Goldman lecture and had just time to turn anarchist before the presses closed."[31] (See fig. 6.1.) In Anderson's assessment, anarchism was a philosophy accessible to all enlightened people: "the goal for which they are striving—namely, individual human freedom—is one for which we might all strive with credit." Anarchists were not violent in acts, Anderson argued, but in speech: "dynamite is a part of their intellectual, not physical, equipment."[32] Such fearlessness and pluck on the part of a female rebel proved irresistible to Anderson.

Anderson's article on Goldman appeared in the third issue of the *Little Review*, with two notable consequences. The primary financial backer of the *Little Review* pulled his support from the magazine over fears that he might be associated with the anarchist movement, a gesture that only strengthened Anderson's resolve to feature anarchism as a key component of the magazine. This resolve paid off when Goldman herself wrote to Anderson at the *Little Review*, pleased with the article, and especially happy that "it was a woman who demonstrated such depth and appreciation of the cardinal principles of my work."[33] This initiated both a friendship between the women and a relationship between their magazines, each helmed by women editors and committed to exploring avant-garde ideas in the arts and politics.

In their respective memoirs, Anderson and Goldman share a remarkably similar recall of their first meeting at the Lexington Hotel, although the exact date of this meeting is unknown. Goldman recalls turning her back on the "*chic* society girl" emerging from the elevator; and in Anderson's recollection, "[Goldman] wore a flowered summer dress and a straw hat with a ribbon. She was made all of one piece. When I stepped from the elevator she turned her back on me."[34] Both women's instant class-based assessment of the other's clothing was quickly overcome by Anderson's extroverted invitation for Goldman to stay with her, her sister Lois, and lover Harriet Dean in the nearly empty apartment facing Lake Michigan the women rented. Lacking furniture, apart from a piano, Anderson urged Goldman "not to worry about capitalism while she was with us."[35] Goldman recognized the lesbian relationship between Anderson and Dean, noting that Dean was "athletic, masculine-looking," while Anderson was "feminine in the extreme," and valued how both "girls" (as Goldman referred to them) were "strongly individualized."

Unlike the radical women in Goldman's anarchist milieu, Anderson and Dean's radicalism was not—in Goldman's estimation—motivated by

FIGURE 6.1. "Light occupations of the editor, while there is nothing to edit" (*The Little Review* 3.6, September 1916): 14.

social injustice. But "as rebels for their own liberation," Anderson and Dean "had broken the shackles of their middle-class homes to find release from family bondage and bourgeois tradition."[36] Goldman's call for "modern women" found a strong example in the young lesbian couple who so charmed her. After meeting Anderson, Goldman's resolution not to be so judgmental about female dress can be seen in an interview she gave around the time she met Anderson, when she proclaimed: "Every time I see a woman who has dared to be independent in dress—even if she is extremely dressed—I am glad of it. I know she has brains and has dared to prove it."[37]

The affection Goldman felt for the "girls" is undeniable; when she returned to Chicago later in 1914 for a second lecture tour, she claimed that her stay "was lent charm by my two young friends Margaret and Deansie. Both consecrated themselves to me and turned the office of the *Little Review* over to my needs."[38] Goldman's affection was very much a function of the work the two younger women were willing to do to aid and support their older mentor. Again, this was a common pattern in Goldman's relationships with women (and men), especially during these busy years when she toured America constantly: Goldman tended to demand rather than ask for the support of other women, thinking of it as her due for the long years of labor she had put into the cause of liberation.[39] This dynamic would evolve in Goldman's relationships with women in her later years, as Goldman's own star waned and the younger women took center stage. But during this second trip to Chicago, Goldman accepted the tribute of Anderson and Dean as her due. Once again, Goldman split her time between afternoon drama lectures, primarily at the Fine Arts Building, and evening political topics ("the propaganda ones" in Anderson's words) at labor halls like the Workman's and Hod Carriers' halls. Their professional relationship was solidified when Goldman's *Mother Earth* published Anderson's review of the Fine Arts Lectures in its December issue.

Anderson's review in *Mother Earth* is significant for it establishes a major line of thought about Goldman's legacy. Historians of anarchism and Goldman have had to reckon with Anderson's assessment that "Emma Goldman's genius is not so much that she is a great thinker as that she is a great woman; she preaches, but she is a better artist than she is a preacher."[40] In this review, Anderson suggests that Goldman's power and authority derives from the force of her personality rather than from her ideas. Although Goldman had recently published *The Social Significance of the Modern Drama* (1914), and was, for all intents and purposes, engaged on a book tour, Goldman's aesthetic ideas struck her more sophisticated listeners as obvious; as suffragist Sara Bard Field quipped of Goldman's drama lectures, "I think Ibsen would groan in spirit and Hauptmann hold up his hands in horror."[41] The problem with Goldman's drama talks, for Anderson, was that they lacked "her special function," which—for Anderson, and for Goldman's audiences—was to serve as a symbol of the advanced ideas emerging in America in both arts and politics. As we will see, however, this progressive America, which looked to Goldman as a figurehead, was under increasing threat from reactionary forces emerging in response to the threat of World War I, a reaction that would eventually suppress both Goldman's *Mother Earth* and Anderson's *Little Review*.

The relationship between Emma Goldman and Margaret Anderson is often viewed as a balancing act between their respective commitments to the political and the aesthetic avant-garde. Some historians, such as Christine Stansell, believe that their relationship ultimately breaks down over these issues: according to this line of thought, Goldman scorns Anderson's embrace of modernism, while Anderson ridicules Goldman's insistence on evaluating art on the basis of its politics. Certainly, the *Little Review* changed dramatically under Jane Heap's influence beginning in 1916: once Ezra Pound became its European editor in 1917, the journal's focus evolved dramatically from cultural progressivism to high modernism. From 1917, James Joyce, W. B. Yeats, and the Baroness Elsa von Freytag-Loringhoven took aesthetic precedence over Goldman's old-school radicalism in the pages of the *Little Review*. Indeed, as the editors of *The Little Review "Ulysses"* point out, there are twenty-five references to Goldman in the *Little Review* prior to 1917, and only one after that date.[42] That single reference comes from Heap's ironic response to Goldman's deportation in 1919: "I feel that the Government was right in deporting Emma Goldman and Alexander Berkman. They had become a tradition. Kind, loving, intelligent, intense, they had made anarchism a harmless, respected, even fashionable word in every kind of American home."[43] Goldman's anarchism was perceived as old hat to the new generation of cultural rebels, prompting Heap's dismissal.

But this line of argument ignores the evidence that Anderson happily disagreed with Goldman about art from the first: in Anderson's words, "Miss Goldman and I will sometime have a long and heated argument about this matter of form. She believes it is of second importance; I think it is first."[44] Historian Kathy Ferguson parses the aesthetic differences between Goldman and Anderson generationally: in Ferguson's reading, the two women occupy different "compositional logics." While Goldman's aesthetic choices reflect the "romantic-realism" of the 1890s, Anderson's privilege high modernist form.[45] For Ferguson, Goldman's "daily lifework" is the more important influence on Anderson. Both Goldman and Anderson were "social artists," merging their domestic lives with their political and artistic commitments: Anderson's 1915 experiment living in a women's tent camp on the bank of Lake Michigan is a case in point.[46] If Goldman inspired Anderson to make radical personal life choices, so too did Anderson inspire Goldman to read from the new modernist experiments in literature. Goldman mentions "not minding" being in jail in May 1917 awaiting her upcoming trial, for Anderson has sent her James Joyce's *A Portrait of the Artist as a Young Man* (1916), and Goldman finds it powerful and "original."[47]

I would argue that the most important influence Goldman had on Anderson concerns the fight for free speech. While Heap and Pound were shaping the *Little Review*'s new modernist focus, Anderson returned to the pages of *Mother Earth* to protest Goldman and Berkman's 1917 trial. In "'The Immutables'" (a reference to Anderson's 1914 article with a similar name), Anderson documented her furious response to the trial that would result in Goldman and Berkman's imprisonment and deportation. Officially charged with protesting forced conscription upon the entrance of America into World War I, Goldman and Berkman were effectively prosecuted for the free expression of their radical politics. Anderson attended their trial daily and by her own account lunched with Goldman and Berkman each day. In Anderson's account of their trial, which she called "this very latest of our American atrocities," she roundly disputes the judge's charge to the jury not to consider the "issue of free speech," but to prosecute Goldman and Berkman as criminals expressing "doctrines opposed to law and order."[48] "Shaking with the hideousness and absurdity" of their trial, Anderson claims that the prosecution's law and order line of argument had the opposite effect, converting the audience (if not the jury) to anarchism: as one audience member says in Anderson's report, "Now I'm afraid of the law, of the judge, and of his kind. I'm going to study the philosophy of anarchism."[49] Preceding the trial, the offices of Goldman's journal *Mother Earth* were raided, and afterward the journal was suppressed by the U.S. Postal Service: *Mother Earth* ceased publication in 1918. Through her attendance at Goldman's trial, Anderson clearly saw that free speech and free press were under attack.

Goldman and Berkman's imprisonment and deportation were part of a larger government crackdown on immigrants and so-called radicals. In 1918, the U.S. Congress authorized the deportation of undocumented immigrants belonging to radical organizations (including the Industrial Workers of the World). But even American citizens, like Margaret Anderson and Jane Heap, whose nationality was unquestioned, suffered from the suppression of free speech under the Espionage Act of 1917. In October 1917, just after Goldman's trial, the *Little Review* was also suppressed by the U.S. Post Office for publishing Wyndham Lewis's story "Cantleman's Spring Mate"; while the censorship was supposedly motivated by obscenity, the primary motivation was political, as the *Little Review* was by then listed as a "Publication of Anarchistic tendency" by the Post Office.[50] But despite the threat of prosecution, Anderson and Heap persisted and began publishing *Ulysses* in March 1918. Their courage and commitment to publishing *Ulysses,* despite the real threat of prosecution, grows out of Anderson's dedication to Goldman's example. Thus, when Anderson and Heap went on trial for publishing *Ulysses* in December 1920, they were directly following in Goldman's footsteps.

Following Ferguson's argument, the differences between Goldman and Anderson primarily emerge because of the generation gap between them: Goldman's radical youth in the 1890s offered a different set of aesthetic choices than Anderson's "millennial" aesthetic education in the 1910s.[51] Focusing on the aesthetic-political binary to define their relationship ignores the greater similarities between the two women; both occupied gendered positions outside the familiar social and "human categories," and both constructed larger-than-life personalities as an act of self-definition.[52] Utterly opposed to the doctrine of modernist impersonality, both women made life choices that merged the personal with the political. Further, as editors of little magazines committed to publishing ideas and work that challenged the status quo, both Goldman and Anderson faced censorship and prosecution with courage, humor, and grit. Perhaps the biggest difference between the two is that while Anderson could learn from, critique, and outgrow Goldman's example, Goldman's self-invention was sui generis.

"A Natural Rebel and Anarchist"

Because of the generational divide between Emma Goldman and the modernist women she knew, Goldman confronted the stark financial and emotional stresses of aging outside patriarchal safety nets twenty years sooner than they did. Thus, in the 1920s, while many American modernists—Margaret Anderson and Jane Heap among them—were voluntarily transplanting themselves to the aesthetic and social whirl of expatriate life in Europe, Goldman found herself in unhappy exile from America. Goldman's loss of public identity left her feeling financially and emotionally vulnerable, without the audiences and speaking tours that had sustained her in America. She found it difficult to rebuild her career as a lecturer and writer in Britain, when her negative views on Soviet Russia (her book *My Disillusionment in Russia* was published in 1923) flew in the face of a burgeoning Bolshevist movement.[53] Attempts at giving a lecture tour on drama in the industrial north of England left Goldman feeling further deflated and uninspired. Her angst was exacerbated by a sense that she had given her all to the anarchist movement, and now she looked to her former comrades for help, even as she found the process of asking for it "humiliating."[54] Goldman's loss of citizenship reinforced her sense of being a woman without a country and made travel difficult, until an old comrade, Welsh miner James Colton, came to Goldman's aid by marrying her.[55] For much of the 1920s and 1930s, until the Spanish Civil War when she immersed herself in the partisan effort to defeat fascism, Goldman would struggle to redefine her purpose as a revolutionary activist.

Goldman attributed much of her personal turmoil to the consequences of living a modern woman's life. In a letter to Sasha Berkman in 1925, Goldman expressed what made her exile and deportation different from his. She approached the comparison through invoking a mutual friend, M. Eleanor Fitzgerald ("Fitzi"):

> Fitzi's main tragedy . . . is really the tragedy of all of us modern women. It is a fact that we are removed only by a very short period from our traditions, the traditions of being loved, cared for, protected, secured, and above all, the time when women could look forward to an old age of children, a home and someone to brighten their lives. Being away from all that by a mere fraction of time, most modern women, especially when they see age growing upon them,

and if they have given out of themselves so abundantly, begin to feel the utter emptiness of their existence, the lack of *the man*, whom they love and who loves them, the comradeship and companionship that grows out of such a relation, the home, a child.[56]

Whether or not Fitzi, a key behind-the-scenes organizer for both Goldman and Berkman and, at the time of Goldman's letter, the manager of the Provincetown Players, actually felt this way is a moot point. Goldman felt that she herself was living out a modern woman's "tragedy."[57] The melodramatic tone was characteristic of Goldman in these years of exile. After having devoted her life to the cause of liberty, what could she look forward to in her old age?

Tragedy, as such, was averted by Goldman's friends and supporters in New York, who began organizing financial support for Goldman while she wrote her autobiography. An economically diverse group of men and women helped fund Goldman's next steps. In 1926, Frank and Nellie Harris—who were living in the south of France—found a rental cottage for Goldman and Berkman in St. Tropez. They introduced Goldman to Peggy Guggenheim and Laurence Vail, and an informal network of expatriate New Yorkers began to take shape along the French Riviera. Meanwhile back in New York, Fitzgerald and lawyer Arthur Ross formed a committee to raise funds for Goldman's autobiography: donors included W. S. Van Valkenburgh, Howard Young, Mark Dix, and Guggenheim. Later in 1928, once Goldman had settled in St. Tropez, Ross and Dix negotiated the sale of Bon Esprit to Goldman, with Guggenheim and Dix as major donors.[58] Although Guggenheim would claim in her memoirs that she was the one who "bought" Goldman the cottage, the truth is that it took a village to house Emma Goldman.

Once settled in St. Tropez with Emily Coleman as roommate, Goldman continued to ponder the life choices available to modern women as she observed the arc of Coleman's personal life. Like Anderson, Coleman—despite having been a wife and mother—lived outside the traditional patriarchal categories, a woman whose distinctive individuality would be best expressed through the hypomanic and voluminous diaries she kept throughout her life.[59] Goldman found in Coleman a "natural rebel and anarchist" who challenged the status quo through her personal life.[60] By choosing to focus on work rather than her child, Coleman embodied Goldman's idea of the "modern mothers," those independent, creative women who were "forerunners of a new culture in the United States."[61] Goldman seems to be thinking of Coleman in a letter she writes during Coleman's tenure as her secretary: "I prefer the modern woman, the modern mother. . . . she knows that in order to be of any help to her child she herself must grow and develop—to give her own life purpose and meaning."[62] Goldman's notion that a mother must retain her individual identity may seem commonplace now, but was shockingly bold at the time.

For Goldman, the symbolic term "Mother" (as in "Mother Russia") represented female power and authority, and was separate from biological motherhood. Throughout her life, Goldman had enjoyed playing this symbolic "Mother": early on, she resolved to sublimate her "mother-need in the love of *all* children."[63] Subsequently, Goldman's ideas about mothers, biological and symbolic, permeate her work, from the title of her journal *Mother Earth* to the love-talk she engaged in with Ben Reitman (she was his "Mommy").[64] In her relationship with Coleman, we find another significant example of Goldman's maternal displacement; their bond was close, emotional, and expressed through food and drink. Throughout her diaries, Coleman refers to Goldman's cooking as an expression of love. Goldman ("Hero" in the diaries), emerges as a lost mother figure for Coleman:

> At noon Hero made me a salad of old. It was sweet to see her bending over a kitchen table with an onion in one hand and a knife in the other, nipping with her mouth the onion. Hero rushing an omelette on the table at the last minute, made of nothing, with Jewish sausages. I crying "Hero there you are, you always did that." She liked that, she is my mother and that is why I love her.[65]

In this quote, Goldman is mother as "hero" to the motherless Emily, whose own mother had died when Coleman was a child. The bond between the two women is bittersweet, with the "nipped" onion suggesting tears. Modern women ambivalent about motherhood, Goldman and Coleman form a new woman-centered family unit, emblematized by the symbolic meal of eggs and "nothing," with "Jewish sausages," an odd detail that positions Goldman as ethnic other, a beloved nurse to the hungover Coleman. (See fig. 6.2.)

Their rich and complex bond was fostered by time spent working on Goldman's autobiography in the garden at Bon Esprit. Although Coleman

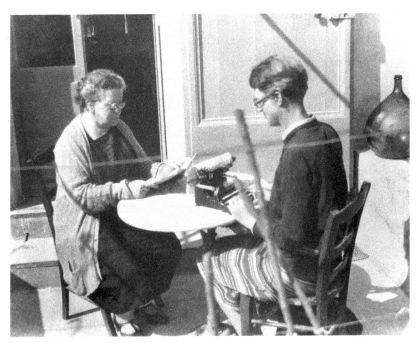

FIGURE 6.2. "Emma Goldman and Emily Coleman in St. Tropez, Publicity Photo (Oct. 19, 1931)." ©Bettman Collection/Corbis Getty Images.

was a terrible amanuensis, her editorial work on Goldman's *Living My Life* appears to have been substantial.[66] While we do not know how much direct influence Coleman exerted over the finished manuscript of *Living My Life*, we do know that it was shaped by the conversations and arguments the two women enjoyed during their year living together, and that Coleman continued to edit chunks of the manuscript after leaving St. Tropez. Coleman's shaping hand is obvious in the letters Goldman writes at this time; her puckish insertion of marginal commentary in Goldman's letters is expressed via parenthetical references and word choices. For example, in a letter written to Juliet Soskice, a friend who offered her own services as secretary, Goldman assured her that she would not enjoy the job very much. Coleman, who is apparently transcribing the letter from dictation, offers an interjection: "(She has just called out, 'There are too many people after my job!') I continue to tell her that if she will continue to do nothing as nobly as she had done it in the past, no one shall take her place."[67] A letter written to the American novelist Evelyn Scott is liberally spiced with Coleman's commentary: "A propos of my secretary, she is really no good as an ordinary typist (lie)—she not only thinks while I dictate but she corrects me every time I say anything she doesn't agree with."[68]

Emily Coleman would insist that she was "not Goldman's secretary," but an equal participant in the process of writing.[69] In this way, Coleman's parenthetical presence in Goldman's letters can be seen as precursor to her later editorial relationship with Djuna Barnes during the composition of *Nightwood* (1936). Whether secretary or editor, Coleman's opinionated insertions amount to a form of dialogic collaboration.[70] In both editorial relationships, Coleman never held back praise or blame. Goldman, in particular, suffered from the wrath of Coleman's unvarnished opinions: "I feel I cannot go through another page of her clichés and mis-wrought words and sentences. She brims with sentimentality, her style is like the villain writers of the Victorian age."[71] Goldman was in good company though. Finding a copy of *Mrs. Dalloway* (1925) in Goldman's Paris studio, Coleman similarly trashes Virginia Woolf: "It was silly, and long-drawn-out, and purposeless."[72] As with Barnes, however, Coleman's affection for Goldman wins out in the end: "I do love Hero, but damn her soul, she cannot write the English language."[73] Goldman passed tribute to Coleman's temper in the acknowledgments to *Living My Life*: "We clashed furiously, often to the point of wishing each other in Saint-Tropez Bay."[74]

Peggy Guggenheim, with her husband, Vail, and lover, John Holms, was another important part of this year in St. Tropez. Guggenheim and Vail, who lived nearby, frequently joined Goldman for dinner. In Guggenheim's memoirs, she passes tribute to Goldman's cooking: "she was a Jewish *cordon bleu* and her gefüllte fish was her *pièce de résistance*."[75] For New Yorkers craving proper Jewish food, Goldman offered the best kitchen in the south of France. Here again we see Goldman's instinct to mother younger women with food, an emotional arc Guggenheim recognized in Goldman's relationship with Coleman: "Emma adored [Emily] and mothered her and spoiled her."[76]

This dynamic also characterized Goldman's own decisive actions protecting Guggenheim when her volcanic personal life exploded late in 1928. After witnessing Vail's violence toward Guggenheim on multiple occasions during the summer and fall, Goldman proved instrumental in helping her escape this abusive marriage.[77] Acting as an intermediary between Guggenheim and Vail, Goldman tried to reason with Vail, who was outraged that Guggenheim had fled to Paris and was consulting lawyers: "you seem to have frightened and terrorized her into silence."[78] Writing to her nephew Saxe Commins, who had counseled Goldman to stay out of the ugly battle, Goldman insisted on her obligation to help: Guggenheim was "the friend who has contributed the largest sum for my book."[79]

Emma Goldman's relationship with Guggenheim was complicated by this admixture of friendship and patronage. Indeed, even as Guggenheim hid out in Paris, using Goldman as a go-between with Vail, negotiations helmed in New York by Mark Dix and Arthur Ross were underway to buy Bon Esprit outright. In letters written at the time, Goldman mentions Vail's resentment of her influence over Guggenheim "because of my free ideas regarding women's independence."[80] Goldman was adamant however that she was not helping Guggenheim because of her opposition to marriage, or out of any sense of financial obligation. Indeed, Goldman mentions in several letters how sickened she would feel were Vail to believe that Guggenheim's offer to help buy the house was in payment for Goldman's aid with the divorce.

Emma Goldman also agonizes over how this drama has disrupted her own work on the autobiography, for she has written 100,000 words already and hopes to finish in time for her sixtieth birthday the following June. To be fair to Goldman, she seems to have been caught up in an impossible situation. And we should note that helping a woman escape domestic violence is consistent with Goldman's lifelong advocacy of birth control, free love, and a woman's right to sexual self-expression. The bottom line is that helping Guggenheim was the right thing to do, *and* may have also led Guggenheim to promise her financial support.

In these complex, human, and imperfect relationships, Goldman no longer stands on the pedestal where Margaret Anderson had placed her in 1914. Although Goldman is still a "great woman," even a "Hero," she is less hierarchical in her interactions with Coleman and Guggenheim. She expects support from both, but she also offers help—and indeed love—in return. As such, Goldman's friendship with Coleman can be seen as a form of the "affectional patronage" interwoven in the networks of female modernism.[81] Marked equally by emotional commitment and intellectual critique, their collaboration is a good example of how women's literary networks developed to serve and promote the work of one another.

Emma Goldman's relationship with Guggenheim is more complicated and less happy; Guggenheim would become known for both her generosity and insecurity as a female patron of modernism.[82] Indeed, as Guggenheim would later claim of another female recipient of her largesse: "I think

Djuna [Barnes] the most ungrateful & spoilt person I have ever helped except Emma [Goldman]."[83] Guggenheim, Goldman, and Coleman all had "big" personalities; but while Coleman and Goldman could enjoy their clashes, Guggenheim and Goldman would permanently fall out with one another. Perhaps the millionaire and the anarchist were each used to being the most important person in the room.

Emma Goldman's intersections with modernist women and modernism were extensive, more than has previously been recognized.[84] Inevitably, scholarship on Goldman has focused on her American years and on her distinguished career as an anarchist speaker and political activist. Goldman's biographers, particularly Candace Falk, have also contended with the fascinating relationship between her strong public presence and her sometimes abject private romantic life with men. But there is much more to learn about Goldman's myriad relationships with women, from her intense attractions to fellow anarchists like Voltarine de Cleyre, her passionate respect for Helen Keller, and her friendships with the modernist women analyzed here. This essay has endeavored to show how two generations of modern women learned to fashion personalities and personal lives in woman-centered networks outside traditional patriarchal social structures.

Although Goldman's aesthetic preferences often differed from those of her modernist friends, her life as a "social artist" preceded and helped shape theirs. Like Goldman, modernist women were actively engaged in creating "new mediums" for partnerships, and in learning to negotiate between independent self-development and relationship with others. While some modernist women—such as Mina Loy and Jane Heap—dismissed Goldman's ideas as obvious, others—such as Margaret Anderson, Emily Coleman, and Rebecca West—felt a deep sense of kinship with "mother" Emma. Her anarchist feminism was a part of their rebellion, and her deepest questions were theirs. As Goldman articulated it, the primary question modern women faced was "how to be oneself, and yet in oneness with others?"[85] Goldman's presence in modernist women's communities testifies to her continued relevance for their lives and work, and for ours.

Notes

1. Goldman to W. S. Valkenburgh, June 10, 1928, in *The Emma Goldman Papers: A Microfilm Edition*, reel 20. Hereafter cited as *EGP*.

2. Goldman to Evelyn Scott, June 26, 1928, *EGP*, reel 20.

3. Ibid.

4. Ibid.

5. Goldman to Evelyn Scott, June 26, 1928, *EGP*, reel 20.

6. Goldman to Arthur Ross, June 25, 1928, *EGP*, reel 20.

7. Goldman, "Louise Michel," in Wilbur, *Anarchy and the Sex Question*, 126.

8. Ferguson, *Emma Goldman*, 9. Ferguson contextualizes the history and usage of this apocryphal representation of Goldman.

9. Mannin, *Red Rose*, 15.

10. See Falk, *Love, Anarchy, and Emma Goldman*, 344.

11. Anderson, "Challenge of Emma Goldman," 6.

12. Anderson, "'The Immutable,'" 20.

13. Goldman to Arthur Ross, June 9, 1928, in *EMG,* reel 20. Throughout her life, Goldman cited Thomas Paine's quote, "the world is my country," to expose the perils of nationalist thinking. After deportation, this favorite quote became an ironic refrain. See Catherine W. Hollis, "'The World is My Country,'" 15–21.

14. Goldman quoted in Falk, *Love, Anarchy, and Emma Goldman*, 340–41.

15. Kowal, *Tongue of Fire*, xiii.

16. Falk, "Let Icons Be Bygones!," 45.

17. Anderson, "Challenge of Emma Goldman," 6.

18. These essays are all collected in Wilbur, *Anarchy and the Sex Question*.

19. Goldman, "Marriage and Love," in *A Documentary History of the American Years, Vol. 3*, 270.

20. Ibid., 266–68.

21. Goldman, "Victims of Morality," in *A Documentary History of the American Years, Vol. 3*, 417.

22. Francis coins the terms "gender rebels" in *Secret Treachery of Words*, 42.

23. Antliff, *Anarchist Modernism*, 1. Antliff persuasively describes Goldman's anarchism as a "project of individual liberation" and argues that early twentieth-century anarchism "generated a farflung cultural rebellion encompassing lifestyles, literature, and art as well as politics" (1).

24. Delap, *Feminist Avant-Garde*, 103.

25. Goldman, "The Tragedy of Woman's Emancipation," in *A Documentary History of the American Years, Vol. 2*, 185.

26. Delap, *Feminist Avant-Garde*, 9. Mina Loy is a good example of a female modernist who, like Goldman, rejected suffrage and conceived of female modernity as existing outside conventionally gendered roles. See Parmar, *Reading*

Mina Loy's Autobiographies, 31. Ironically, Loy is also a good example of a female modernist who found Goldman laughably old-fashioned. See Coleman, *Rough Draft*, 29.

27. Anderson, *My Thirty Years' War*, 4. Anderson begins her autobiography with this statement, declaring her lifelong estrangement from her middle-class, Midwestern family: "I liked my home and disliked my family" (7).

28. Anderson, "Challenge of Emma Goldman," 9.

29. Falk and Pateman, "Chronology," in *A Documentary History of the American Years, Vol. 3*, 653.

30. Anderson, "Challenge of Emma Goldman," 5.

31. Anderson, *My Thirty Years' War*, 54.

32. Anderson, "Challenge of Emma Goldman," 5.

33. Goldman, "The Reader Critic," 54.

34. Goldman, *Living My Life*, 530; Anderson, *My Thirty Years' War*, 70.

35. Anderson, *My Thirty Years' War*, 72.

36. Goldman, *Living My Life*, 531.

37. Goldman, "Emma Goldman in Defense of Modern Women's Fashions," in *A Documentary History of the American Years, Vol. 3*, 489. Francis interprets Anderson's markedly femme "personal style" in the matter of her famous blue suit as an expression of "bohemian avant-gardism," which was only "precariously" feminist, in *Secret Treachery of Words*, 50–54.

38. Goldman, *Living My Life*, 547.

39. Hemmings unpacks the significance of Goldman's "frequent unpleasantness to women" in *Considering Emma Goldman*, 12.

40. Anderson, "Emma Goldman in Chicago," 322. See also Wilbur, introduction to *Anarchy and the Sex Question*, 1, and Ferguson, *Emma Goldman*, 4–8, for more examples of this discussion.

41. Quoted in Stansell, *American Moderns*, 134.

42. See Gaipa, Latham, and Scholes, *The Little Review "Ulysses,"* xiii.

43. Jane Heap quoted in Gaipa, Latham, and Scholes, *The Little Review "Ulysses,"* xiii.

44. Anderson, "An Inspiration," 435, 435–36.

45. Ferguson, *Emma Goldman*, 190.

46. Ibid., 8. The phrase "social artist" is used in the *Little Review* to describe Goldman, but applies equally to Anderson. See Falk's discussion of this term in her introduction to *A Documentary History of the American Years, Vol. 3*, 54–55.

47. Goldman, *Living My Life*, 612.

48. Anderson, "'The Immutables,'" 173, 170.

49. Ibid., 167, 170.

50. Vanderham, *James Joyce and Censorship*, 18.

51. Stansell in *American Moderns* charts the difference between the 1890s Bohemians and the 1910 avant-gardists as a question of access: "if you came of age in the first decade of the century, there was available, for the first time, a road map to American Bohemia" (41). We might compare this to the divide between Generation X and Millennials in our own time. While Goldman invented herself through male mentors when she sought out the anarchist scene in the Yiddish-speaking lower East Side of New York City in 1890, millennial Anderson could look to Goldman as a "rebel girl" role model.

52. As in Melissa Bradshaw's discussion of "public femininity" in *Amy Lowell, Diva Poet.*

53. For Goldman's struggles in the 1920s, see Alice Wexler, *Emma Goldman in Exile.* Rebecca West was one of the few British leftists who supported Goldman's "Anti-Bolsh" stance; see Scott, *Refiguring Modernism*, 31.

54. Goldman to W. S. Van Valkenburgh, November 15, 1928, in *EGP*, reel 20.

55. For more on marriage, nationality, and Goldman, see Hollis, "'The World Is My Country,'" 17.

56. Goldman quoted in Falk, *Love, Anarchy, and Emma Goldman*, 340–41.

57. Wexler notes that Goldman was not alone in experiencing the "difficulties faced by older, unmarried, heterosexual women in a society organized around marriage and motherhood" (*Emma Goldman in Exile*, 113).

58. See Falk with Stephen Cole and Sally Thomas, *Emma Goldman*, 94–95.

59. For biographical information on Coleman's marriage and experience of motherhood, see Podnieks, introduction to *Rough Draft*, xi–xlvi. By the time she came to work for Goldman, Coleman had separated from her husband and placed her son in the care of a governess.

60. Goldman, *Living My Life*, vi.

61. Goldman to Max Nettlau, March 9, 1929, in *EGP*, reel 21.

62. Ibid.

63. Falk, *Love, Anarchy, and Emma Goldman*, 30.

64. See Wexler, *Emma Goldman in Exile*, 117, 145; and Falk, *Love, Anarchy, and Emma Goldman.*

65. Coleman, *Rough Draft*, 22.

66. Podnieks, introduction to *Rough Draft*, xxvii.

67. Goldman to Juliet Soskice, June 25, 1928, in *EGP*, reel 20.

68. Goldman to Evelyn Scott, June 26, 1928, in *EGP*, reel 20.

69. Guggenheim, *Out of This Century*, 96.

70. See Hollis, "No Marriage in Heaven."

71. Coleman, *Rough Draft*, 33.

72. Ibid.

73. Ibid., 20.

74. Goldman, *Living My Life*, vi.
75. Guggenheim, *Out of This Century*, 96.
76. Ibid.
77. For a fuller narrative, see Dearborn, *Peggy Guggenheim*, 70–72.
78. Goldman to Laurence Vail, December 7, 1928, in *EGP*, reel 20.
79. Goldman to Saxe Commins, December 5, 1928, in *EGP*, reel 20.
80. Goldman to M. Eleanor Fitzgerald, December 8, 1928, in *EGP*, reel 20.
81. McCabe, "Bryher's Archive," 118–25.
82. McCabe, "Bryher's Archive," 119. McCabe argues that Guggenheim's money, like Bryher's, "fueled (and preserved) a significant portion of modernist culture." See also Julie Vandivere's essay in this volume.
83. Herring, *Djuna*, 201.
84. Recent work on anarchism and modernism maps the extensive interconnections between the movements, although not specifically from a gendered standpoint. See especially Antliff, *Anarchist Modernism*.
85. Goldman, "The Tragedy of Women's Emancipation," in *A Documentary History of the American Years, Vol. 2*, 178.

Works Cited

Anderson, Margaret C. "The Challenge of Emma Goldman." *Little Review* 1, no. 3 (May 1914): 5–9. Modernist Journals Project.

———. "Emma Goldman in Chicago." *Mother Earth* 9, no. 10 (December 1914): 320–24.

———. "'The Immutable.'" *Little Review* 1, no. 8 (November 1914): 19–22. Modernist Journals Project.

———. "'The Immutables.'" *Mother Earth* 12, no. 5 (July 1917): 167–73.

———. "An Inspiration." *Mother Earth* 10, no. 1 (March 1915): 435–36.

———. *My Thirty Years' War*. New York: Horizon Press, 1969.

Antliff, Allan. *Anarchist Modernism: Art, Politics, and the First American Avant-Garde*. Chicago: University of Chicago Press, 2001.

Bradshaw, Melissa. *Amy Lowell, Diva Poet*. Burlington, VT: Ashgate, 2011.

Coleman, Emily Holmes. *Rough Draft: The Modernist Diaries of Emily Holmes Coleman, 1929–1937*. Edited by Elizabeth Podnieks. Lanham: University of Delaware Press, 2012.

Dearborn, Mary. *Peggy Guggenheim: Mistress of Modernism*. London: Virago, 2006.

Delap, Lucy. *The Feminist Avant-Garde: Transatlantic Encounters of the Early Twentieth Century*. Cambridge: Cambridge University Press, 2007.

Falk, Candace. "Let Icons Be Bygones! Emma Goldman: The Grand Expositor." In *Feminist Interpretations of Emma Goldman*. Edited by Penny A. Weiss and

Loretta Kensinger, 41–69. University Park: Pennsylvania State University Press, 2007.

———. *Love, Anarchy, and Emma Goldman: A Biography*. New York: Holt, Rinehart, and Winston, 1984.

Falk, Candace, with Stephen Cole and Sally Thomas. *Emma Goldman: A Guide to Her Life and Documentary Sources*. Alexandria, VA: Chadwyck-Healey, 1995.

Ferguson, Kathy E. *Emma Goldman: Political Thinking in the Streets*. Plymouth, UK: Rowman and Littlefield, 2011.

Francis, Elizabeth. *The Secret Treachery of Words: Feminism and Modernism in America*. Minneapolis: University of Minnesota Press, 2002.

Gaipa, Mark, Sean Latham, and Robert Scholes, editors. *The Little Review "Ulysses."* By James Joyce. New Haven: Yale University Press, 2015.

Goldman, Emma. *A Documentary History of the American Years, Vol. 1: Made for America, 1890–1901*. Edited by Candace Falk, Barry Pateman, and Jessica Moran. Berkeley: University of California Press, 2003.

———. *A Documentary History of the American Years, Vol. 2: Making Speech Free, 1902–1909*. Edited by Candace Falk, Barry Pateman, and Jessica Moran. Berkeley: University of California Press, 2005.

———. *A Documentary History of the American Years, Vol. 3: Light and Shadows, 1910–1916*. Edited by Candace Falk and Barry Pateman. Palo Alto: Stanford University Press, 2012.

———. *The Emma Goldman Papers: A Microfilm Edition*. Edited by Candace Falk with Ronald J. Zboray et al. Alexandria, VA.: Chadwyck-Healey, 1990. Cited throughout as *EGP*.

———. *Living My Life: In Two Volumes*. 1931. New York: Dover, 1970.

———. "The Reader Critic." *Little Review* 1, no. 6 (September 1914): 54. Modernist Journals Project.

Guggenheim, Peggy. *Out of This Century: The Informal Memoirs of Peggy Guggenheim*. New York: Dial, 1946.

Hemmings, Clare. *Considering Emma Goldman: Feminist Political Ambivalence and the Imaginative Archive*. Durham, NC: Duke University Press, 2018.

Herring, Phillip. *Djuna: The Life and Work of Djuna Barnes*. New York: Viking, 1995.

Hollis, Catherine W. "No Marriage in Heaven: Editorial Resurrection in Djuna Barnes's *Nightwood*." *Text* 13 (2000): 233–49.

———. "'The World is My Country': Emma Goldman among the Avant-Garde." In *Virginia Woolf and Her Female Contemporaries*. Edited by Julie Vandivere and Megan Hicks, 15–21. Clemson, SC: Clemson University Press, 2016.

Kowal, Donna M. *Tongue of Fire: Emma Goldman, Public Womanhood, and the Sex Question*. Albany: State University of New York Press, 2016.

Mannin, Ethel. *Red Rose: A Novel Based on the Life of Emma Goldman ("Red Emma")*. London: Jarrolds, 1941.

McCabe, Susan. "Bryher's Archive: Modernism and the Melancholy of Money." *English Now: Selected Papers from the 20th IAUPE Conference in Lund 2007.* Edited by Marianne Thormählen, 118–25. Lund: Lund University, 2008.

Parmar, Sandeep. *Reading Mina Loy's Autobiographies: Myth of the Modern Woman.* London: Bloomsbury, 2013.

Podnieks, Elizabeth. Introduction to *Rough Draft: The Modernist Diaries of Emily Holmes Coleman, 1929–1937.* Edited by Elizabeth Podnieks, xi–xlvi. Lanham: University of Delaware Press, 2012.

Scott, Bonnie Kime. *Refiguring Modernism: The Women of 1928, Volume 1.* Bloomington: Indiana University Press, 1995.

Stansell, Christine. *American Moderns: Bohemian New York and the Creation of a New Century.* Princeton: Princeton University Press, 2010.

Vanderham, Paul. *James Joyce and Censorship.* New York: New York University Press, 1997.

Weir, David. *Anarchy and Culture: The Aesthetic Politics of Modernism.* Amherst: University of Massachusetts Press, 1997.

Wexler, Alice. *Emma Goldman in America.* Boston: Beacon Press, 1984.

———. *Emma Goldman in Exile.* Boston: Beacon Press, 1989.

Wilbur, Shawn P. Introduction to *Anarchy and the Sex Question: Essays on Women and Emancipation, 1896–1926.* Edited by Shawn P. Wilbur, 1–14. Oakland, CA: PM Press, 2016.

7

Fantasies of Belonging, Fears of Precarity

MELISSA BRADSHAW

Returning to *Women of the Left Bank* at the news of Shari Benstock's death in May 2015, over twenty years after I first read it, I was moved, once again, by the world it creates. The material object of the book itself brings the names, and in its picture sections, the faces, of an unprecedented assemblage of modernist women writers together in one place. How many hours did I spend in my early twenties tracing my finger over the women's names listed on the cover? How many hundreds of times did my attention wander to the picture sections, leafing through the glossy pages, staring at their glamorous, inscrutable faces? I spent more time, perhaps, than on the text itself, which made me impatient, as it wrestled with its competing desires to be both biographical and analytical. Djuna Barnes, H.D., Mina Loy, Nancy Cunard. Which ones would I align myself with? Which ones would I build my academic world around? For twenty-something me, Benstock's book was the ultimate Sears catalog of feminist modernist desire. I suspect I am not alone in this, and that many in my generation of modernist scholars came of age dreaming over those pictures, indulging in fantasies of future careers spent writing about a collaborative, woman-centric modernism.

Benstock's book changed my life, as it propelled me toward a master's thesis, written as a young, married Mormon woman at Brigham Young University, pushing back against cultural and familial expectations that I shouldn't be getting an advanced degree. I wrote my thesis on feminist utopias and called my project "Doing Away with Man Altogether," a line I took from Barnes's *Ladies Almanack* (1928), one of the texts I studied alongside H.D.'s *Asphodel* (1921–22), and a piece of Woolf juvenilia called "Friendship's Gallery" (1907). Within a year of completing my master's degree, just as I began doctoral work, I broke from Mormonism, divorced my husband, and came out as a lesbian, a series of ruptures I experienced as primarily joyful. My life went from impossibly constrained, to impossibly mine. Twenty years later, I remain grateful for the life Benstock's book gave me, and for the books like it that filled the syllabi of our modernist seminars in that early 1990s moment of feminist possibility.

I foreground my comments here in the personal as a form of confession and observation, aware that drawing a causal effect between my understanding of a woman-centered modernism and dramatic changes in my personal life might read as self-indulgent. I am cringing a bit even as I write this, but stronger than my self-consciousness is my belief that feminist scholars need to own our personal investment in the women and the works we study, as well as recognize our complicity in constructing the narratives that weave their way through our scholarship, which in turn shape our modernist canon.

As I have grown into my career, I have had to reckon with *Women of the Left Bank*'s project of narrating a modernism where women wrote, painted, sculpted, took photographs, editorialized, and socialized together as precisely that: a narrative. Reading Benstock at twenty-two, I understood the connections she was making to be archaeological, her critical intervention a refocusing of attention on once significant women authors and editors and pointing us toward major works we should know. Most important, of course, I saw her redrawing the forgotten lines that connect these women, theorizing a modernist literature dependent on friendship and collaboration among women.

But as we know, connections that have been made can be unmade. Or rather, sidelined, undermined, ignored. In this moment when feminist approaches to modernism remain precarious, either deeply marginalized or solidly canonical, depending on which conference room you walk into or which journal you pick up, we need to think about the ways in which the connections Benstock made were architectural, as well as archaeological. This is not to say that *Women of the Left Bank* is inaccurate or exaggerated. Rather, the stories Benstock pulls from the raw material of the archive and shapes into a cogent narrative, one we are invited to plot along with her on the map printed across the book's first pages, reflect her priorities and politics.

Shari Benstock's refashioned modernism is all about gatherings, in bookstores and salons and nightclubs. She invites us to imagine stylish, urban women making a world for other women, and each other, an intoxicating dance-party modernism best represented by Natalie Clifford Barney's Académie des Femmes. Other feminist modernist scholars tell different stories. Jane Marcus, for example, chooses from among Virginia Woolf's many roles to emphasize her as a woman writing in a room alone, exulting in the freedom to have her own thoughts without being disturbed. Or think about the many Gertrude Stein scholars, women and men, who fondly sketch a jocular bohemian in hippy clothing, passing around Alice B. Toklas's magical brownies to a charmed circle before getting down to the serious business of taste-making. Archives, as we know, are not neutral, and neither is the work we do in them.

I want to think about which women were included in Benstock's study (given the limited choices of its focus on expatriates in Paris) as well as in other significant works of feminist modernist recovery, like Bonnie Kime Scott's *The Gender of Modernism*, and Sandra Gilbert and Susan Gubar's three-volume *No Man's Land*. These wide-ranging explorations of women excluded from canonical modernism launched many feminist dissertations, as graduate students like me saw modernism's canon crack open. Often, in the richness of these new-to-us voices we perceived a connection to literature beyond the aesthetic and the intellectual, a connection rooted in identification and aspiration.

But I am even more interested in the many prolific women artists who were doubly left behind, first by the New Critics, who, in assembling the modernist canon dismissed them as minor, if they even noticed them, and then, several generations later, by feminist scholars who, in their work recovering women artists lost to New Criticism's masculinist narrative could not find a place for them in what quickly became a narrow feminist canon. As early as 1989, Celeste M. Schenck asked us to think hard about which women were finding their way into heavy rotation in the new modernist canon. Pointing to the experimental poetry of H.D., Gertrude Stein, and Mina Loy as exemplary of the kind of female-authored poetry most likely to make it onto course syllabi—dense, experimental, often difficult—she asks "whether we feminist critics, in privileging those female poets who broke form with the boys (even if, as it turns out, they broke form *for* the boys) have reproduced the preferences of dominant critical discourse and extended the hegemony of an exclusive, in this case antigeneric, prejudice."[1] Our new modernist studies are more flexible in defining modernism—as a set of formal aesthetics, or a time period, or a mindset—but still, we find ourselves circling around the same few modernist women writers.

The Leftovers

The two modernist figures I keep returning to in my research, poet-editor-impresarios Amy Lowell and Edith Sitwell, are precisely the kinds of "experimenters . . . form-breakers . . . and vers-librists" Schenk argues are more likely to be the subject of feminist recovery work than women poets writing in traditional genres, and yet they only make cameo appearances in those important early works of feminist recovery (230). Decades later, they continue to slip through the cracks of modernist studies. Both have been recovered just enough to have representation in most literary anthologies; few reference works on twentieth-century Anglo-American literature leave them out anymore. But years go by without papers on them at the Modern Language Association Conference, or even at our more period-focused conferences like the Modernist Studies Association Conference or the annual meetings of The Space Between: Literature and Culture, 1914–1945.

The slowness of their return to modernist conversations, in fits-and-starts more than anything, means their work does not get the steady, sustained reevaluation necessary for substantive readings of their work. Instead, scholarship on them remains stuck in a loop of excited rediscovery and preliminary introductions, never getting much further than their origin stories: who were they and why should we care? Lowell and Sitwell's exclusion from that early moment of concentrated feminist recovery work, and their continued lack of representation in new modernist studies, perplexes me, given their investment in just the sort of aggressively experimental modern poetics that should have guaranteed their position in that first wave of reclamation. But it is actually a very useful exclusion, because it can tell us as much about the identifications and interests that drove late twentieth-century feminist recovery work as it does about the inclusion of more now-canonical figures.

In many ways, their careers parallel each other: both were poets, critics, and editors who waged very public wars against an older, more conservative poetics in America and Britain, respectively. Through their poetry and criticism, as well as through the more immediate occasions of their popular lectures, they offered themselves as the public face of avant-garde poetics. Most important, each edited a popular poetry anthology that brought modern poetic aesthetics to a larger audience—Lowell, the three volumes of *Some Imagist Poets* (1915, 1916, 1917), Sitwell the six "cycles" of *Wheels* (1916–1921).

These highly visible and mostly powerful roles as critics and editors offered them opportunities to promote, as well as to denigrate, the work of their female contemporaries. Given the forum and the audience, then, whose work did they publish, and whose books did they review? Which, if any, women did they mentor? Were there women whose work they actively sought to undermine? Which, if any, did they publicly disagree with? What about privately? These questions lead to bigger questions about how they formed their aesthetics and how they employed them to evaluate other women. Is the way they view other women fair, or are their critiques of other women self-serving? Are they interested in supporting and writing about other women *because* they are women?

The truth is, despite rich personal relationships with women, neither Sitwell nor Lowell had significant or lasting professional relationships with other women, and I have found little evidence that they went out of their way to regularly mentor them.[2] Perhaps Lowell and Sitwell operated at a remove from gendered oppressions and experienced unprecedented freedom from worrying about gender, but not only is this unlikely, if it were true, the fact that they somehow did not find as many women to praise or mentor or support as men is hard to ignore.

Edith Sitwell and the Allure of the "Strange"

I most expected to find Edith Sitwell working with other women writers in *Wheels*, the provocative poetry anthology she edited from 1916–1921, and so when I was asked to write a chapter on it for a volume on women's periodical culture in Britain, I jumped at the chance to spend a summer reading and writing about the controversial modernist annual. Unapologetically avant-garde and antiwar, *Wheels* caused an uproar when it appeared, with detractors describing it as morbid and overwritten, while enthusiasts welcomed it as a reprieve from the cloying sentimentality of Edward Marsh's *Georgian Poetry* anthologies (1912–1922) and applauded its vehement antiwar politics.

The anthology featured work by Aldous Huxley, Arnold James, both of Sitwell's brothers, Osbert and Sacheverell, and most notably, Wilfred Owen, whose trench poetry, edited by Sitwell, was first published in the 1919 volume, shortly after his death. But only five women appear in its six cycles, out of twenty total contributors, including Nancy Cunard, Iris Tree, and Sitwell herself. Though Cunard helped develop *Wheels*, which takes its title from one of her poems, she only appears in that first issue. Tree and Helen Rootham, who contributes translations of Arthur Rimbaud, as well as her own poetry, are featured through the fourth cycle, but by the final cycle the only female poet left standing is Sitwell.

When *Wheels* was not the vehicle for publishing and promoting the work of women I had hoped it would be, I struggled to find something to say about it that would make it relevant to a volume on women's periodical culture. What made this even more challenging was that those *Wheels* poems written by women seldom touched on women's issues. Jane Dowson, one of very few critics to write about *Wheels*, describes the periodical as uniquely non-gendered. "There was nothing woman-centered about the poems," she explains, "and, unusually, reviewers rarely mentioned gender," instead discussing the poets as a group, often using the name they used for themselves, "cyclists," without differentiating between male and female contributors.[3] Except for the fact that a woman edited it, then, *Wheels* frustrated my feminist intervention. And apparently, I am not alone: *Wheels* has received very little critical attention, even as work on women's periodical culture flourishes.[4]

Sitwell's highest critical praise of other women is reserved for the American poets Gertrude Stein, Marianne Moore, and H.D., who write in ways that she claims surprise her by shaking up, or even better, breaking down language. Importantly, she praises these artists for producing art that is wholly original, without traces of any obvious influences, describing their work as "strange." Sitwell biographer Richard Greene attributes her preference for these poets in part to her somewhat jealously guarding her position as "England's leading woman poet," but the greater reason for ignoring the work of her British contemporaries, he argues, is because they disappoint her: "she did not believe that women poets in Britain had lived up to the challenges of modernism and that instead they had tended to weep like minor Victorians."[5] The challenges of being a poet in "this age, the most warlike, various, and tragical that our country has ever known," Sitwell explains in her study *Poetry and Criticism* (1926) include taking a hard look at "the claims of tradition, as far as the technique of poetry is concerned" and "defend[ing] innovations."[6]

Gertrude Stein, in particular, serves as an example of the kind of innovative work Sitwell finds worth defending. Their brief professional relationship ended badly when Sitwell read her own poems, rather than Stein's, at a Shakespeare and Company gathering in Stein's honor, but during its honeymoon period, their relationship showed how far Sitwell was willing to go when another poet's work engaged her. After writing a lukewarm review of *Geography and Plays* in the *Nation and Athenaeum* in 1923, Sitwell spent several months studying Stein's work, and within a year had written an appreciative piece on her for *Vogue*, followed by a longer retrospective piece on her work the following year, again in *Vogue*. Sitwell wrote effusively in that October 1925 piece of Stein's importance: "In the future it is evident that no history of the English literature of our time could be of any worth without a complete survey of [her work]. . . . She is, I am convinced, one of the most important living pioneers."[7] She arranged Stein's 1926 visit to England, where she lectured at Oxford and Cambridge, and invited her to join her and her brothers on the dais for a poetry reading that marked her first public appearance in England. When Contact Press published *The Making of the Americans* (1925), Sitwell praised it in the *Criterion* as "the product of one of the richest, and at the same time most subtle, minds of our time."[8] And although she was unable to convince Leonard and Virginia Woolf to bring out an edition through Hogarth Press, they eventually agreed to publish Stein's lectures in England as *Composition as Explanation* (1926).

Not surprisingly, Sitwell values Stein's originality, the way she uses words as a medium for creating abstract patterns, like modern composers and painters have done in their mediums. The Sitwell siblings played an important role in introducing high modernist art to the British public, proselytizing for Diaghilev's Ballets Russes, and organizing an important early exhibition of modern French art that brought new work by Amedeo Modigliani, Pablo Picasso, Henri Matisse, and Fernand Léger to England. Sitwell understands Stein to be part of the artistic movement she simultaneously recognizes and curates, a movement which, in forcing a "fresh perception of natural objects comes, sometimes, as a shock to people who are used to taking their impressions at second-hand—to people who want comfort and not the truth."[9] She even includes Stein's "The Portrait of Constance Fletcher" as the only other positive example of contemporary work she cites in *Poetry and Criticism*, besides her own poem "Aubade" (which she discusses at length without identifying as her own).

Amy Lowell and the Search for the Virile

Amy Lowell, similarly, most approves of her female contemporaries when they produce highly original work that breaks from tradition in both form and subject. She especially appreciates work that validates her aesthetic choices. She is, of course, an early and enthusiastic supporter of H.D., the only other female contributor of the six poets in the three volumes of *Some Imagist Poets*, and the only woman of the six poets Lowell singles out in her 1917 book *Tendencies in Modern American Poetry*. She praises H.D. for creating a poetic world that, while drawing themes and images from classical literature, creates a "world of her own longings . . . [that] resembles nothing but itself" (257). She describes her as "a true artist" because her inspiration comes from "internal mental and emotional experiences, not . . . external events" (252). But often her celebration of H.D.'s work points the reader back to her own, as, in writing about her first volume, *Sea Garden* (1916), Lowell praises H.D.'s descriptions of "beauty . . . so sharp as to be painful, delight so poignant it can scarcely be borne" (257). Readers of Lowell's love lyrics will recognize in her praise a reflection of her own aesthetic of masochism, which involves lovers shrinking from, shielding their eyes from, even cutting themselves on the "too bright beauty" of their beloveds.

Lowell again centers her praise in identification when she responds to the then-common critique that H.D.'s poetry is cold. She urges her readers to not think that this coolness reflects a lack of feeling: "Let me mix my similes," she suggests, "let me liken H.D.'s poetry to the cool flesh of a woman bathing in a fountain" (276). Here she invokes the poetic image most closely associated with her own poetry, the bathing woman, as seen most notably in the poem "In a Garden," which earned her a place among the Imagists when Ezra Pound included it in his anthology, *Des Imagistes* (1914).

Even as she praises H.D., Lowell ends her section on her in *Tendencies* by criticizing her poetry as "a narrow art [that] has no scope, it neither digs deeply nor spreads widely." She claims that it "bears with it the seeds of over-care, of something bordering on preciosity," and that H.D.'s greatest strength is in her technique, even if that "is perhaps monotonous to those who are not concerned with its excellence." As a poet herself, she reminds her readers, one who understands and values technique, Lowell decrees that although "H.D. is not a great poet, . . . she is a rarely perfect poet" (279).

Lowell makes this distinction between greatness and technical virtuosity often when describing the work of other women. She draws this contrast in a 1922 letter she writes to literary columnist May Lamberton Becker, when she worries that a younger generation of American poets has not come near the achievement of her generation, "the old guard."[10] While she singles out Edna St. Vincent Millay and Elinor Wylie as the most technically sophisticated poets of this group, she complains that Millay "attempts nothing beyond the personal," which is "the hall-mark of minor poetry."[11] She takes this criticism public the following year in the essay "Two Generations of American Poetry," published in the *New Republic* (republished in *Poetry and Poets*, [1930]). Including herself in the first generation, she writes at length about the courage she and her peers demonstrated when they broke from the moralizing and strict versification of Victorian poetry. Her generation "endeavour[ed] after a major utterance," she explains, one with which they could, collectively, "voice America." Importantly, she describes "this new poetry, whether written by men or women, [as] in essence masculine, virile, very much alive" (117, 114, 116).

The second generation, however, has been a disappointment, Lowell writes, failing to build on the successes of their immediate elders. While she expresses disappointment in a few schools of younger poets, notably the "Secessionists" whose work, she complains, takes an overly mathematical approach to poetry, she saves her most aggressive criticism for a somewhat arbitrary grouping of poets she calls Lyrists because, she says ruefully, while "all poets write lyrics, . . . these poets write practically nothing else" (119). Again she singles out Millay, of all the younger poets, for criticism. While Millay is, in fact, much younger than Lowell, in order to claim her as a poet who has benefited from her success, Lowell must ignore the fact that Millay shot to fame in 1912 with the publication of her poem "Renascence" the same year Lowell published her first, almost completely ignored volume of poems, *A Dome of Many-Coloured Glass*. She condescendingly characterizes Millay as a "delightfully clever exponent of the perennial theme of love," noting "where emotion is the chief stock in trade, we should not expect a high degree of intellectual content." She concedes, at least, that Millay exemplifies a group of uncommonly good poets whose "expertness is really amazing" (120).

This weak compliment comes with a major qualification: the poets of the younger generation are good, she explains, primarily because Lowell and her contemporaries have already won the public over to the New Poetry:

> They have profited by the larger movement in finding an audience ready-made to their hands, a number of magazines eager to welcome them, and a considerable body of critical writing bearing on the poetical problems of the moment—aids to achievement that the older group lacked. (120)

With no public battles to fight, all they have to do is write poetry. And yet, Lowell complains, they have wasted the advantage conferred on them by only writing "minor" poetry, a word she claims is not a critique of their poetry, for "in matters of versification there is scarcely a fault to be found with their work," but rather a critique of its aims. "Major and minor refer to outlook, and it is a fact," she says, "that this younger group deliberately seeks the narrow, personal note." This attention to the personal makes the work of the Lyrists "a feminine movement, and remains such even in the work of its men" (120–21). That Lowell relies on gendered categories is not surprising—poetry rooted in the personal, in the domestic, is feminine; poetry rooted in intellectual exploration of historical themes, or abstract experimentation is masculine—but her unselfconsciousness in using them here to try to describe and delineate disparate strains of contemporary American poetry is important because it shows her actively grappling with the costs of the personal in poetry, or in her words, "femininity," and weighing them too high.

Lowell's refusal to help edit the late poet Adelaide Crapsey's dissertation on poetic metrics, unpublished at her untimely death at thirty-six, further complicates understanding what she hoped to find in the work of other women. Certainly, it suggests how impossible it is to be a woman artist Lowell approves of. Crapsey was a lyric poet known for inventing the cinquain—a 22 syllable, 5-line poem, similar to a tanka or a haiku. A graduate of Vassar, she taught at Smith, published a few poems during her lifetime, and was working on a graduate degree at Columbia University when she died from tuberculosis.[12] Lowell read and admired her collection

Verse, published posthumously in 1915, describing it to Carl Sandburg as "that dreadful book of hers, so poignant and so in a way abortive, so horrible to die with one's work half accomplished."[13] But when one of Crapsey's professors at Columbia asked Lowell to help edit her dissertation for publication she declined. In refusing the invitation, she dismissed Crapsey's comparative study of polysyllabic words in the verse of poets from John Milton to Lord Alfred Tennyson to contemporary poets as "superfluous" and "depressing," its use of academic methodology to interpret poetry "outmoded" and "pathetic."[14] Crapsey's dissertation was eventually published by Knopf in 1918 as *A Study in English Metrics*, despite Lowell's objection to it as a distraction from what the older poet saw as her true vocation. "Miss Crapsey was an artist," Lowell explains to the professor, "and that she should have felt obliged to mould her thought into this unspeakable form, as being the one more sure to gain her admittance in the great 'company of educated men' is a terrible comment on the company."[15]

I am struck by the bitterness of Lowell's backhanded compliment, as she accuses Crapsey of wasting her poetic talent looking for respect and admiration from the "company of educated men." Lowell was no stranger to academia, or educated men: her ancestors, among the first English colonists to arrive in America, were among that group of men who founded American higher education; her brother Lawrence Lowell served as president of Harvard for over thirty years. But Lowell women were not allowed formal schooling past grammar school. An autodidact who relied on her father's library and the Boston Athenaeum for any learning past the tutoring she received as a young woman, she singles out this trait as demonstrating true intellectualism in others, as when she praises H.D. and Richard Aldington as self-styled scholars who "read Greek for fun," and for whom "the so-called dead languages are very living."[16] However, Lowell dismisses Crapsey's research, which her biographer describes as her first love, the thing that "gave her purpose, a sense of significance, a reason to live," as a waste of time, unable to allow that she might have experienced that work, as much as her poetry, as satisfying and creative.[17]

So, what does Amy Lowell want? She argues that artistic drive should be deeply felt and intuitive, and yet she disparages women who write from a worldview of feminine domesticity, critiquing them for not aspiring toward "a major [masculine] expression." At the same time, she does not approve of Crapsey working from within the male world of the academy, where intellectualism is "smothered under the weight of academic tradition."[18] Lowell's disapproval, like her praise, almost always mirrors her own experiences and strengths.

Tellingly, one of the women for whom Lowell reserves her most unequivocal approval is not quite a woman. She lavishes praise, in print and from the lectern, on the child poet Hilda Conkling, a prodigy who published her first volume of poetry at nine years old. She even wrote the preface to Conkling's first volume, *Poems by a Little Girl* (1920). This preface is no puff piece; it offers a serious introduction to the volume, giving background on the poet and her methodology, and highlighting what she thinks are important tropes and themes. It is far more generous, in fact, than Lowell's writing on H.D. Not surprisingly, however, she attributes much of Conkling's poetry to the workings of her subconscious. Pointing out the irony in one poem she asks, "Did she quite grasp its meaning herself? We may doubt it. In this poem, the subconscious is very much on the job."[19] By characterizing Conkling as too young to have control of her artistic choices, Lowell effectively wrests control of the volume from her, installing herself as mediator between the young poet and her public.

Anxieties of Influence

I want to frame Lowell's need to position herself as older, wiser, and more sophisticated than her female peers as something other than professional jealousy, though it is difficult to read criticisms like "she has the ambition to be a minor poet," as anything else. I have often wondered how to read Lowell's tone when she says things like this. Defensive, of course. She has a lot invested in "major utterances," in writing what she calls "big" poetry, and she fully expected to be remembered for her long, experimental poems in critically acclaimed volumes like *Men, Women, and Ghosts* (1916) and *Can Grande's Castle* (1918), not for her lyrics. I imagine her feeling threatened by, and competitive toward, women flourishing in a genre she does not feel she can afford to indulge in without being stereotyped as a "woman poet." And she is not wrong. Her frustration and impatience with Millay et al. shows prescience, after all, since the Lowell poems most likely to make their way into anthologies and course syllabi are the protofeminist "Patterns," with its meditation on the bonds, literal and figurative, that limit women, and tender love lyrics such as "Venus Transiens," which contemporary critics have read as offering glimpses of lesbian domesticity.

But I also hear righteous indignation in her words: skip the sonnet and venture out on your own. Experiment with technique. Take up history as your subject, not love. Be braver, think bigger, want more.

Sitwell is just as prickly as Lowell when she makes generalizations about female poets. And, too, she seems to want more for them, wants them to push past familiar forms and content and develop a unique poetics. Like Lowell, she offers more damnation than encouragement, noting in a particularly scolding 1925 piece in *Vogue*, "Some Observations on Women's Poetry," that "most of the rules for women poets begin with a 'Don't' or an 'Avoid'" (189). But where Lowell urges women to embrace a more "masculine" poetics, Sitwell argues that "women poets will do best if they realize that male technique is not suitable to them. No woman writing in the English language has ever written a great sonnet, no woman has ever written great blank verse" (189). Lest readers think her claim that women cannot write using traditional forms "not because of inspiration, but because technically it does not lie within her muscles" is figurative, using "muscles" as a metaphor for temperament, she continues with a long diatribe against Elizabeth Barrett Browning ever having written *Aurora Leigh* (1856), linking "the general weakness of her poetry" to the "feeble state of her health" (191). (Remember, Lowell also struggled with Barrett Browning as a poetic ancestor, confessing in "The Sisters" that "literary sisters left her feeling 'sad and self-distrustful / For older sisters are very sobering things.")[20] Sitwell writes here for a broad audience, and her tone is brisk, emphatic, perhaps sarcastic, but her hyperbole makes it difficult to find the serious critique in her condemnation.

Twenty years later, in a 1944 letter to critic Maurice Bowra, she sounds the same note, complaining that "most women's poetry" is "simply awful—incompetent, floppy, whining, arch, trivial, self-pitying." She argues that women must try to "write in as hard and glittering a manner as possible, and with as strange images as possible—(strange, but believed in)."[21] This turning from tradition is what Lowell values in H.D., what Sitwell praises in Stein, and in Marianne Moore, about whose 1921 *Poems* she writes, "they are strange and I believe them to be entirely new. I can see no trace of influence."[22] Given Lowell and Sitwell's antipathy to feminine domesticity, and in the context of careers with little connection to other women, their need to disassociate from earlier generations of female poets in their search for just the right form and aim in woman-authored poetry jars. They respond to the everyday denigration of femininity by joining in on the scorn—retreating from rather than repurposing its clichéd softness, its "ghastly wallowing."[23]

Conclusion

I find it ironic that these women who, to a certain degree, resisted aligning themselves with feminism, wanting to be evaluated as artists first, not as women, have been forgotten by both male and female scholars. The ideological alliances and aesthetic choices they hoped would keep them relevant were not enough. They wanted to compete with men on their own terms, but men could not, and still today, will not see them, while the women who might have recovered them have perhaps been alienated by their hostility. I am sympathetic to Lowell and Sitwell. I do not agree with it, but I think I understand their anxiety about being evaluated fairly and their reluctance to align themselves with or work in genres identified with women. I also understand that they both come from male-dominated worlds, that, nonetheless, in various ways made room for them that they did not for other women writing at this moment. My point here is not to excoriate them. But given their reluctance to imagine a female-oriented poetics, it should not surprise us that they have not captured the imagination of feminist critics. After all, our feminisms impress themselves onto the materials we pull from the archive, shaping the stories we tell. Not that we shape them exactly, but that we are selective and strategic, if subconsciously, in what we connect.

It is not hard to imagine, then, a causal effect between Lowell and Sitwell's relatively weak support for other women artists and the disinterest of contemporary feminist scholars in writing about them. You cannot save everyone, after all. When the walls closed in on that intense flourishing of feminist modernisms sooner even than we expected, as universities turned corporate and humanities programs, and subsequently, humanities publishing, shrank and resources became scarce, why would not the few female artists who made the canonical cut either fit into institutionalized narratives of modernism, or share a feminist commitment to subverting them, or both? This narrowing coincides, of course, with a loss of interest in a more inclusive modernism by the only stakeholders who ultimately matter: English department hiring committees, tenure and review boards, and academic press acquisitions editors. The junior scholar who engages in feminist recovery work today takes the risk of becoming an exile from the institutions that support and subsidize literary criticism.

In a 1998 article originally delivered at the Eighth Annual Conference on Virginia Woolf, Madelyn Detloff warned of the temptation in feminist reclamation work to turn iconic writers into "a kind of historical fetish, the feminist icon: a symbolic representative of difficulties that women encounter in the present." She suggested that we should be cautious, or at least have self-knowledge about the ways in which we look to our most loved women modernists for guidance.[24] We are almost thirty years out from *Women of the Left Bank*, forty from *The Madwoman in the Attic*. At this point we are past "opening the canon." And as the institutions that house the canon erode, we are uniquely free. Who is there to open the canon for?

In the face of apocalypse, I am asking that we be more historical, that we pull back from the now-familiar and let our gaze pan over a wider landscape. This work is already happening, thanks to the digitizing of archives and the flourishing of sub-foci such as magazine studies, which insist we expand what we mean by "modernism" and thereby significantly expand who we mean by "modernist." In this more historical, more material modernism, we will be meeting many new women, playing roles in cultural production we may not yet recognize as generative and creative. May we have the intellectual curiosity and joy in our research to greet them warmly, however ornery they may be, and pull them into our fold.

Notes

1. Schenck, "Exiled by Genre," 230.

2. Lowell's early mentorship of Bryher stands out as a brief exception. The two heiresses corresponded for several years, after Bryher wrote an early appreciation of Lowell's work (*Amy Lowell, A Critical Appreciation*, Second edition, London: Eyre and Spottiswoode, 1918). Lowell read and commented on Bryher's earliest work, wrote the preface to her first novel, *Development* (1920), and encouraged her not to try to hide her wealth. "Is it not just as snobbish to pretend downward as it is to pretend upwards?" she cautioned (qtd. in Bradshaw, *Amy Lowell, Diva Poet*, 15). But a face to face meeting in New York in 1920 ended their initial closeness, when, as Bryher recounts in her 1962 memoir *The Heart to Artemis*, "Amy Lowell was disappointed in me," not only because, according to Bryher's fictionalization of their meeting in her novel *West* (1925) the younger writer declined the older woman's invitation to represent the New Poetry in England, but because of

her unconventional lifestyle, what the Lowell character, Miss Lyall, disparages as "wild." "The greatest poet is the man who lives as other people live," she warns. "Conventional in all save words" (qtd. in Radford, "A Transatlantic Affair," 49).

3. Dowson, *Women, Modernism and British Poetry,* 94.

4. *Wheels* is routinely discussed in biographies of Sitwell, and is allotted a few paragraphs in histories of modern poetry, but with the exception of my essay, "Wheelpolitik: The Moral and Aesthetic Project of Edith Sitwell's *Wheels*, 1916–1921" in *Women, Periodicals and Print Culture in Britain, 1890s–1920s: The Modernist period,* eds. Faith Binckes and Carey Snyder (University of Edinburgh Press, 2019), Kathryn Ledbetter's 1995 "Battles for Modernism and *Wheels*" in the *Journal of Modern Literature* (Fall 1995) is the only journal article or book chapter to focus exclusively on the anthologies. Dowson includes a chapter on *Wheels*'s female contributors in *Women, Modernism and British Poetry, 1910–1939,* and Aaron Jaffe discusses it in his chapter on modernist anthologies, "Promotional Marketing," in *Modernism and the Culture of Celebrity* (Cambridge University Press, 2005).

5. See Greene, *Edith Sitwell,* 135–36.

6. Sitwell, *Poetry and Criticism*, 3.

7. Quoted in Perloff, *Poetics of Indeterminacy*, 79.

8. Sitwell, review of *The Making of Americans*, by Gertrude Stein, *New Criterion*, April 2, 1926, 391.

9. Sitwell, *Poetry and Criticism*, 22.

10. Quoted in Damon, *Amy Lowell,* 635.

11. Ibid.

12. See Alkalay-Gut, *Alone in the Dawn.*

13. Quoted in Damon, *Amy Lowell,* 367.

14. Ibid., 412, 413.

15. Ibid., 412.

16. Lowell, *Tendencies in Modern Poetry*, 253.

17. Alkalay-Gut, *Alone in the Dawn,* 283.

18. Damon, *Amy Lowell,* 414.

19. Lowell, introduction to *Poems by a Little Girl*, xviii.

20. Lowell, "The Sisters," 26.

21. Sitwell, *Selected Letters,* 243.

22. Quoted in Greene, *Edith Sitwell,* 160.

23. Sitwell, *Selected Letters,* 243.

24. Detloff, "Imagined Communities of Criticism," 51.

Works Cited

Alkalay-Gut, Karen. *Alone in the Dawn: The Life of Adelaide Crapsey*. Athens: University of Georgia Press, 1988.

Bradshaw, Melissa. *Amy Lowell, Diva Poet*. Surrey: Ashgate, 2011.

Damon, S. Foster. *Amy Lowell, A Chronicle with Extracts from her Correspondence*. Boston: Houghton Mifflin Company, 1935.

Detloff, Madelyn. "Imagined Communities of Criticism: 'Wounded Attachments' to the Icons of H.D., Gertrude Stein, and Virginia Woolf." In *Virginia Woolf and Communities: Selected Papers from the Eighth Annual Conference on Virginia Woolf*. Edited by Jeanette McVicker and Laura Davis, 50–56. New York: Pace University Press, 1999.

Dowson, Jane. *Women, Modernism and British Poetry, 1910–1939*. Aldershot: Ashgate, 2002.

Greene, Richard. *Edith Sitwell, Avant-Garde Poet, English Genius*. London: Virago, 2011.

Lowell, Amy. Introduction to *Poems by a Little Girl*. New York: Frederick A. Stokes, 1920.

———. "The Sisters." In *Selected Poems of Amy Lowell*. Edited by Melissa Bradshaw and Adrienne Munich. New Brunswick: Rutgers University Press, 2002.

———. *Tendencies in Modern American Poetry*. Boston: Houghton Mifflin, 1917.

———. "Two Generations of American Poetry." In *Poetry and Poets*, 111–22. Boston: Houghton Mifflin, 1930.

Perloff, Marjorie. *The Poetics of Indeterminacy: Rimbaud to Cage*. Evanston: Northwestern University Press, 1999.

Radford, Jean. "A Transatlantic Affair: Amy Lowell and Bryher." In *Amy Lowell, American Modern*, edited by Adrienne Munich and Melissa Bradshaw, 43–58. New Brunswick: Rutgers University Press, 2004.

Schenck, Celeste. "Exiled by Genre: Modernism, Canonicity, and the Politics of Exclusion." In *Women's Writing in Exile*, edited by Mary Lynn Broe and Angela Ingram, 225–50. Chapel Hill: University of North Carolina Press, 1989.

Sitwell, Edith. *Poetry and Criticism*. New York: Henry Holt, 1926.

———. Review of *The Making of the Americans*, by Gertrude Stein. *New Criterion*, April 2, 1926.

———. *Selected Letters of Edith Sitwell*, Edited by Richard Greene. London: Virago, 1997.

———. "Some Observations on Women's Poetry." In *Edith Sitwell: Fire of the Mind*. Edited by Elizabeth Salter and Allanah Harper. London: Michael Joseph, 1976.

8

Virginia Woolf and Mina Loy

Modernist Affiliations

ERICA GENE DELSANDRO

Virginia Woolf has long been an anchor for and an exemplar of feminist modernist studies. Although only a footnote in the early monographs on modernism, Woolf, thanks to the efforts of feminist scholars, has assumed her place in the pantheon of modernist writers. Moreover, Woolf has become a literary, artistic, and political icon not only in the academy but also in Western popular culture.[1] For many, Woolf has become synonymous with modernist literary innovation, gender politics, and feminist aesthetics. Mina Loy, however, holds a very different place in modernist studies, if she holds one securely at all. In fact, Loy is all but absent from the dominant accounts of modernism, despite helping to shape and challenge its contours. And yet, there has been enough sustained interest in her life and work that she has not been completely forgotten or overlooked. Portrayed as more of a myth than a modernist, Loy resides on the margins of modernist studies.[2]

Consequently, Woolf and Loy, their lives and their work, are viewed through very different lenses. And understandably so, as these two modernists led very different lives and made their mark on the literary landscape in very different manners. However, what happens when the scholarly examination of Woolf and Loy tells two distinctly different stories about modernism, despite the fact that both women were integral in shaping the historical moment and the aesthetic movement? In this essay, I intend to "trespass freely," to borrow a phrase from Woolf's essay "The

Leaning Tower" (1940), across the boundaries that maintain two distinct scholarly narratives for Woolf and Loy, and consequently, that buttress narratives of modernism oriented around singular icons, especially among female modernists.[3] My aim is to encourage feminist scholars to explore and cultivate the "common ground"—again, borrowing from Woolf's essay—that our icon-oriented modernisms share.

Although they are exact contemporaries—both born in 1882—Woolf and Loy are hardly ever brought together in the scholarly discourse that has come to define and interrogate modernism.[4] Let us consider their respective trajectories briefly. Woolf was born into the Victorian intellectual aristocracy and, after an adolescence marked by loss and struggles with her mental health, lived a measured life with her husband, Leonard, managing her social circles and acquaintances carefully, establishing reliable routines oriented around writing, the Hogarth Press, and their Bloomsbury friends. Loy was born into the emerging middle class, struggled with the religious tensions that characterized her family life, fought for an artistic education, and sought escape, first, in marriage, and, subsequently, in art, continental philosophy, Christian Science, intense friendships, and dramatic love affairs. Whereas Woolf spent her whole life in England, Loy lived in England, Europe, and the Americas. Whereas Woolf had two significant romantic partnerships in her life—Leonard and Vita Sackville-West—Loy had several intense romantic relationships. Both women were scripted in female-female rivalries, Woolf with Katherine Mansfield and Loy with Marianne Moore, although to what extent they actually participated in these rivalries is up for debate.[5] And although both Woolf and Loy were considered beautiful, Loy's cultivation of an avant-garde albeit recognizably traditional femininity won her the "prize" of being a muse and artistic mother to many modernist men.

Arguably, these two female modernists are so divergent in their lives that a comparison of the two should result in a study of contrasts. And yet, the differences highlighted here only make the affiliations more significant. That two women with such distinct experiences can express mutually engaging gender politics in their work and life suggests that there is another story to be told about modernism, one motivated by affiliations rather than antagonisms, by synthesis rather than singularity.

In this essay, by reading Woolf and Loy together, I suggest that the scholarly distance between the two reveals more about the priorities and presumptions of literary critics than it does about these two modernist writers. Ultimately, I would like to encourage feminist scholars to examine the various networks and affiliations, tenuously associative as well as formally organized, that connect female writers and artists as ostensibly different as Woolf and Loy in service of a more nuanced and more feminist vision of modernism. With these aims in mind, I will take a first step toward a new literary dimensionality, one that moves associatively, privileging affiliations and affinity, rather than moving vertically, creating linear narratives of artistic singularity. My strategy consists of tracing some biographical, literary, and political affiliations between Woolf and Loy, charting their responses to a few "modernist motifs" with the intention of illuminating new ways to read these two modernists in tandem and, by extension, new ways to narrate—and to teach—a feminist inflected modernism.[6]

To begin, I explore mothers, maternity, and family memory in the life and work of the two writers. Drawing motivation from Woolf's well-known declaration in *A Room of One's Own* (1929) that we think back through our mothers if we are women, this section offers an initial foray into tracing the maternal: where is it and how is it portrayed? For Woolf, who lost her mother when she was thirteen and was not a mother herself, the maternal, although often present in her writing, is hardly ever the focal point. For Loy, whose mother was a powerful if unpleasant influence and for whom motherhood was fraught, the maternal emerges as a significant force, as in "Parturition" (1914) and "Anglo-Mongrels and the Rose" (1923–25), and is a theme Loy engages with through most of her life.[7]

Next, I will highlight the filters through which Woolf and Loy construct their relationship to the nation and national identity. Neither writer treats national identity with priority; rather, each understands their place in the national project as vexed, mediated by other identity vectors. Consequently, both women consider themselves outsiders to national discourse: gender and Jewishness impact Woolf and Loy to varying degrees and, thus, play pivotal roles in each author's self-conception in relation to issues of national, political, and cultural belonging. Realizing the power of the outsider, Woolf and Loy cultivate unique positionalities that provide a crucial angle of vision for critiquing patriarchal structures in political life and in art. And it is this angle of vision that supports their respective feminisms. Although neither author claimed the feminist label, to readers—then and now—their work reveals a deep investment in questions about the power of gender roles and the construction of femininity. In the third section, I discuss Loy's virgins and Woolf's Angel of the House, emphasizing the feminist undercurrents of their work and, ultimately, suggesting that despite their differences, both authors share similar gender-inflected concerns.

The last two sections present a scholarly and pedagogical meta-reflection. Here I encourage modernist scholars and teachers to refocus our feminist attentions by listening for resonances and looking for affiliations within the canon and beyond. The work of recovery continues, but also let us take up the mantle of revision, cultivating reading and teaching practices that challenge the traditional conventions and patriarchal standards that have kept us confined to reproducing restrictive structures of scholarly value and knowledge creation. Ultimately, this essay advocates for postures of feminist possibility in service of seeing both our scholarly subjects and our scholarly selves anew.

Biography: Mothers, Maternity, and Familial Memory

Mothers loomed large for both Woolf and Loy. Their relationships with their mothers influenced their portrayal of the Victorian age of their birth and shaped their conceptions of the maternal and the role of family in their writing. Woolf, who lost her mother as she entered adolescence, often portrays motherhood sympathetically if obscurely. Never a mother herself, Woolf keeps a certain narrative distance from mothers and motherhood in her fiction, foregoing detailed explorations of that aspect of her characters, thus keeping motherhood mostly out of the narrative spotlight. (Mrs. Ramsay in *To the Lighthouse* [1927] is Woolf's most direct and in-depth portrayal of motherhood.) And although Loy was a mother, she rarely gives voice to her own experience, choosing to keep the mother figure imprisoned in a Victorian past.[8] For Loy, her feelings toward female sexuality and gender identity are inextricably linked to her mother's conservative Victorian outlook. As I hope this brief introduction suggests, to examine Woolf and Loy through the lens of mothers, motherhood, and familial memory provides a rich field to traverse, highlighting surprising sympathies and revealing important distinctions, thus reorienting Woolf's oft-quoted sentiment in *A Room of One's Own*: perhaps we should think back through mothers if we are feminist scholars.

Woolf's mother, Julia Stephen, haunted her, fueling reflections on home, family, and their role in the creation of individual identity, themes that are woven throughout Woolf's writing. The maternal functions as an origin point as well as a point of return, and as such, is a generative, if also complex, source for narrative, in structure as well as content. For Woolf, the maternal is an elusive but foundational bedrock for identity creation and self-reflection. The significance of the maternal is recognizable throughout much of Loy's oeuvre as well, although in quite a different manner. Mothers often represent and give voice to restrictive traditions that, for Loy, restrict female agency and foster both guilt and self-doubt. (Loy's "Anglo-Mongrels and the Rose" is exemplary.) Taking childbirth as her subject in "Parturition," Loy assumes the role of mother-to-be, the "I" of the poem who muses, "I should have been emptied of life / Giving life," thus associating motherhood with loss, a fracturing of wholeness that familial narratives attempt, but fail, to fill.[9] And yet, Loy dedicates much of her autobiographical writing—most of which remains unpublished—to determining the significance of the maternal influence in the formation of the self.[10]

"Sketch of the Past" (1985) is Woolf's only sustained attempt at autobiography and, beginning with a memory of her mother, it provides readers with a glimpse into Woolf's earliest associations with the maternal. The image of Julia Stephen's dress, close up, recalled from the vantage point of child on her mother's lap, leads Woolf to a formative memory of St. Ives, where, as a child in the nursery, Woolf listened to the waves break and heard the pull from the window blind slide across the floor. The light, the sound, the feelings are, Woolf declares, "the purest ecstasy I can conceive."[11] "If life has a base that it stands upon, if it is a bowl that one fills and fills and fills," Woolf explains, "then my bowl without a doubt stands upon this memory."[12] Autobiographical memory, for Woolf, is anchored by the maternal, a connection strengthened by Julia Stephen's untimely death in 1895. *To the Lighthouse* is often read as an elegy to her mother, an interpretation supported in an epistolary exchange between Woolf and her sister, Vanessa Bell: "You have given a portrait of mother which is more like her to me than anything I could ever have conceived of as possible," writes Bell after reading *To the Lighthouse* for the first time.[13] Pleased at Bell's response, Woolf responds: "I'm in a terrible state of pleasure that you should think Mrs. Ramsay so like mother." Woolf continues, skeptical regarding her knowledge of Julia Stephen yet convinced of her mother's influence: "At the same time it is a psychological mystery why she should be: how a child could know about her; except that she has always haunted me."[14]

Whereas Woolf's foundational memory is familial, made comforting by the proximity of her mother, Loy's earliest memories are disconcerting and rife with conflict. Loy's first memory, with which Carolyn Burke begins her biography of Loy, *Becoming Modern*, finds Loy among strangers. Held in the arms of an unfamiliar man, Loy is startled by a flash of colored light that dazzles her young eyes: "She blinked and stared at the fiery reds and yellows, barely making out the colored bottles that stood in a row behind the fanlight. The sun was shining through the layers of glass and straight at her, as if she had caught fire, as if shards of color had entered her body. But as she stretched her arms towards the brilliance, the force that gripped her like a clamp kept on going down the stairs" (13). Loy's first memory expresses the acute pleasure and pain of an awakening self-consciousness, realizing that although the glow of the colored lights shined upon her, they were not her. Her desire to be one with the lights was only heightened by the circumstances surrounding this memory: she had been sent to stay with the doctor's family while her sister, Dora, was born. Taken away from her mother for the birth of her sister, Loy would never return to the position of only child. Ambivalence dominates Loy's earliest memories as, in retrospective analysis, it is obvious that she will not regain the comfort of her mother's arms as the sole object of maternal affection. As Burke suggests, "the discovery of the self was linked not only with the enchantment of light and color but also with the loss of 'home'" (14).

For Loy—born Mina Gertrude Löwy—her mother, Julia Bryan Löwy, was less of a fond memory—fodder for reflective musings and memorial excavations, as was the case for Woolf—and more of an inescapable psychological hazard. Many of Loy's adult choices seem to betray her conflicting desires simultaneously to distance herself from her mother and to gain her attention. Even in childhood, Loy felt acutely the contradictory pressures her mother exerted upon her. Conceived prior to marriage, young Loy was, at best, a reminder to her mother of moral indiscretion and, at worst, a punishment issued upon Julia for her female sexuality. Moreover, Sigmund Löwy, Loy's father, was a Jewish tailor and, although he eventually joined the ranks "of the highly skilled English tailors" who attired the upper classes, Julia would never be able to erase what she perceived as the anti-Semitic stain of trade from her perception of her family (*Becoming Modern*, 17). Julia's personal insecurities and her paranoid attention to class markers indelibly marked Loy. In her powerful autobiographical poem, "Anglo-Mongrels and the Rose"—penned when she was in her thirties, the same age as Woolf when she wrote *To the Lighthouse*—Loy critiques and satirizes her mother and her repressive family circumstances:

> New Life
> when it asserts itself into continuity
> is disciplined
> by the family
> reflection
> of national construction
> to a proportionate posture
> in the civilized scheme
>
> deriving
> definite contours
> from tradition . . .
>
> Suburban children
> of middle-class Britain
> ejected from the home
>
> are still connected
> with the inseverable
> navel-cord of the motherland
> and
> need never feel alone[15]

In these stanzas, readers discern Julia's discomfort with the tensions inherent in her class position as seen through her daughter's eyes: although eventually well ensconced in middle-class respectability, Julia (according to Loy) could never forget that her family's social status derived from her husband's needle and thread, an inexcusable tarnish to any luster a place in the growing business class had to offer Loy's mother.

Loy absorbs her mother's ambivalence toward her father and, by extension, herself, growing to understand her position in the family as indictment, punishment, and inescapable witness to Julia's sin of slumming:

To the mother
the blood-relationship
is a terrific indictment of the flesh

under cover
of clothing and furnishing
"somebody" has sinned
and their sin—
a living witness of the flesh—
swarms with inquisitive eyes[16]

As these lines of "Anglo-Mongrel and the Rose" reveal, Loy's conception of her mother is related to the risks of female sexuality and class
climbing, not only cultivating a vexed relationship between mother and
daughter but also between Loy's own sexuality and its veiled commodification within a traditional Victorian family structure. Consequently, for Loy
to think back through her mother is to struggle against the constraints of
her strict Victorian upbringing, an indictment of her class and her sex.

As this brief foray into the maternal makes visible, mothers are forces
motivating personal reflections for the two writers. Both perceive their
mothers as foundational in their perceptions of self while recognizing
the powerful role of the mother figure within traditional Victorian family structures. This portrayal of motherhood in their work offers feminist
scholars an entry point for analysis, linking life-writing and gender studies
productively in modernist studies, which has been long dominated by the
patriarchal anxiety of influence.

Outsiders Within: National Identity, Art, and Authorship

This section highlights the ways Woolf and Loy fashioned themselves as
outsiders to dominant cultural norms buttressing national identity and
contributing to particular conceptions of the artist and his art. Gender
plays a significant role in the way these two women understood their positionality vis-à-vis national and emerging modernist discourses, but also
important is how their respective affiliations with Jewishness shaped their
self-fashioning. By privileging the figure of the outsider, Woolf and Loy
recognize and champion the political and artistic benefits of residing on
the periphery of dominant gender and national discourse.

In *A Shrinking Island*, Jed Esty characterizes Woolf's writing in the 1930s as participating in an "anthropological turn" that, in the guise of modernist form, allowed the literary innovators of the nineteen-teens and twenties, such as T. S. Eliot, E. M. Forster, and Woolf, to embrace their emerging "little Englander" in the subsequent decade.[17] However, Woolf's *Three Guineas* (1938) asserts that although her attentions might be taking an anthropological turn, her politics remain critical of the national establishment. Linking domestic patriarchy with national patriarchy, Woolf famously positions herself as an "outsider" within both structures. Employing a hypothetical letter that inquires, "How in your opinion are we to prevent war?," as the vehicle for her sharp examination of national and gender politics during the rise of fascism, Woolf inaugurates the "Outsiders Society": "Let us then draw rapidly in outline the kind of society which the daughters of educated men might found. . . . If name it must have, it could be called the Outsiders Society."[18]

As scholars have comprehensively documented, Woolf's understanding of herself as an outsider evolved throughout her life. From an early age, Woolf was excluded from the male-dominated realm of formal education which, as highlighted in *Three Guineas*, perpetuates the "procession of educated men," constituted by those who go on to don the robes of the professoriate, take seats in Parliament, and assume positions of colonial administration. This gendered exclusion had consequences in terms of her national identity, and by extension, her civic and political efficacy. Ultimately, Woolf came to value her role as an outsider, exemplified by her refusal of honorary degrees and of the insider position that such honors afforded.

Although intimately connected to her gender politics, Woolf's theorization of the outsider does not derive from her gender position alone. Married to a Jewish man, Leonard Woolf, and a business partner with him in the Hogarth Press, Woolf was well acquainted with the anti-Semitic sentiment found in Britain and on the Continent, although perhaps not so aware as to consistently recognize her own internalized anti-Semitism.[19] Natania Rosenfeld examines Woolf's outsider position in relation to her marriage to Leonard with a focus on the way Leonard's Jewishness and Woolf's gender created an intellectual reciprocity that cultivated an outsider perspective.[20] In "Thinking Back through Our Mothers," Jane Marcus, too, examines the link between Woolf's self-identified outsider status and the position of the Jewish intellectual: "Nevertheless, Woolf's *feelings* about women's oppression match those of her German Jewish contemporaries. Even as they felt that as Jews they were administering the intellectual property of a people who denied them the right to do so, Virginia Woolf felt as a woman literary critic that she stood in the same untenable position in relation to British culture."[21]

By the 1938 publication of *Three Guineas*, Woolf had claimed the outsider position in the context of Englishness. As England careened closer to military conflict with Germany, and as the plight of the Jewish people in Germany became more dire, Woolf was certain that being outside the national establishment offered intellectual clarity and political creativity. As portrayed in Woolf's powerful "Thoughts on Peace in an Air Raid" (1940), the outsider is vulnerable but powerful and, ostensibly, holds the answer to the question of peace in the future: "Up there in the sky young Englishmen and young German men are fighting each other. The defenders are men, the attackers are men. Arms are not given to Englishwomen either to fight the enemy or to defend herself. She must lie weaponless tonight. . . . How far can she fight for freedom without firearms? By making arms, or clothes or food. But there is another way of fighting for freedom without arms; we can fight with the mind."[22] For Woolf, women have the most important weapon at their disposal, their minds. As outsiders, women are not invested in war and national identity the same way men are since the military and national establishment have largely excluded them.

Loy, also, felt acutely the outsider aspects of her identity. Although raised under the strict Christianity of her mother, Loy always struggled with an ambivalent identification with her Jewish father. In Loy's eyes, Sigmund Löwy was the parent from whom she inherited her aesthetic sensibility as well as her skill as a craftswoman, an inheritance she perceived (however stereotypically) as derived from her father's Jewishness and which she privileges in "Anglo-Mongrels and the Rose." However, because of his success in the business realm, Sigmund also represented that which continued to keep Loy on the outside of what her mother, Julia, considered respectable society. In fact, throughout her life, Loy would oscillate between her desire to go into the trades—her lampshade shop, with Peggy Guggenheim as her patron, was surprisingly successful—and her distaste, passed down from her mother, of all things commercial. Even her self-given name, Loy, attests to the impact of her mother's anti-Semitism by removing the original umlaut and eliding the "w" in order to fashion herself as both sui generis and not Jewish. Despite her position as a self-proclaimed outsider in her own (already-outsider) family, Loy remained emotionally tethered to her family, often returning to the vexed familial dynamics in her autobiographical reflections. In the late 1920s and early 1930s, Loy engaged in a life-writing project, similar to her better-known "Anglo-Mongrels and the Rose," in which she examined her contradictory inheritance: Julia's "'vocal shrapnel'" made her a "wrathful god" as much as a woman "of another generation," cultivating in Loy a deep-seated insecurity; similarly, Sigmund's "'pedigree'" and "'racial memory'" had created in Loy "'a wanderer infinitely more haunted than the eternal Jew: a bi-spirited entity.'"[23]

One way that Loy negotiated her familial inheritance was to leave the country of her birth, England, for a more cosmopolitan existence through which her identity as an expatriate would trump what she perceived as her mixed heritage. And in this, she succeeded: Loy lived in Berlin, Florence, Paris, New York, and Aspen, and in each fashioned herself as an alluring outsider by rejecting British propriety (associated with her mother) in favor of an avant-garde sensibility.[24] After her first marriage to Stephen Haweis, which ostensibly protected her from social scandal, Loy cultivated an expatriate community that existed on the fringes of polite society. Although a list of her friends reads like a "Who's Who of Modernism," many were plagued by poverty, marginalized within their artistic professions, positioned on the edges of mainstream politics and philosophy, and, in terms of the women, regarded with social suspicion by the arbiters of traditional society.

Ultimately, vacillating between famous and infamous, Loy's expatriate community was a collection of outsiders.[25] Which was perhaps by design: Loy always sought the outsiders because, as "Apology of Genius" (1922) suggests, Loy associated outsider status with genius:

Ostracized as we are with God—
    The watchers of the civilized wastes
    reverse their signals on our track

Lepers of the moon
all magically diseased
we come among you
innocent
of our luminous sores

. . . .

Our wills are formed
by curious discipline
beyond your laws

You may give birth to us
or marry us
the chances of your flesh
are not our destiny—[26]

Thus, Loy crafts her own Outsiders Society: a Society of Geniuses. Similar to Woolf, Loy imagines this marginal position as one of unrealized power, not explicitly political or national, but inherently revolutionary—culturally, artistically, and literarily.[27]

Underappreciated by modernist scholars, Loy's theorization of the outsider as genius offers feminist scholars yet another framework through which to read the work of women modernists, linking writers and artists seemingly unrelated through their shared outsider status. Moreover, whereas Woolf's outsiders are positioned thus because of their gender identity,[28] Loy's outsider-as-genius troubles the dominance of the gender binary since Loy neither reinforces the mythology of the male genius nor leverages gender as a vector in determining who can attain genius status. Thus, when Woolf's and Loy's theorization of the outsider are studied in tandem, they provide a productive example of the ways in which two binary structures and their attendant hierarchies—men and women, insider and outsider—can disrupt each other concurrently, destabilizing the primacy of national identity in discussions of modern art, opening up a new space for scholarly inquiry.[29]

Making It New: *Feminist Manifesto* and *A Room of One's Own*

Published in 1929, *A Room of One's Own* reached readers one year after the full enfranchisement of women in England. However, the vote does not seem to be the answer for Virginia Woolf, who, throughout her feminist treatise, advocates for educational, economic, and cultural equality by examining and critiquing the patriarchal ideologies that, regardless of women's suffrage, continue to reinforce and perpetuate gender inequality. One might go as far as to apply the opening line of Mina Loy's 1914 "Feminist

Manifesto" to Woolf's feminism as articulated in *A Room of One's Own*: Loy's manifesto begins "The feminist movement as at present instituted is *Inadequate*."[30] Loy, inspired by her contact with Futurist aesthetics—though she differed with Futurism distinctly on issues of gender—pens her polemic not in essay form, as Woolf does, but in manifesto form, positioning herself among more famous manifesto writers such as the Futurist Filippo Marinetti and the Vorticist Wyndham Lewis. Like Woolf, she challenges the restrictions of patriarchy in regard to gender roles: "Leave off looking to men to find out what you are *not*—seek within yourselves to find out what you *are*. As conditions are at present constituted—you have the choice between *Parasitism*, & *Prostitution*—or *Negation*."[31]

Readers of Woolf will recognize resonances between this passage from Loy and Woolf's reflections on the Angel of the House in her essay "Professions for Women" (1931/1942),[32] not to mention how Loy's lines support a reading of many of Woolf's female characters who negotiate their way through a social structure that casts them either as mistresses or mothers—or, perhaps worse, as irrelevant. (*The Years* [1937] is exemplary here with its ensemble cast of female characters.) And yet, despite their trenchant critiques of patriarchy, both women were wary of being labeled a feminist and of organized feminism.[33] Ambivalence toward feminism as well as a distrust of patriarchy and the structural olive branches it extends to women, such as the vote, notwithstanding, one cannot argue that Woolf and Loy share the same approach to gender politics. However, I suggest that Woolf and Loy, when placed in conversation with each other, offer feminist scholars fresh ways to approach the gendered history of modernism.

Reading for affiliations leads us to the authors' pointed critique of traditional gender roles for women and the commodification implicit in the heterosexual relationships buttressing patriarchal structures both private and public. Born in 1882, both women entered a world dominated by Victorian values, which were especially restrictive for women. Coming of age at the turn of the century, both women reflected on the lingering strength of Victorian gender expectations in regard to traditional roles, such as the wife, and more progressive roles, such as the professional woman. In "Virgins Plus Curtains Minus Dots" (1915), Loy tackles outdated gender commodification in the marriage market in modernist verse form. Portraying the family home as a kind of prison, Loy imagines unwed virgins without dowries (dots) looking out from behind the curtains, seeking potential suitors in the crowd. Virginal but not naïve, these women recognize that without a marriage portion, their chances of transforming themselves from daughters to wives is nearly impossible:

Houses hold virgins
The door's on the chain

'Plum streets with hearts'
'Bore curtains with eyes'

Virgins   without dots
Stare   beyond probability[34]

Confined in their fathers' homes, these virgins struggle with competing narratives, one romantic and the other economic. As Loy explains, although "We have been taught / Love is a god," women know full well that their romantic prayers will remain unanswered without proper financial backing: "Virgins for sale / Yet where are our coins / For buying a purchaser" (22). The narrative reveals the tension between romance and the gendered economics of the marriage market: "Love is a god / Marriage expensive / A secret well kept" (22). First published in *Rogue*, "Virgins Plus Curtains Minus Dots" was written after the dissolution of Loy's marriage to Haweis, suggesting that although a virgin no longer, Loy was very much considering the structures of romance and marriage from the other side of the curtain.

Although Woolf never took up the particularities of the marriage market and female sexuality as explicitly as Loy did, she does investigate the evolution of gender expectations fifteen years after "Virgins Plus Curtains Minus Dots" in her essay "Professions for Women" (1942). A catalyst for some of Woolf's arguably most feminist undertakings, this short essay, which was originally read to members of the Women's Service League, directly attacks the continued presence and power of the Victorian concept of femininity as it manifests in the life of professional women. In "Professions for Women," Woolf commits one of the most famous literary murders: she kills the Angel of the House. This sympathetic phantom is "immensely charming," "sacrificed herself daily," and "never had a mind or wish of her own, but preferred to sympathize always with the minds and wishes of others" (237). And above all, Woolf reminds her readers, "she was pure" (ibid.). In other words, the Angel of the House was the ghost of the

Victorian Woman, the virginal daughter and the dutiful wife, obedient, caring, and altogether selfless. And yet, a figure so amenable and arguably necessary to traditional masculinity is fatal to the professional woman Woolf addresses: "Had I not killed her she would have killed my writing. For, as I found, directly I put pen to paper, you cannot review even a novel without having a mind of your own, without expressing what you think to be the truth about human actions, morality, sex" (238). Thus, the patriarchal economy of gender is Woolf's subject, too. A woman cannot succeed in her profession if she cannot think for herself, and to do so, she must destroy all vestiges of the Angel of the House.[35]

Very different in form and tone, Loy's poem and Woolf's essay seem to speak to each other across the years that separate them. Woolf laments that women writers have not yet been able to overcome "the extreme conventionality of the other sex" ("Professions," 240). "Men, her reason told her, would be shocked" if she wrote about the body, about the passions (ibid.). Although Woolf believes the problem of the Angel of the House can be solved—murder is the answer—the problem of "telling the truth about my own experiences as a body, I do not think I solved" (241). And yet, if Woolf had read the poetry Loy was writing (which we have no indication she did) between 1914 and 1920—especially Loy's "Parturition" published in 1914 in *The Trend* or "Love Songs" published in 1915 in *Others*—she may have recognized a compatriot in arms, not only killing the Angel of the House but also telling the truth about her experiences as a body.

Woolf writes that inwardly there are still many obstacles for women in the professional world, "many ghosts to fight, many prejudices to overcome" (ibid.). And yet is not that exactly what Loy was undertaking in her poetry? She fights the ghosts of Victorian femininity that keep virgins locked within their fathers' homes. Loy calls out the economic prejudices that reduce women to commodities in financial exchanges masquerading as romantic narratives. And in doing so, she tells the truth about women's experiences as bodies: the false power of purity, the economic value of virginity, and the forbidden desires of female sexuality. "So much flesh in the world / Wanders at will," Loy muses, revealing the existence and knowledge of sexuality, even by those who are "wasting their giggles / For we have no dots" ("Virgins," 22). For Woolf, it is the cheapness of paper that opened the door of authorship to women,[36] and for Loy, it is the high price of virginity that manages to keep them confined behind curtains.

A New Modernist Baedeker

Despite their dramatic differences in form and style, both women blaze trails through an otherwise male-dominated modernism. Woolf studies has an overabundance of novels, stories, and essays—not to mention the collected letters and diaries—upon which to anchor such an argument about Woolf's work. Loy scholars, conversely, are faced with an archive of unpublished material when seeking additional evidence to support the claim of Loy's position within modernism. Loy published only one collection of poetry during her lifetime, titled *Lunar Baedecker* (1923). Ironically, Robert McAlmon's titular spelling mistake has become integral to Loy's identity as a modernist poet, making it new through the revision of poetic form and content. As Burke explains, "The title evoked the old-fashioned, opinionated, and reliable Baedeker, the handbook familiar to all European travelers. Whatever country it described, Baedeker's reassuring format—red cloth jacket, marbled edges, cream pages, and elegant maps—implied that one was in good hands: its authoritative tone lulled the traveler into accepting the author's tastes and prejudices."[37] But with its notable misspelling and its self-consciously modern content, Loy subverted the old-fashioned reliability of its namesake.

The title poem, "Lunar Baedeker," maps modern terrain, one that privileges the lunar over the solar, sleeping over waking:

A silver Lucifer
serves
cocaine in cornucopia

To some somnambulists
of adolescent thighs
draped
in satirical draperies
. . . .

Delirious Avenues
lit
with the chandelier souls
of infusoria
from Pharoah's tombstones

lead

to mercurial doomsdays[38]

A critique of the "decadent tradition from which it arises," the poem "deploys short jazzy stanzas in a recognizably modern landscape."[39] Loy, through her poetic "I," explores a kind of night world, walking the delirious avenues like a nocturnal flaneuse, watching "Immortality" mildew "in the museums of the moon."[40] The landscape is both recognizable and strange, a simultaneity highlighted by the large breaks between stanzas, forcing the reader to tread carefully through what might seem like, but is obviously not, familiar poetic territory.

Reading Loy's "Lunar Baedeker" sends me to Woolf's novel, *The Waves* (1931). Bernard's narration concludes the novel, expressing his own kind of mercurial doomsday: "What enemy do we now perceive advancing against us, you whom I ride now, as we stand pawing this stretch of pavement? It is death. Death is the enemy. It is death against whom I ride with my spear couched and my hair flying back like a young man's, like Percival's, when he galloped in India. I strike spurs into my horse. Against you I will fling myself, unvanquished and unyielding, O Death!" (297). The last section of *The Waves* begins with a description of twilight turning to night: "Now the sun had sunk" (236). Bernard's final soliloquy, thus, takes place at night. He, too, like Loy's poetic "I," must make his way in the dark. And like Loy's poetry, *The Waves* takes a recognizable form, the novel, and reveals its potential for newness by subverting readerly expectations, temporally and structurally. Temporal conventions are both emphasized and exploited as each chapter begins with a description of a single moment in the duration of a single day (twenty-four hours) while the book's duration spans the life of its characters (thirty-some years). Structurally, Woolf employs third-person narration, but rather than portraying actual speech, the quoted passages convey the character's innermost thoughts, disrupting readerly assumptions about the objective reality of experience and interpersonal relations.

Rather than continuing these close readings in order to craft an argument about Woolf's *The Waves* and Loy's "Lunar Baedeker," their influence or innovation, I want to pose a challenge for modernist feminist scholars. It is through resonance and association that I link these two texts, and I do so in service of encouraging us to follow the traces, the subtle resonances, and the intuitive associations that we, as attentive readers of modernist literature, explore with keenness and care—a skill especially paramount to feminist modernist scholars who, for so long, have had their ears close to the ground of the texts we study, listening for reverberations and echoes, silenced cries for help, and muffled calls for revolution, that have been nearly lost under the white noise of traditional, male-oriented modernism. Woolf has secured a place in canonical modernism because of scholars who did not adhere to the academic party line but rather listened closely to the texts, the histories, and the archive, who unearthed connections buried and brought to the light writers and artists languishing in the shadows of great men. And Loy, although well mythologized as muse, mistress, and mother to modernist men, is only just beginning to be integrated into feminist portrayals of modernism, not as a feminine accessory to the male-dominated canon, but as an object worthy of feminist study whose life and work can teach us something about modernism and about our process of constructing it.[41]

That said, we must continue to examine the institutions of modernism, as characterized by Lawrence Rainey, tracing the material conditions and social structures that mark "neither the straightforward resistance nor an outright capitulation to commodification but a momentary equivocation that incorporates elements of both in a brief, necessarily unstable synthesis."[42] For Woolf and Loy, modernism's relationship to commodification plays a significant role in their careers: Woolf and her husband chose to own and operate the means of their literary production, controlling how their work was produced and sold, whereas Loy existed on the fringes of modernist commodification, oscillating between commercial success and more traditional patronage, always struggling to thrive as a working artist in the early twentieth century. Both Woolf and Loy were attentive to what Rainey identifies as modernist strategies "for reputation building—involving theatricality, spectacle, publicity, and novel modes of cultural marketing and media manipulation—[that] responded to increasingly international cultural interchanges."[43] But because of their respective positions as outsiders within these male-dominated modernist institutions, Woolf and Loy are often overlooked in analyses that do not recognize informal, perhaps even intangible, networks of inspiration, affiliations around shared experiences, and constellations of correspondence and allusion. Even feminist scholarship, in its desire to become legible and creditable, has reproduced reading and interpretive practices that buttress traditional structures of valuing, like icons and canons.

Reaching back to Hugh Kenner's *The Pound Era* (1971), modernist scholars have worked to elevate and secure literary and cultural icons within the field, positioning them as centers around which modernism revolved. As is well established, it was the modernist men who first presided over the canon. However, feminist scholars made inroads into modernist studies, inaugurating a period of discovery, recovery, and revision. Feminist scholars have rightfully fought fire with fire, cultivating a canon of female icons, each supported by single-author societies, *Cambridge Companions*, and monographs aplenty. Perhaps unconsciously borrowing from a very modernist phenomenon, the culture of celebrity—to appropriate a phrase from Aaron Jaffe—feminist scholars sought to bring female, lesbian, and queer modernists out of the closet, so to speak—or out of the dark, to gesture back to "Lunar Baedeker" and *The Waves*—and in the process, made icons out of a few.[44] And current feminist scholars are indebted to this work as it has opened up a rich world of women writers and marginalized communities, as well as revealed the interdependency between the male icons and male-dominated institutions, on one hand, and the female icons and the female-oriented networks, on the other. The story we tell about modernism has, thankfully, become more nuanced and complex, and in the process, more responsible as well.

Yet I encourage feminist scholars to push beyond a modernist landscape characterized by towering icons, men and women. I want us to ask and explore: What exists in the shadows cast by these icons? What happens if we alter our vantage point? Instead of standing atop our towers of iconicity, what happens when we traverse the ground in their wake? Perhaps, instead of seeing only the distance between Woolf and Loy, to take the example at hand, we seek out the affiliations at their foundations, the shared ground upon which their work and lives reside.

To do so might be to acknowledge and challenge "the limits of critique" that Rita Felski examines in her book by that title. To do so might be to undertake a version of weak theory, as eloquently presented in Paul K. Saint-Amour's book, *Tense Future*, and as thoroughly explored in the September 2018 special issue of *Modernism/modernity*.[45] To do so might be to rewrite our syllabi to reflect not canons but constellations, to encourage not only close reading but also creative reading. To do so might be to create a new home for innovative and unconventional scholarship which will allow us, borrowing from Loy's "Apology of Genius," to "forge the dusk of Chaos" "in the raw caverns of the Increate" "to that imperious jewelry of the Universe /—the Beautiful—."[46] To do so might be to tell a new story about modernism. A story in which there is not just one or two or even three versions of modernism, each anchored by their own icon, but rather a mutually informing plethora of voices, a harmonious cacophony, that, like Bernard, flings itself, "unvanquished and unyielding," against our own presumptions, prejudices, and preoccupations.

Teaching Feminist Modernism

Given all that I have suggested above about affiliations and affinities, reading resonances and seeking synthesis in feminist modernist scholarship, how do we translate this approach into our classrooms? The majority of modernist scholars are teachers as well, and given the importance of feminist pedagogy for many, it seems incongruent to reproduce traditional models of modernism in our syllabi when we could leverage the kinds of reading practices showcased in this collection to reimagine the modernist classroom. And here I turn to Sandeep Parmar's *Reading Mina Loy's Autobiographies* as a guide. Parmar's approach to Loy's autobiographical writing offers insight for those of us interested in examining the efficacy of our feminist modernist teaching in tandem with our scholarship.

What stands out most for me in *Reading Mina Loy's Autobiographies* is Parmar's commentary on the Loy archive, housed at Yale University's Beinecke Rare Book and Manuscript Library, as it offers teachers of modernism a lens through which to reexamine our work in the classroom. For Parmar, the archive does not bequeath a "nugget of pure truth to wrap up between the pages of your notebooks and keep on the mantelpiece forever," to borrow from *A Room of One's Own*.[47] Rather, it is both a magnifying glass and a mirror: on one hand, providing a close look at unpublished material, and, on the other hand, reflecting back to attentive scholars the values and presuppositions employed in the retrospective creation of an author's life and work. Parmar is as interested in the archive *as a mirror* as she is in the archive as a magnifying glass; her study of Loy's autobiographical writing revealing as much about modernist studies as it reveals about Loy's writing life. The myth of completion and the context of the canon are two aspects of the archive that Parmar addresses that can be applied to the teaching of modernism in a feminist context.

First, Parmar's reading of the archive. Although the Beinecke foregrounds "biographical completeness," the archivists at the Beinecke do so,

Parmar argues, through an extension of the definition of archive: "Today it is the author's personal papers that are of more interest than the fair copy of a poem or an appealing group of letters. The papers that bear witness to the creative process—an author's notes, drafts, setting copies, corrected proofs, and the documentation, such as correspondence, which surrounds them—are chiefly to be desired."[48] In light of this definition, the archive represents "the writer's private, 'creative' self" and "commemorate[s] their place within literary communities of their era." Such an approach to the archive implies that Loy's papers "are of greater significance [to scholars] alongside those of her contemporaries and vice versa" and, consequently, the archive "resituates itself in a distant past" (5).

I would extend Parmar's analysis even further, suggesting that in addition to resituating itself in a distant past, the archive contributes immensely to the recreation of that past. Considering the other authors with whom Loy is contextualized—Gertrude Stein, Marianne Moore, and Ezra Pound, for example—not only is a particular modernist canon privileged and reinforced but also Loy's life and oeuvre is understood as *complete* only within the context of these iconic modernists, thus limiting the analytical imagination of modernist scholars looking for new ways to approach writers, like Loy, relegated to the margins of the modernist canon.

How are our modernist classrooms like this archive? How often do we, as teachers of modernist literature, endorse the myth of completion at the cost of our students'—and our own—imaginations? How often do we, in the service of course objectives and assessment goals, privilege a canonical contextualization, presenting modern authors and their works as pieces to a puzzle finished only when every chosen writer and every chosen text fits together neatly, creating a—culturally and politically—coherent picture of modernism? These are the questions Parmar's analysis of the archive make imperative for teachers of modernism. The Loy archive, on the one hand, is an "idiosyncratic collection of typescripts, handwritten drafts, address books, letterhead and graph paper that illustrates the fantasy of a modern writer at work," and, on the other hand, is a system of "carefully ordered folders [that] are at odds with their, at times, chaotic contents."[49] This is but one of the challenges for Loy scholars approaching the archive, and it corresponds to a challenge that teachers of modernism—whether their research takes them to the archive or not—encounter regularly as they draft syllabi, choose texts, and craft lectures: how to negotiate our need to narrate modernism while simultaneously allowing for multiple stories?

In troubling the stories we tell about modernism—recognizing their exclusivity, their tethers to the canon, and their limited imagination—I am reminded of Loy's critique of the romance narrative in "Songs to Joannes" (1917):

Spawn   of   Fantasies
Silting the appraisable
Pig Cupid   his rosy snout
Rooting erotic garbage
"Once upon a time"
Pulls a weed   white star-topped
Among wild oats   sown in mucous membrane[50]

Provocative at the time of its publication, "Songs to Joannes" begins with an unexpected juxtaposition: love and garbage. The Pig Cupid of the poem roots around in the erotic waste of "once upon a time." Romance narratives and tropes are evacuated of meaning in this arresting image, compelling the reader to replace the rose-colored glasses of romantic fantasy with a rosy snout, able to sniff out the ripest pieces of garbage.

As teachers of modernism, we should look to the literature we study as a model and a mentor, and "Songs to Joannes" reminds us of the power of the unexpected pairing. Love and garbage, pig and cupid: these are not the "famous marriages" Woolf references in her 1937 essay "Craftsmanship."[51] Rather, these words, when paired together, reinforce Woolf's suggestion that "it is [words'] nature *not* to express one simple statement but a thousand possibilities." Words have "done this so often that, at last," Woolf admits, "happily, we are beginning to face the fact" (200; emphasis mine).

Let us happily face the fact, in terms of the teaching of modernism, that despite our sincerest attempts at constructing completeness and coherence under the reign of canonicity and iconicity, modernism presents more possibilities than it does conclusions, more complexity than coherence. And if we approach our syllabi, reading lists, and lecture notes with a commitment to possibility and multiplicity, affiliation and affinity, new narratives will emerge out of the unexpected juxtapositions offered. Is not this our challenge as feminist teachers and scholars, to reimagine, reinterpret, and revise? Our feminist revisions should be directed at readings of canonical texts as well as at the very concept of canonicity and iconicity. Moreover, with the modernist writers we study as our mentors and models, we should revise our reading practices, too, through a revision of our interpretative acts, modeling to students the value of creativity as well as mastery. Although we may be scholars and teachers of modernism, we are always students of literature, and if this constellation of Woolf and Loy shows us anything, it is that modernist texts have much more to teach us.

Notes

1. Mina Loy poems used by permission of Roger L. Conover. Examples range from the July 2008 cover of *Vanity Fair* upon which a close-up of Angelina Jolie featured a quote from Woolf's *Three Guineas* tattooed on her arm, to a short video essay (2015) on the website NOWNESS featuring an insider tour of Florence Welch's apartment during which an early photo of Woolf adorns her staircase wall (https://www.nowness.com/series/my-place/florence-welch-barbara-anastacio). Although Woolf's appearance in *Downton Abbey* made it only as far as the editing room floor, she and the Bloomsbury Group are referenced in season six. See Nesbitt, "Absent Presence of Virginia Woolf," 250–70.

2. Although not granted a significant role in the making of modernism, Loy is often mythologized in more male-centered accounts of modernism as an enigmatic muse, thus imbuing her with a larger-than-life persona that overshadows her artistic experimentation and innovation. Sandeep Parmar's book *Reading Mina Loy's Autobiographies* is an example of new scholarship that intends to give Loy's life and work the critical examination it deserves by taking as one of its subjects the very mythology that has constrained Loy to the margins of modernist scholarship:

> Despite increasing interest in Loy both within and outside of academia, assumptions made about her life and her character, at times, overshadow critical interpretations of her writing. . . . And yet mythmaking serves a dual purpose in the process of historical revision . . . provid[ing] an existing aesthetic framework in which to recontextualize their contribution, while also heightening a sense of his or her uniqueness. In Loy's case, modernist scholarship must call for a deeper analysis of this mythmaking. (2)

Or, as Suzanne Hobson and Rachel Potter explain in their introduction to *The Salt Companion to Mina Loy*: "By maintaining her aesthetic position within and on the margins of the avant-garde, her texts help us to re-evaluate what we understand by Anglo-American modernism" (5).

3. Woolf, "The Leaning Tower," 154.

4. Parmar does address Loy and Woolf in tandem in *Reading Mina Loy's Autobiographies*. In her chapter surveying Loy criticism, she reminds feminist scholars of Shari Benstock's *Women of the Left Bank*, in which Benstock briefly compares

Loy's portrayal of women's lives to Woolf's investigation of female experience in her novels (68). Parmar elaborates and problematizes Benstock's connection of the two writers—citing Rachel Bowlby—challenging the usefulness of perceiving both as "case studies," as Benstock does. What strikes me as curious, though, is how Parmar quickly rejects the notion that studying the two writers in tandem could be productive to modernist studies, suggesting that their separate "circles of influence" and differences in "class, family, maternity and marital status" are obstacles to envisioning them within a shared modernist discourse (68). Conversely, in her essay, in *The Salt Companion to Mina Loy*, Parmar suggests that, in fact, "Loy's and Woolf's autobiographical writings . . . merit comparison in the ways both authors construct and subsequently reflect on their selves." "Mina Loy's 'Unfinishing' Self: 'The Child and the Parent' and 'Islands in the Air'" (London: Salt Publishing, 2010), 91.

5. In the case of Loy and Moore, the rivalry is more a construction of their male editors and advocates. The two women were mutually admiring if wary of each other. Moore supposedly immortalizes Loy in her poem "Those Various Scalpels." See Moore, *Complete Poems* (New York: Penguin, 1994), 51–52.

6. Although I have found passing reference to Woolf in the Loy literature—Carolyn Burke, Loy's most recent biographer, mentions their shared birth year and their constellation vis-à-vis Roger Fry's first Post-Impressionist exhibition in 1910, and the late Shari Benstock places their work in conversation in *Women of the Left Bank*—what connects them more so in my mind is the way in which each responded to familial circumstances, historical events, cultural shifts, and, particularly, gender politics.

7. Parmar's *Reading Mina Loy's Autobiographies* makes the case for the significance of Loy's mother in her autobiographical writing and, by extension, her self-reflection and self-fashioning.

8. Loy gives birth four times, the initial experience immortalized with fierce ambivalence in her poem "Parturition," originally published in 1914, exploring the birth of her first daughter, Oda Janet, who only lived for a year. Loy did not spend much time with her three subsequent children, turning their care over to governesses, and she was estranged from her son, Giles, during his adolescence when he was with his father. She did not cultivate close relationships with her two daughters, Joella and Fabienne, until the late 1920s and early 1930s when they lived in Berlin and Paris. See Burke, *Becoming Modern*.

9. Loy, "Parturition," in *The Lost Lunar Baedeker*, 6.

10. See Parmar's *Reading Mina Loy's Autobiographies*, especially chaps. 3 and 4, pp. 85–134.

11. Woolf, "Sketch of the Past," in *Moments of Being*, 65. "This was of red and

purple flowers on a black ground—my mother's dress; and she was sitting either in a train or in an omnibus, and I was on her lap" (64).

12. Ibid., 64.

13. Woolf, *The Letters of Virginia Woolf, Volume Three*, 572.

14. Ibid., 383.

15. Loy, "Anglo-Mongrels and the Rose," in *The Last Lunar Baedeker*, 153–54.

16. Ibid., 147.

17. Esty, *A Shrinking Island*, 1–23.

18. Woolf, *Three Guineas*, 126. The quotation continues:

> That is not a resonant name, but it has the advantage that it squares with facts—the facts of history, of law, of biography; even, it may be, with the still hidden facts of our still unknown psychology. It would consist of educated men's daughters working in their own class—how indeed can they work in any other?—and by their own methods for liberty, equality and peace. Their first duty, to which they would bind themselves not by oath, for oaths and ceremonies have no part in a society which must be anonymous and elastic before everything would be not to fight with arms. (126)

Three Guineas is composed as a response to three letters seeking the narrator's support, the first of which being about the prevention of war.

19. Many critics have examined the anti-Semitism in Woolf's writing, such as the depiction of Sara's Jewish neighbor's bathing habits in her 1937 novel, *The Years*. For more on Woolf and anti-Semitism, see *Woolf Studies Annual* 19 (2013).

20. See Rosenfeld, *Outsiders Together*.

21. Marcus, "Thinking Back through Our Mothers," 2–3.

22. Woolf, "Thoughts on Peace in an Air Raid," 243–44.

23. This passage is quoted from Burke who refers to the unpublished manuscript, "The Child and the Parent." See Burke, *Becoming Modern*, 375–76. In *Reading Mina Loy's Autobiographies*, Parmar examines "The Child and the Parent," leveraging archival material to make an argument about how the "juxtaposition of religious and scientific languages impacts on her construction of selfhood in her prose works of the 1930s and 1940s" (87).

24. Loy lived the last thirty years of her life in America, first in New York and then in Colorado, where she died in 1966 at age eighty-three.

25. Matthew Hart concludes his book, *Nations of Nothing But Poetry*, with an epilogue titled "Denationalizing Mina Loy." In this succinct and sharp examination, Hart explores the ways in which Loy and her work has been subsumed under the umbrella of American poetry. Beginning with Ezra Pound's well-known characterization of Loy as American and reaching to her eventual American citizenship in 1936, scholars have often considered Loy's poetry under the rubric of

American poetics in large part because her cosmopolitan existence aligned with conceptions of American freedom and liberty from forced allegiances. Moreover, as Alex Goody reminds us, Loy identified "'the muse of modern literature'" with the American "'melting pot'" in her 1925 article "Modern Poetry." Goody, "Empire, Motherhood and the Poetics of Self in Mina Loy's *Anglo-Mongrels and the Rose*," *Life Writing* 6, no. 1 (2009): 64. Hart's intervention is as follows: "I don't intend, then, to reclaim Mina Loy for England. I want, rather, to argue that while her cosmopolitanism cannot escape the political horizon of the nation-state, neither can it be annexed to qualities of any national culture" (178).

26. Loy, "Apology of Genius," in *The Lost Lunar Baedeker*, 77. Rachel Potter, in "Obscene Modernism and the Wondering Jew," reminds readers of Loy's poetry of one significant context informing her writing, especially in the 1920s: censorship of modernist writing, such as the obscenity trial of James Joyce's *Ulysses* in 1921, the same year she wrote "Apology of Genius." Hobson and Potter, *The Salt Companion to Mina Loy*, 50.

27. Related to but different from being an outsider, for Loy, was being an outcast. Burke explains that Loy's attention to and sympathy with the outcast—fallen women and Bowery bums are two notable examples from Loy's life—derives from her fear of "outcasting": unlike the empowerment that can come from choosing to be on the outside, outcasting is a process through which those who are in positions of power and privilege decide who is in and who is out. Burke, *Becoming Modern*, 412.

28. Gender is paramount for Woolf, but equally significant to her project in *Three Guineas* is class. Woolf's class focus is particular, in that she is speaking to the daughters of educated men, and nuanced, as she perceives class as inextricable from her gender analysis.

29. This reading is deeply indebted to Caroline Levine's book, *Forms: Whole, Rhythm, Hierarchy, Network* (2015), especially her chapter "Hierarchy" (82–111), which examines Sophocles' *Antigone*.

30. Loy, "Feminist Manifesto," in *The Lost Lunar Baedeker*, 153.

31. Ibid., 154.

32. "Professions for Women" was first composed as a speech for the National Society for Women's Service in 1931. The essay version was posthumously published in 1942 in *Death of the Moth*, 235–42.

33. Through the correspondence between Woolf and Dame Ethel Smyth, a prominent suffragist in the Pankhurst's Women's Social and Political Union, readers get a glimpse into Woolf's personal reflections on feminism, especially the organized variety. The letters from the early 1930s traverse the nascent days of their friendship. See Woolf, *The Letters of Virginia Woolf, Volume Five, 1932–1935* and *Volume Six, 1936–1941*. For Loy, it was her intense interactions with Marinetti—colored by romantic attraction—that motivated her most direct ruminations on

gender equality and national politics. See also Benstock, *Women of the Left Bank*, 381–86. For both Woolf and Loy, personal relationships are vehicles for honing their gender politics.

34. Loy, "Virgins Plus Curtains Minus Dots," in *The Lost Lunar Baedeker*, 21–23.

35. Nor can a professional woman succeed without five hundred pounds and a room of her own, Woolf had argued just a few years earlier. Class is a still under-developed line of inquiry in Woolf studies considering much of Woolf's gender analysis, in her fiction and nonfiction, relies upon an angle of vision derived from a certain secure class position. See Alison Light's *Mrs. Woolf and the Servants* (2007) and Mary Wilson's *The Labors of Modernism* (2016).

36. Woolf, "Professions," 235.

37. Burke, *Becoming Modern*, 321.

38. Loy, "Lunar Baedeker," in *The Lost Lunar Baedeker*, 81.

39. Burke, *Becoming Modern*, 322.

40. Loy, "Lunar Baedeker," in *The Lost Lunar Baedeker*, 82.

41. Loy's star seemed to be on the rise in modernist studies in the 1980s and 1990s with a few important publications: Virginia Kouidis's *Mina Loy: American Modernist Poet* (1980), Carolyn Burke's, *Becoming Modern: The Life of Mina Loy* (1996), and Maeera Shreiber and Keith Tuma's *Mina Loy: Woman and Poet* (1998) are exemplary. And, of course, the publication of Roger Conover's *The Lost Lunar Baedeker* in 1996 influenced Loy's visibility in modernist studies. *The Salt Companion to Mina Loy*, edited by Suzanne Hobson and Rachel Potter, *Reading Mina Loy's Autobiographies* by Sandeep Parmar, and *Poetic Salvage: Reading Mina Loy* (2017) by Tara Prescott are examples of the new attention directed at Loy's work and life by modernist scholars in the twenty-first century. In Parmar's book there is a comprehensive overview of Loy studies in chapter 2, "From Modern to Mystic to Marginal: Loy Criticism from 1918 to the Present."

42. Rainey, *Institutions of Modernism*, 3.

43. Ibid., 4.

44. See Brenda Silver, *Virginia Woolf Icon*.

45. Saint-Amour theorizes weak modernism in "Introduction: Traumatic Earliness," the initial chapter of his book, *Tense Future*. He continues this work in the introduction to the *Modernism/modernity* special issue on weak theory. In it, Saint-Amour suggests "that instead of anchoring a strong, all-or-nothing, unified theory of its field, modernism now functions in local and provisional ways, as an auxiliary term that supports other lines of argument not endogenous to its problem-space. In the house of modernist studies, *modernism* has left off playing bouncer and started playing host" ("Weak Theory, Weak Modernism," 437–59).

46. Loy, "Apology of Genius," in *The Lost Lunar Baedeker*, 78.

47. Woolf, *A Room of One's Own*, 4.

48. Parmar, *Reading Mina Loy's Autobiographies*, 4–5. Parmar, in a note to the introduction explains that "group[s] of letters" are not considered part of "an author's 'personal papers'" (178) as personal papers, according to the Beinecke's perception of "bibliographical completeness" (4), designate "those items that are involved in the processes of drafting and publishing" (178).

49. Ibid., 5.

50. Loy, "Songs to Joannes," in *The Lost Lunar Baedeker*, 53.

51. Woolf, "Craftsmanship," in *Death of the Moth*, 203.

Work Cited

Benstock, Shari. *Women of the Left Bank: Paris, 1900–1940*. Austin: University of Texas Press, 1986.

Burke, Carolyn. *Becoming Modern: The Life of Mina Loy*. Berkeley: University of California Press, 1997.

Esty, Jed. *A Shrinking Island*. Princeton, NJ: Princeton University Press, 2003.

Felski, Rita. *The Limits of Critique*. Chicago: University of Chicago Press, 2015.

Goody, Alex. "Empire, Motherhood and the Poetics of Self in Mina Loy's *Anglo-Mongrels and the Rose*." *Life Writing* 6, no. 1 (2009).

Hart, Matthew. *Nations of Nothing But Poetry: Modernism, Transnationalism, and Synthetic Vernacular Writing*. Oxford: Oxford University Press, 2010.

Hobson, Suzanne, and Rachel Potter, eds. Introduction to *The Salt Companion to Mina Loy*. London: Salt Publishing, 2010.

Jaffe, Aaron. *Modernism and the Culture of Celebrity*. Cambridge: University of Cambridge Press, 2005.

Kouidis, Virginia. *Mina Loy: American Modernist Poet*. Baton Rouge: Louisiana State University Press, 1980.

Levine, Caroline. *Forms: Whole, Rhythm, Hierarchy, Networks*. Princeton, NJ: Princeton University Press, 2015.

Light, Alison. *Mrs. Woolf and the Servants: An Intimate History of Domestic Life in Bloomsbury*. New York: Bloomsbury, 2007.

Loy, Mina. *The Last Lunar Baedeker*. Edited by Roger Conover. Highlands, NC: Jargon Society, 1982.

———. *The Lost Lunar Baedeker: Poems of Mina Loy*. Selected and edited by Roger Conover. New York: Farrar, Straus and Giroux, 1996.

Marcus, Jane. "Thinking Back through Our Mothers." In *The New Feminist Essays on Virginia Woolf*. Edited by Jane Marcus. Lincoln: University of Nebraska Press, 1981.

Moore, Marianne. *Complete Poems*. New York: Penguin, 1994.

Nesbitt, Jennifer. "The Absent Presence of Virginia Woolf: Queering *Downton Abbey*." *Journal of Popular Culture* 49, no. 2 (April 2016): 250–70.

Parmar, Sandeep. *Reading Mina Loy's Autobiographies: Myth of the Modern Woman*. New York: Bloomsbury, 2013.

Rainey, Lawrence. *Institutions of Modernism*. New Haven, CT: Yale University Press, 1998.

Rosenfeld, Natania. *Outsiders Together: Virginia and Leonard Woolf*. Princeton, NJ: Princeton University Press, 2000.

Saint-Amour, Paul K. *Tense Future: Modernism, Total War, and Encyclopedic Form*. Oxford: Oxford University Press, 2015.

———. "Weak Theory, Weak Modernism." *Modernism/modernity* 25, no. 3 (September 2018).

Shreiber, Maeera, and Keith Tuma. *Mina Loy: Woman and Poet*. Chicago: National Poetry Foundation, 1998.

Silver, Brenda. *Virginia Woolf Icon*. Chicago: University of Chicago Press, 1999.

Wilson, Mary. *The Labors of Modernism: Domesticity, Servants, and Authorship in Modernist Fiction*. New York: Routledge, 2016.

Woolf, Virginia. "Craftsmanship." *Death of the Moth*. New York: Harcourt Brace Jovanovich, 1942.

———. "The Leaning Tower." In *The Moment and Other Essays*. New York: Harcourt Brace Jovanovich, 1975.

———. *The Letters of Virginia Woolf, Volume Three, 1923–1928*. Edited by Nigel Nicolson and Joanne Trautmann. New York: Harcourt Brace Jovanovich: 1977.

———. *The Letters of Virginia Woolf, Volume Five, 1932–1935*. Edited by Nigel Nicolson and Joanne Trautmann. New York: Harcourt Brace, 1979.

———. *The Letters of Virginia Woolf, Volume Six, 1936–1941*. Edited by Nigel Nicolson and Joanne Trautmann. New York: Harcourt Brace Jovanovich, 1980.

———. "Professions for Women." In *Death of the Moth*. New York: Harcourt Brace Jovanovich, 1942.

———. *A Room of One's Own*. 1929. Edited by Susan Gubar. New York: Harcourt, 2005.

———. "Sketch of the Past." In *Moments of Being: A Collection of Autobiographical Writing*. Edited by Jeanne Schulkind. New York: Harcourt, 1985.

———. "Thoughts on Peace in an Air Raid." In *Death of the Moth*. New York: Harcourt Brace Jovanovich, 1942.

———. *Three Guineas*. 1938. New York: Harcourt, 2006.

———. *The Waves*. New York: Harcourt, 1931.

———. *The Years*. New York: Harcourt, 1937.

9

Iconic Shade . . . and Other Professional Hazards of Woolf Scholarship

MADELYN DETLOFF

Prologue: On Modernist Literary Criticism as Feminist Palimpsest

This essay originated as spoken performance for a plenary dialogue with Melissa Bradshaw. I have chosen to retain the colloquial tone and dialogic nature of the argument, complete with a few hypothetical scenarios presented in italics meant to engage the audience (and I hope the reader). I happen to study one of the few female modernists currently (but not always) considered one of the prime "makers" of modernism—Virginia Woolf. My apprehension about writing on a "major" modernist in a volume that attends to how and why women writers are relegated to "minor" roles in dominant conceptions of literary modernism is somewhat allayed by my own historical perspective on Woolf's reception. I had already graduated from college when Hugh Kenner described Woolf as a relatively trivial novelist of manners: "an English novelist doing the English novelist's traditional business—elucidating for her readers the manners and mores of England."[1] Bonnie Kime Scott examines this parochializing reading of Woolf and other female writers in *Refiguring Modernism, Volume 1: The Women of 1928*, and an illustrious cast of feminist scholars such as Brenda Silver (among many others) have illuminated the masculinist values that contributed to the earlier reception of Woolf as unworthy of the attention given to modernist "greats" such as Ezra Pound, T. S. Eliot, and James Joyce.[2] There are many, many scholars I could list alongside

Silver and Scott whose recovery of female modernist writers such as H.D. and Gertrude Stein, along with Woolf, has reshaped the field of modernist studies. Susan Stanford Friedman, Marianne DeKoven, Rachel Blau DuPlessis, Linda Wagner-Martin, and Diana Collecott would begin the litany, but the more people I list, the more aware I am of those I have left out.[3] Indeed, the unfinished list above highlights the greatest source of my apprehension regarding this essay—the sense that I am not saying anything startlingly new in a realm (academic publishing) where newness is a paramount measure of value. Rather, I am scratching my twenty-first-century perspective onto a richly layered palimpsest of feminist literary history and criticism. The imperative to be new leaves the feminist and social-justice-oriented critic in a conundrum when seemingly "old" issues such as racism, (hetero)sexism, ableism, and classism resurface with disappointing regularity. It can be difficult to say (again) what is necessary when the new is not only alluring, but also institutionally obligatory.[4] Nevertheless, I take the risk of rearticulating familiar arguments here because they bear repeating, and moreover, because, as literary history and criticism evolve, our own positions (literally our institutional positions and conceptually our rhetorical positions) coevolve. Evolution does indeed bring about change, but that change is often subtle and always informed by a complexly contextualized past. With that in mind, I offer this essay in the spirit of a deep commitment to our continuous coevolution as scholars, readers, and cultural critics.

Iconic Shade . . . and Other Professional Hazards of Woolf Scholarship

The original title for this essay was "But don't you have Woolf fatigue?," a phrase that was inspired by a conversation Melissa Bradshaw and I had in 2014. It was a texted conversation, on Facebook, which I mention to signify that I fully inhabit the twenty-first century, even though I often feel like a remnant of the 1990s—especially with my students, whom I secretly suspect of harboring the idea that 1990 marks the unofficial cutoff between prehistory and the modern age. That ever widening chasm between my own temporality and my students' presents a professional hazard that I try to recognize in the classroom by continually reminding myself that events that are part of my living memory are aspects of unlived history to my students: the ravages of the HIV/AIDS epidemic before the advent of protease inhibitors, for example, or life as a schoolgirl before Title IX, or the murder of Harvey Milk. This autobiographical perspective is one reason I do not suffer from "Woolf fatigue," even though I have been studying Woolf for almost thirty years. For me, Woolf was not always canonical, not always part of the institution of literary or modernist studies, and is often still refreshingly heretical in her approach to traditional pieties.

My autobiographical awareness influences the second professional hazard that I endeavor to avoid—the "I-walked-twelve-miles-uphill-in-the-snow" syndrome that is the bane of so many established scholars' interactions with subsequent generations of scholars. The mantra of that syndrome goes something like this: *"Back when I sat for my MA exam we had to answer questions about a prescribed list of authors (almost exclusively male), and due to the distinctions between 'optional' and 'required' readings, one could pass an entire exam without having read the work of a single female author."* For the record, this was true in 1991 when I sat for my MA exam, but if one goal of feminist scholarship has been to change such exclusionary practices, then repeating a litany of our past exclusions as a means of extracting gratitude from younger generations is a backhanded way of disavowing our progress toward that goal. I think it is more gracious to accept our small victories while admitting that our work is far from done.

Yes, Woolf was not always part of the canon, but she is now, and her status as an unavoidable literary giant percolated behind the question that Bradshaw posed during our conversation back in 2014, "But don't you have Woolf fatigue?," as well as behind Anne Fernald's 2013 special issue of *Modern Fiction Studies* on "Women's Fiction, New Modernist Studies, and Feminism," with its focus on modernist women writers besides the big three—Woolf, Gertrude Stein, and H.D. Many contemporary feminist scholars share Fernald's concern that the long shadows cast by these three iconic writers have the potential to cast shade on other female modernists who deserve more light.

I therefore acknowledge the irony of my writing as a Woolf scholar in a volume dedicated, in part, to drawing other female modernists out from under Woolf's long shadow. This irony is associated with professional hazard number three: becoming the hegemon, the insider to the institution of literary studies, and perhaps academe in general. I have a vague recollection of when Virginia Woolf became canonical—sometime in the early 1990s when studies of modernism could no longer omit her without explanation. But to my chagrin, I seem to have conveniently overlooked the moment when I crossed the border from outsider to insider status within academe. Being situated in a position of relative privilege inside the belly of the institutional beast is fraught with ambivalence. Woolf was a great theorist of such ambivalence. The fictitious letter writer in her epistolary essay, *Three Guineas* (1938), for example, speculates on whether she should send a hypothetical woman's college a guinea "to buy rags and petrol and Bryant & Mays matches and burn the college to the ground?"[5]

For the record, neither Woolf nor I ultimately advocate that incendiary action, for if we take the lessons of *Three Guineas* to heart, we still need the institution of higher education (flawed as it may be) because it is still one of the most accessible pathways for developing the critical aptitudes, the cultural capital, and the material resources necessary for flourishing in a complex contemporary world. As Christopher Newfield argues in *The Great Mistake: How We Wrecked Public Universities and How We Can Fix Them*, "generalized *creativity learning* is the necessary (though not sufficient) condition of prosperity and justice."[6] Accessible higher education is an endangered public good, despite understandable concerns about the potentially hegemonic effects of academic institutionalization and elitism. These concerns about the hegemonic effects of a radical discourse's assimilation within dominant institutions are not new. Over thirty-five years ago in her 1982 *Signs* essay, "Storming the Toolshed," Jane Marcus identified what she saw as radical differences between insider academic criticism and "Lupine" criticism by lesbian feminists and Marxist feminists. Since Marcus wrote that essay, feminist criticism and theory (not to mention Marxist theory) have become more accepted within academe. Even so, it is very possible that Marcus, were she still alive, would decry the taming effects that institutionalization has had upon radical "Lupine" thought. Such is the dilemma facing social-justice-oriented scholars within the university.

Incorporation by mainstream academe is both a sign of progress and a disciplining process. As Robyn Wiegman notes, "institutionalization transforms identity's political calculus."[7] This is not to say that institutionalization is an unambiguous betrayal of political aims (feminist, Marxist, queer, and so on) but rather that being absorbed into a power structure necessarily changes one's relation to power, and that must be accounted for rather than disavowed. Moreover (and this is professional hazard number four), as Newfield suggests, higher education appears to be trending in the direction of greater separation of the classes, with the well-resourced Oxbridges and Ivies offering strong liberal arts education to the wealthy, and the struggling Fernhams or Morleys charged with educating on the cheap a precarious class of workers to serve the people who graduate from Oxbridge and the Ivies.[8] I do not want public education to become (more of a) proving ground for the replication of social class and cultural privilege, thus like Woolf's guinea-giver, I have chosen to fight for the soul of the institution rather than let it burn down.

With that fight in mind, I want to explore two dilemmas presented by the institutional absorption of Woolf and Woolf Studies into academe. These dilemmas include the effects of canonicity—becoming a "literary giant" who may overshadow other authors deserving of our attention—and the material realities of educational institutions in the era of neoliberal instrumentalization that Newfield describes in *The Great Mistake*. The two dilemmas are not unrelated, but rather complexly entwined. As John Guillory noted in 1993, canonical inclusion does not necessarily translate into social inclusion: "Given the only partially successful social agenda of educational democratization in the last three decades, we may conclude that it is much easier to make the canon representative than the university."[9] Nevertheless, Woolf herself observed in 1928 that readers and writers with different experiences (in Woolf's case, men and women) would be likely to communicate different values in their fiction: "This is an important book, the critics assumes, because it deals with war. This is an insignificant book because it deals with the feelings of women in the drawing-room."[10] If this is the case, then reading and teaching works by authors who may have different experiences from writers who are dominantly situated provides a means of disrupting the seeming neutrality of dominant social scripts and values.

There are two conceptual roadblocks in the way of this project of disruption. The first conceptual problem is tokenism (I know this is not a new insight, but unfortunately a necessary one, still) and the second is the problem of professional intelligibility.[11] As an example of the persistence of the former, let's imagine this hypothetical scenario: *We are at a conference on modernism—let's say the Modernist Studies Association. A keynote speaker presents a history of modernism. Let's imagine that it is 2010, a hundred years after Woolf claimed that human relations had shifted in "Mr. Bennet and Mrs. Brown." The speaker proceeds with his history without mentioning a single female scholar of modernism and only one female writer. If someone were to call that speaker out and ask how his history of modernism might look different if female scholars and writers were considered, and if, perchance, he were to answer, "but I mentioned Woolf!" that would be an example of tokenism.*[12]

The tokenist response "But I cited _____!" (fill in the blank with a single canonical female author) understandably elicits groans from scholars who regularly study many and various modernist women writers, from Elizabeth Bowen to Nella Larsen, Victoria Ocampo, Jean Rhys, Dorothy Richardson, Zora Neale Hurston, or any number of interesting woman writers of the early twentieth century. Tokenism works through a contradictory logic of sufficiency and scarcity, where a single example is imagined to represent the whole of a group sufficiently, while the available positions within a set of exemplars is imagined to be scarce. If there *were* only one "woman slot" in a canon of modernist writers, then devoting attention to Woolf would indeed be overshadowing attention to other women writers. But why must we be forced to choose? As no selection of authors, canonical or not, will convey a complete picture of literary modernism, there is room to present a less "skewed" (the term Rosabeth Moss Kanter uses to describe unbalanced demographics ripe for tokenism) version of the field.[13]

This is a simple and elegant solution, and I presume that one of the aims of this volume is to provide scholarship on less well-known female modernists that we can use to help "unskew" our syllabi, our talks, and our publications. I know many of us already do that, however, and that this seemingly simple, elegant solution may not be as simple as it sounds. The problem of scholarly intelligibility can make the simple solution risky— even impossible—for academics in vulnerable (that is, nontenured) positions. Now that Woolf is recognized as part of the canon, researching Woolf's work does grant those scholars who focus on her a measure of intelligibility in academe. While intelligibility in academe is certainly no guarantor of cultural intelligibility at large, it can help one secure enough gainful employment to pay the bills. *Imagine telling a dean, provost, or university trustee that you're doing research on Kate Bornstein or Butch/FTM masochism in "The Well of Loneliness" and "Stone Butch Blues." Imagine their faces as you mention this. Then imagine saying, "I study Virginia Woolf" and the sense of relief that washes over their faces as they latch on to something familiar—Virginia Woolf? Wasn't there a movie about her starring Elizabeth Taylor? Or was that Nicole Kidman? Phew. Woolf scholarship is legit.*

This intelligibility problem is connected to the institutional structures—notably hiring, promotion, tenure, and curriculum priorities—and attending to those structural issues requires difficult and often thankless work. And tokenism, which is far too often the strategy of choice where institutional diversity is concerned, tends to let the institution off the hook, absolving those of us in the institution of the responsibility to transform it, to transform the curriculum, to match our words about diversity and inclusion with deeds. As Sara Ahmed notes in *On Being Included,* her study of diversity work in academic institutions, "if institutionalizing diversity is a goal for diversity workers, it does not necessarily mean it is the institution's goal. I think this 'not necessarily' describes a paradoxical condition that is a life situation for many diversity practitioners. Having an institutional aim to make diversity a goal can even be a sign that diversity is not an institutional goal" (5).

Devoting one's self to transformative work in one's own institution tends to release a maelstrom of ambivalence, especially if one has become absorbed into the institution. The institution changes us even as we aim to change the institution. Moreover, as Ahmed notes, diversity workers who are from marginalized groups often "become" the person who embodies the difference that diversity lauds. In other words, one becomes the token who represents institutionalized diversity. Ahmed explains that "Becoming the race person means you are the one who is turned to when race turns up. The very fact of your existence can allow others not to turn up" (5). Institutions also are prone to reproducing what Ahmed (following Joan Acker) calls "inequality regimes"—"a set of processes that maintain what is supposedly being redressed" (8).

I would like to keep the dynamics of tokenism and intelligibility in mind as I shift now to consider Woolf herself as a canon maker and breaker. Focusing attention on her practices, her deeds as well as words, might give us some strategies to avoid as well as emulate. I aggregate them here as context for what I hope will be a more prolonged critical conversation about Woolf's appraisal of her contemporaries, her leveraging of privilege, and her precarious but powerful position as a *metic,* an outsider within the belly of the beast.[14]

For Woolf was a modernist *metic*—a privileged outsider in her country and culture. As a woman, as a queer person, as someone with a neuroaffective atypicality, she occupied a precarious position in relation to dominant cultural power.[15] Yet, at the same time, she had the privilege of intellectual and cultural status by way of her family connections: through Leslie Stephen and his milieu on her father's side, but also through her mother's side, if we remember that her great aunt Julia Margaret Cameron, the pioneering photographer, was friend of Alfred Lord Tennyson among other literati. To top it off, her godfather, James Russell Lowell, was the cousin of Amy Lowell, whom Bradshaw discusses in this volume. Woolf was more than one of the "daughters of educated men," a term she uses to describe her class position in *Three Guineas* (4). She was a daughter of the intelligentsia.

She was also a prolific reviewer for the *Times Literary Supplement* and other venues, a co-owner of the Hogarth Press, and the author of two volumes of literary criticism (the first and second *Common Readers* [1925, 1929]) as well as a "Hogarth Pamphlet" (*Letter to a Young Poet* [1932]) in her lifetime. She was not always complimentary to fellow women writers—her remarks on Katherine Mansfield smelling like a "civet cat that had taken to street walking," for example, strike one as simply mean.[16] Mary Jean Corbett argues convincingly that Woolf unfairly—perhaps unconsciously or uncannily—overlooked literature written by late Victorian women, despite her claim that "a woman writing thinks back through her mothers."[17]

Virginia Woolf also corresponded generously and constructively with a number of aspiring female writers, not to mention common readers. Beth Rigel Daugherty's collection of "Letters from Readers," for example, demonstrates that Woolf had a diverse and widespread readership (beyond the highbrows Q. D. Leavis presumed were her readership), and that she corresponded with her "common readers," many of whom were aspiring or successful female authors.[18] As Patricia Laurence notes in *Lily Briscoe's Chinese Eyes*, Woolf corresponded with writer and artist Ling Shuhua, advising her on her autobiography and offering to read drafts (282). And as Helen Southworth's wonderful collection on *The Hogarth Press and the Networks of Modernism* attests, the Woolfs' press published a number of women writers, including Vita Sackville-West and Hope Mirrlees as well as what Melissa Sullivan calls "a network of middlebrow women writers."[19] I could go on with examples of Woolf's active engagement with women writers who were her contemporaries, but I think Anne Fernald sums it up well when she explains, in *Virginia Woolf: Feminism and the Reader*, "what critics have seen as inconsistencies in Woolf can more properly be

explained by our unease with her ambitions as an artist (and her conse-
quent unwillingness to make less than sisterly judgments about women
writers whose work she did not admire)" (1).

In terms of Woolf's own canonicity, it is probably wise to remember
Woolf's insight that "masterpieces are not single and solitary births; they
are the outcome of many years of thinking in common, of thinking by the
body of the people, so that the experience of the mass is behind the single
voice."[20] The very notion of a "masterpiece" is of course problematic. One
could as easily say that the experience of the elite, rather than the masses,
is behind the single voice that ascends to the status of "masterpiece." This
is implicit in Woolf's focus on the material conditions necessary to foster
good writing ("a woman must have money and a room of her own if
she is to write fiction").[21] I am less interested here in the "masterpiece"
part of Woolf's claim than her emphasis on the importance of "thinking
in common." Community, Woolf seems to be saying, can manifest itself
diachronically as well as synchronically. What would it mean to apply this
insight to contemporary readers and critics who not only inherit a living
past but actively reshape it?

By living past, I mean something like our embodied, temporally specific, and locational relationship to that which comes before us. That relationship looks something like the dynamic imagined by T. S. Eliot in his
assertion that "No poet, no artist of any art, has his [sic] complete meaning
alone."[22] Eliot, however, is concerned with the poet or artist's individual
virtuosity in relation to artistic works of the past, while Woolf, as I noted
above, has something more communal in mind when she speaks of the
"experience of the mass behind the single voice."[23]

While Eliot does say that the old "ideal" order is modified by the introduction of the "really new," there is yet something necrotic in his (un-
marked, male) poet's relationship with tradition, represented by Eliot as
"dead poets and artists":

> No poet, no artist of any art, has his complete meaning alone. His
> significance, his appreciation is the appreciation of his relation to
> the dead poets and artists. You cannot value him alone; you must
> set him, for contrast and comparison, among the dead. . . . The ne-
> cessity that he shall conform, that he shall cohere, is not one-sided;
> what happens when a new work of art is created is something that
> happens simultaneously to all the works of art which preceded it.

> The existing monuments form an ideal order among themselves, which is modified by the introduction of the new (the really new) work of art among them. (37)

While his words describe a symbiotic relationship between the living poet and past works of art, Eliot's language, evoking "dead poets," "among the dead," figures that past as lifeless, sepulchral—"existing monuments" rather than something very old, yet living. Woolf differs from Eliot in her figuration of our relationship to tradition as living rather than necrotic. "Think[ing] back through our mothers" implies a live heritage, a bloodline that is still present in the thinker.[24] This may seem like a semantic point about Eliot's choice of language because tradition, for Eliot, is clearly something that changes, reordered by interaction with the new. But if we look at Eliot's famous description of the poet's mind as a catalyst—a "filament of platinum" that remains "inert, neutral, and unchanged" as it "digest[s] and transmute[s] the passions which are its material"—the motif of digestion, of chemical combination, is rather one-sided, with the poet in control (41). Passions do not consume him; he consumes them and, well, if we follow Eliot's metaphorical logic to its end we arrive at a very scatological conclusion: if you are a true poet your poetry does not stink of your own personality. Eliot—to avoid the crude scatology that his metaphor suggests—has to imagine the poet's personality as disembodied in order to keep our focus on cool scientific materials like platinum and oxygen and sulfur dioxide and not on the usual, inevitable byproducts of digestion.

Woolf is not so crude as I have been, but her recognition of "thinking by the body of the people" acknowledges both the importance of embodiment to our thinking (embodied epistemology, we might say, if we were philosophers) and the significance of community, "many years of thinking in common," to our creative endeavors. My aim here is not to show how Woolf differentiated herself from Eliot, or even how she herself perceived literary history, but how her work today, in the twenty-first century, articulates the importance of the "common world" (a term used by Hannah Arendt to denote a figurative public space where ideas circulate) to our communal flourishing. The "common world" is a collective space that has been encroached on for centuries by the "private" and by the "social," which Arendt describes as the extension of the familial into the public with increasing reach. In Arendt's "social" realm, nations are imagined as vast families with kinship bonds and economies (once regulated to the household by ancient Greeks) and structures of belonging that are dependent upon a form of group cohesion or, in other words, normativity.

Hannah Arendt herself notes that "society expects from each of its members a certain kind of behavior, imposing innumerable and various rules, all of which tend to 'normalize' its members, to make them behave, to exclude spontaneous action or outstanding achievement."[25] She goes on to say,

> The public realm, as the common world, gathers us together and yet prevents our falling over each other, so to speak. What makes mass society so difficult to bear is not the number of people involved, or at least not primarily, but the fact that the world between them has lost its power to gather them together, to relate and to separate them. The weirdness of this situation resembles a spiritualistic séance where a number of people gathered around a table might suddenly, through some magic trick, see the table vanish from their midst, so that two persons sitting opposite each other were no longer separated but also would be entirely unrelated to each other by anything tangible.[26]

Arendt's table is not quite Mr. Ramsay's table from *To the Lighthouse* (1927), or any of the many other tables that Ann Banfield describes as "the long paradigmatic object of knowledge in 'the history of English thought' . . . planted squarely in the center of Woolf's novelistic scenery, standing for the 'stuff of the physical world.'"[27] Arendt's table, rather, is a metaphor for a tangible world that lies between individual subjects, demarcating a gathering space for relationality.

"Gathering," according to feminist epistemologist Gaile Pohlhaus Jr., is a material, embodied practice that influences "relational knowing," epistemic "situatedness," and "interdependence."[28] As Pohlhaus notes, "situatedness" is significant "insofar as the knower's social position draws her attention to particular aspects of the world," and "interdependence" is significant "insofar as epistemic resources, needed to make sense of those parts of the world to which she attends, are by nature collective."[29]

Woolf is keenly aware of our interdependence. In "How Should One Read a Book?" (1925) she asks, "How far . . . is a book influenced by its writer's life—how far is it safe to let the man interpret the writer? How far shall we resist or give way to the sympathies and antipathies that the man himself rouses in us—so sensitive are words, so receptive of the character of the author?" (263). Moreover, she admits that our judgments are temporally situated, consisting of a relationship between present reader and past writer. Our passions are not consumed or burned out or made "impersonal," as Eliot's poet-as-catalyst motif suggests. Instead, our personalities, or "identity," as Woolf describes it, cannot be wholly effaced:

> We may stress the value of sympathy; we may try to sink our identity as we read. But we know that we cannot sympathise wholly or immerse ourselves wholly; there is always a demon in us who whispers, "I hate, I love," and we cannot silence him. Indeed, it is precisely because we hate and we love that our relation with the poets and novelists is so intimate that we find the presence of another person intolerable. (268)

To be fair, Woolf is describing the reading process, and Eliot is describing the writing process. But both are describing an attempt, impossible in Woolf's account and necessary in Eliot's, to achieve a depersonalized relationship to affective stimuli. Moreover, Woolf calls the encounter with another's creative work a "relation," even an "intimate" one. Affect is thus both relational and a source of knowledge. "Even if the results are abhorrent and our judgments are wrong," she explains, "still our taste, the nerve of sensation that sends shocks through us, is our chief illuminant; we learn through feeling; we cannot suppress our own idiosyncrasy without impoverishing it" (268).

"We learn through feeling," and we are also motivated to learn through curiosity. Woolf likens the motivation to read to the curiosity piqued by meandering the public streets and witnessing the spectacle of daily life unfolding through the front windows and side yards of one's neighborhood (261). This is an important figuration, because that spectacle unfolds in a public realm—whether it is the street or on the publicly circulated printed page of the book. The bookshelf, as she imagines it, is something like a crowded sidewalk where "biographies and autobiographies . . . lives of great men, of men long dead and forgotten . . . stand cheek by jowl with . . . novels and poems" that may be contemporary, and may not even be "art" (261).

That this crowded bookshelf is something like a commons for Woolf is reinforced by her 1940 project, "Reading at Random," which Brenda Silver excavated and edited in "'Anon' and 'The Reader': Virginia Woolf's

Last Essays." Silver notes in her introduction to those essays that Woolf recorded in her diary that she had "conceived, or re-moulded, an idea for a Common History book—to read from one end of literature including biography; and range at will" (356). Literature provides the basis for a "Common History book." Why is this relevant to our institutional situatedness or the work of canon making and breaking? One of the main critiques of the exclusionary nature of the canon is that it purports to evoke something like universal experience, which is often a code word for dominant cultural worldviews. This is an apt critique if the canon is supposed to represent something universal. But what if we imagine a commons instead of a canon, where the commons is something like Arendt's metaphorical table that lies between us and holds us together? Perhaps literature, history, philosophy, and the humanities in general, can provide a tangible space across which we might think, and even feel, together. This is significant, given the erosion of support for the liberal arts and humanities that we are experiencing in an age (as Newfield might argue) of increased specialization and instrumentalization of knowledge. Perhaps literature has the capacity to provide a commons not because of its content, but because it has the ability to exist between us—temporally, geographically, and culturally?

With that said, I take the disclaimer with which Woolf begins *A Room of One's Own* (1929) seriously. She can not, and what's more, *she will not*, "fulfil . . . the first duty of a lecturer to hand you after an hour's discourse a nugget of pure truth to wrap up between the pages of your notebooks." (I am tempted to call this professional hazard number five.) The most she is willing to do is to "develop in your presence as fully and freely as I can the train of thought which led me to think this . . . to give one's audience the chance of drawing their own conclusions" (4). I submit that this is a helpful practice for those of us in the institution to emulate—leveraging our privilege as *metics*, as Woolf did, to combat structural inequities that mask themselves as differences in aptitude, or talent, or inclination. We cannot burn the institution down (yet) because we need the leverage that the institution provides—but we sure as hell can turn up the heat.

Notes

1. Kenner, *A Sinking Island*, 5.
2. Scott, *Refiguring Modernism, Volume One*, 79–83; and Silver, *Virginia Woolf Icon*, 35–76, 152–58.

3. See Friedman's *Psyche Reborn*; DeKoven's *A Different Language*; DuPlessis's *H.D.*; Wagner-Martin's *"Favored Strangers"*; and Collecott's *H.D. and Sapphic Modernism*.

4. This obligation to be new sets up a structural dynamic that contributes to what I called "the politics of contempt" twenty years ago. While I do not witness contempt as much in 2017 as I did in 1997 (perhaps because of my different institutional location), the structural dynamics of academic publishing, hiring, and promotion still make it difficult to survive in academe without an affective and intellectual investment in the "new" at the expense of the "old." See Detloff, "Mean Spirits," 78.

5. Woolf, *Three Guineas*, 33.

6. Newfield, *The Great Mistake*, 6.

7. Wiegman, *Object Lessons*, 95.

8. Newfield, *The Great Mistake*, 6. In *A Room of One's Own*, Woolf used the euphemism "Oxbridge" to signify prestigious predominantly male institutions of higher education such as Oxford and Cambridge, while "Fernham" was her euphemism for women's colleges such as Newnham and Girton. Woolf, *A Room of One's Own*, 4. Morley College was a college for working-class people for which Woolf taught briefly. For more on Woolf's teaching experiences, see Daugherty's "Morley College, Virginia Woolf and Us," 125–38; and Melba Cuddy-Keane's *Virginia Woolf, the Intellectual, and the Public Sphere*.

9. Guillory, *Cultural Capital*, 7.

10. Woolf, *A Room of One's Own*, 74.

11. Research on tokenism goes back at least forty years. Rosabeth Moss Kanter's *Men and Women of the Corporation* (1977) is often cited as a work that brought the concept of tokenism into wide circulation, although the term was circulating before 1977. The *Oxford English Dictionary* traces the origin of the word to 1962. *OED Online*, June 2017, Oxford University Press, http://www.oed.com.proxy.lib.miamioh.edu/view/Entry/202951?redirectedFrom=tokenism.

12. Although I mention this as a hypothetical example, one might find evidence of such an exchange on the "Keynote Videos" section of the 12th Modernist Studies Association Conference website at https://msa.press.jhu.edu/conferences/msa12/.

13. Kanter, *Men and Women of the Corporation*, 208.

14. On the *metic* status of privileged outsiders in modernism, see Detloff, *The Persistence of Modernism*, 6–8.

15. I use the term neuro-affective atypicality rather than bipolar disorder or mental illness so as not to participate in the normative pathologization of Woolf's affective and cognitive particularity.

16. Simpson and Harvey, "To the Readers," 1.

17. Corbett, "Considering Contemporaneity," 2–7. Corbett provides an even more extended analysis of Woolf's fraught relationship to late-Victorian female authors in *Behind the Times: Virginia Woolf in Late-Victorian Contexts*. Woolf's line "thinking back through their mothers" is from *A Room of One's Own*, 101.

18. Daugherty, "Letters to Readers," 1–3. See also Leavis, *Fiction and the Reading Public*, 5, 51.

19. Sullivan, "Middlebrows of the Hogarth Press," 53.

20. Woolf, *A Room of One's Own*, 65.

21. Ibid., 4.

22. Eliot, "Tradition," 38.

23. Woolf, *A Room of One's Own*, 65.

24. Woolf, *A Room of One's Own*, 76.

25. Arendt, *The Human Condition*, 40.

26. Ibid., 52–53.

27. Banfield, *The Phantom Table*, 66.

28. Pohlhaus, "Relational Knowing and Epistemic Injustice," 716. Pohlhaus develops the notion of "epistemic gathering" in "Knowing without Borders and the Work of Epistemic Gathering."

29. Pohlhaus, "Knowing without Borders," 716.

Works Cited

Ahmed, Sara. *On Being Included: Racism and Diversity in Institutional Life*. Durham, NC: Duke University Press, 2012.

Arendt, Hannah. *The Human Condition*. Second edition. Chicago: University of Chicago Press, 2013.

Banfield, Ann. *The Phantom Table: Woolf, Fry, Russell and the Epistemology of Modernism*. New York: Cambridge University Press, 2000.

Collecott, Diana. *H.D. and Sapphic Modernism 1910–1950*. New York: Cambridge University Press, 1999.

Corbett, Mary Jean. *Behind the Times: Virginia Woolf in Late-Victorian Contexts*. Ithaca: Cornell University Press, forthcoming.

———. "Considering Contemporaneity: Woolf and 'the Maternal Generation,'" in *Virginia Woolf and Her Female Contemporaries: Selected Papers from the 25th Annual Conference on Virginia Woolf*, edited by Julie Vandivere and Megan Hicks, 2–7. Clemson, SC: Clemson University Press, 2016.

Cuddy-Keane, Melba. *Virginia Woolf, the Intellectual, and the Public Sphere*. New York: Cambridge University Press, 2003.

Daugherty, Beth Rigel. "Morley College, Virginia Woolf and Us: How Should One Read Class?" In *Virginia Woolf and Her Influences: Selected Papers from the Seventh Annual Conference on Virginia Woolf*, edited by Laura Davis and Jeanette McVicker, 125–38. New York: Pace University Press, 1998.

———. "'You See You Kind of Belong to Us, and What You Do Matters Enormously': Letters to Readers from Virginia Woolf." *Woolf Studies Annual* 12 (2006): 1–212.

DeKoven, Marianne. *A Different Language: Gertrude Stein's Experimental Writing.* Madison: University of Wisconsin Press, 1983.

Detloff, Madelyn. "Mean Spirits: The Politics of Contempt Between Feminist Generations." *Hypatia* 12, no. 3 (1997): 76–99.

———. *The Persistence of Modernism: Loss and Mourning in the Twentieth Century.* New York: Cambridge University Press, 2009.

DuPlessis, Rachel Blau. *H.D.: The Career of that Struggle.* Bloomington: Indiana University Press, 1986.

Eliot, T. S. "Tradition and the Individual Talent." In *Selected Prose of T. S. Eliot*, edited by Frank Kermode, 37–44. New York: Farrar, Straus and Giroux, 1975.

Fernald, Anne. *Virginia Woolf: Feminism and the Reader.* New York: Palgrave, 2006.

———, ed. "Women's Fiction, New Modernist Studies, and Feminism." Special issue, *Modern Fiction Studies* 59, no. 2 (Summer 2013).

Friedman, Susan Stanford. *Psyche Reborn: The Emergence of H.D.* Bloomington: Indiana University Press, 1981.

Guillory, John. *Cultural Capital: The Problem of Literary Canon Formation.* Chicago: University of Chicago Press, 1993.

Kanter, Rosabeth Moss. *Men and Women of the Corporation.* 1977. Second edition. New York: Basic Books, 1993.

Kenner, Hugh. *A Sinking Island: The Modern English Writers.* Baltimore: Johns Hopkins University Press, 1989.

Laurence, Patricia. *Lily Briscoe's Chinese Eyes: Bloomsbury, Modernism, and China.* Columbia: University of South Carolina Press, 2003.

Leavis, Q. D. *Fiction and the Reading Public.* Kindle edition. London: Chatto and Windus, 1939.

Marcus, Jane. "Storming the Toolshed." *Signs: Journal of Women in Culture and Society* 7, no. 3 (Spring 1982): 622–40.

Newfield, Christopher. *The Great Mistake: How We Wrecked Public Universities and How We Can Fix Them.* Baltimore: Johns Hopkins University Press, 2016.

Pohlhaus, Gaile, Jr. "Knowing without Borders and the Work of Epistemic Gathering." In *Decolonizing Feminism: Transnational Feminism and Globalization*, edited by Margaret A. McLaren, 37–54. London: Rowman and Littlefield, 2016.

———. "Relational Knowing and Epistemic Injustice: Toward a Theory of Willful Hermeneutical Ignorance." *Hypatia* 27, no. 4 (Fall 2012): 715–35.

Scott, Bonnie Kime. *Refiguring Modernism, Volume One: The Women of 1928.* Bloomington: Indiana University Press, 1996.

Silver, Brenda. "'Anon' and 'The Reader': Virginia Woolf's Last Essays." Virginia Woolf Issue *Twentieth Century Literature* 25, no. 3/4 (Autumn–Winter 1979): 356–441.

———. *Virginia Woolf Icon.* Chicago: University of Chicago Press, 1999.

Simpson, Kathryn, and Melinda Harvey, eds. "To the Reader: Virginia Woolf and Katherine Mansfield." In *Virginia Woolf Miscellany* 86 (Fall 2014/Winter 2015): 1.

Southworth, Helen, ed. *Leonard and Virginia Woolf, The Hogarth Press and the Networks of Modernism.* Edinburgh: Edinburgh University Press, 2010.

Sullivan, Melissa. "The Middlebrows of the Hogarth Press: Rose Macaulay, E. M. Delafield and Cultural Hierarchies in Interwar Britain." In *Leonard and Virginia Woolf, The Hogarth Press and the Networks of Modernism*, edited by Helen Southworth, 52–73. Edinburgh: Edinburgh University Press, 2010.

Wagner-Martin, Linda. *"Favored Strangers": Gertrude Stein and Her Family.* New Brunswick, NJ: Rutgers University Press, 1995.

Wiegman, Robyn. *Object Lessons.* Durham, NC: Duke University Press, 2012.

Woolf, Virginia. "How Should One Read a Book?" In *The Second Common Reader,* edited by Andrew McNeillie, 258–70. New York: Harcourt Brace Jovanovich, 1986.

———. *A Room of One's Own.* 1929. New York: Harcourt Brace, 1981.

———. *Three Guineas.* 1938. New York: Harcourt Brace, 1966.

ACKNOWLEDGMENTS

The existence of this collection is the work of Julie Vandivere, and for her energetic inclusion of me in the process of publication I am deeply grateful. With Julie, I had the opportunity to advocate for, organize, and participate in collaborations of inspirational feminist scholarship within new modernist studies. I have learned so much and I have Julie to thank.

Additionally, I owe a deep debt to the feminist modernist scholars included in this volume—not only for their essays presented here but also for their careers of feminist-oriented scholarship, advocacy, and collegiality. Many of the contributors to this volume have figured prominently—whether they know it or not—in my own professional feminist self-fashioning. And some have moved beyond the role of mentor to take on the cherished mantle of friend.

There is a rich community of feminist friends and colleagues beyond the pages of this book that have encouraged and supported me over the years, and listing their names here only scratches the surface of their profound impact on me—professionally, politically, and personally. Thanks to Kristin Czarnecki and Carrie Rohman for being as terrific travel companions as they are second readers. Our friendship is a gift. A huge debt of gratitude is owed to my feminist conspirators and collaborators Lauren Rosenblum, Laurel Harris, and Jennifer Mitchell. Without them, my feminism—and my fashion—would be much less revolutionary. Even from a distance, they keep me laughing, reading, and writing. Similarly, Meghan Fox has been integral to my thinking about feminism, modernist studies, and the academy. Collaborating with Meghan is a dream, and I wish everyone such productive collaborative experiences. There are so many other feminist modernist scholars who have engaged with my presentations, reviewed my submissions, encouraged my work, and, perhaps most important, mentored me indirectly through their example. Your energies and attentions are valued by myself and others.

At Bucknell University, I am privileged to work with outstanding feminist teachers and scholars whose guidance and support have made my work on this collection even more rewarding. Thanks especially to Susan Reed for always emphasizing the importance of my research and believing in my projects. And a particularly tender thank you to Nikki Young whose intersectional feminist praxis is the foundation of our generative working relationship and our wonderful friendship. Another longtime friend and colleague I must recognize is Deirdre O'Connor. She, more than anyone else, has been witness to my evolution as a thinker and a writer. It is a testament to her impact on me that the "editing voice" in my head sounds exactly like her.

My acknowledgments would be incomplete without recognizing the steadfast support of family and friends. My parents have been the presidents of the Erica Gene Delsandro Fan Club for nearly forty years now, and I cannot imagine my life without their unwavering love and encouragement. During the process of bringing this collection to publication, I have been lucky enough to count Brian Donahower as one of my chosen family. Thanks to him, I laugh often and am less likely to lose my sense of work-life balance. In his eyes, I can do it all—and sometimes he convinces even me of that outlandish notion. Also, to my friends Renee Huber and Allen Tran, and to my neighbors Celia Shiffer and Katie Hays, I offer a big thank you: they make the daily comings and goings enjoyable and ensure that the emotional ups and downs of daily life do not threaten to overwhelm me. To my large circle of friends in the United States and beyond: they, too, have been integral to this process, as they compel me to be the best feminist possible. It takes a village, as they say, and I am so grateful to have outposts far and wide cheering me on, giving advice, and making me smile.

Finally, there are many people whose time and attention have helped to transform essays into chapters and chapters into a book, especially Stephanye Hunter, my editor at the University Press of Florida, the insightful and encouraging peer reviewers, and Elizabeth Detwiler, the keen-eyed and kindhearted copy editor. Also, without Regina Marler's eleventh-hour photography mission, Vanessa Bell's painting would not be included in this collection. Similarly, it is with Dr. Sophie Bowness's permission that

Barbara Hepworth's work graces the cover. Roger Conover, too, provided permission to quote Mina Loy's poetry at length. And finally, a note of institutional thanks: from Bucknell University's Office of the Provost I received financial support that assisted in bringing *Women Making Modernism* to fruition.

CONTRIBUTORS

Melissa Bradshaw teaches in the English Department at Loyola University Chicago. Her research focuses on publicity, personality, and fandom in twentieth-century British and American literature. She has published extensively on the American poet Amy Lowell, coediting *The Selected Poems of Amy Lowell* as well as *Amy Lowell, American Modern,* a volume of scholarly essays about the poet. Her book *Amy Lowell, Diva Poet* won the 2011 MLA Book Prize for Independent Scholars. She has also published on Edith Sitwell, Edna St. Vincent Millay, and on divas more generally. She is an associate editor and book review editor for the journal *Feminist Modernist Studies.*

Erica Gene Delsandro is assistant professor in the Department of Women's and Gender Studies at Bucknell University where she teaches courses in gender studies, feminist theory, and literature. Her research interests include modernist women writers, the gender politics of authorship, gender and life writing, as well as the gender politics of literary studies. She has published in *Soundings, Woolf Studies Annual, Clio,* and *Pedagogy,* as well as in several of the Annual International Conference on Virginia Woolf *Selected Papers.*

Madelyn Detloff is professor and chair of English and professor of global and intercultural studies at Miami University (OH). She is the author of *The Value of Virginia Woolf* and *The Persistence of Modernism: Loss and Mourning in the Twentieth Century,* coeditor of *Queer Bloomsbury* and of *Virginia Woolf: Art, Education, and Internationalism,* and the author of essays in journals such as *Hypatia, Women's Studies, ELN, Literature, Compass, Feminist Modernist Studies,* and *Modernism/modernity.*

Jane Garrity is associate professor of English at the University of Colorado at Boulder. She is the author of *Step-Daughters of England: British*

Women Modernists and the National Imaginary and the coeditor of *Sapphic Modernities: Sexuality, Women and National Culture.* Her most recent publication, "Global Objects in *The Waves*," appears in *A Companion to Virginia Woolf.*

Catherine W. Hollis received her PhD from the University of California, Berkeley, where she teaches writing in the Fall Program for Freshmen. She has also worked as an assistant editor for the Emma Goldman Papers Project, a documentary history of Goldman's life and times. She is the author of *Leslie Stephen as Mountaineer* as well as articles on Virginia Woolf, Djuna Barnes, and Jean Rhys. Her reviews of nonfiction, primarily memoir, appear in *Public Books* and *Book Page.* Her current research focuses on Emma Goldman's relationships with modernist women.

Celia Marshik is professor of English, and faculty affiliate of women's, gender, and sexuality studies, at Stony Brook University. She is the author of *British Modernism and Censorship* and of *At the Mercy of Their Clothes: Modernism, the Middlebrow, and British Garment Culture* as well as coauthor of *Modernism, Sex, and Gender.* She is the editor of *The Cambridge Companion to Modernist Culture.* Along with Faye Hammill and Andrew Thacker, she edits the book series Material Modernisms.

Allison Pease is professor of English at John Jay College of Criminal Justice, City University of New York. She is the author of *Modernism, Mass Culture, and the Aesthetics of Obscenity* and *Modernism, Feminism, and the Culture of Boredom*, and also the coauthor of *Modernism, Sex, and Gender* and the editor of *The Cambridge Companion to "To the Lighthouse."*

Emily Ridge is associate professor of English literature at City University of Hong Kong. She is the author of *Portable Modernisms: The Art of Travelling Light* and coeditor of *Security and Hospitality in Literature and Culture: Modern and Contemporary Perspectives.* Her further work has appeared in journals such as *Novel: A Forum on Fiction, Papers on Language and Literature, Literature Compass, Journeys: The International Journal of Travel and Travel Writing, Modernism/modernity*, and *Textual Practice.* She is currently working on a new project on narrative, empathy, and biopolitics in mid-twentieth-century British women's writing.

Julie Vandivere is the director of honors and professor of English at Bloomsburg University. She has written numerous articles and book chapters on women writers, including Emilia Pardo Bazán, Virginia Woolf, H.D., Emily Coleman, and Antonia White. Her work has appeared, among other places, in *Twentieth-Century Literature, Modernism/modernity Print Plus,* and *MLA Publications.* She is the coeditor of the first edition of H.D.'s *The Sword Went Out to Sea.*

INDEX

CPSIA information can be obtained
at www.ICGtesting.com
Printed in the USA
LVHW100820210422
716837LV00002B/4